Glen M. Williford
with Thomas D. Batha

AMERICAN
BREECHLOADING
MOBILE ARTILLERY
1875–1953
An Illustrated Identification Guide

Schiffer Publishing Ltd®

4880 Lower Valley Road • Atglen, PA 19310

Other Schiffer Books on Related Subjects:

500 Years of German Cannon, by Gerhard Taube, 978-0-7643-1308-0

782 Gear: United States Marine Corp and Field Gear and Equipment of World War II, by Harlan Glenn, 978-0-7643-3355-2

9 mm Parabellum: The History and Development of the World's 9 mm Pistols & Ammunition, by Klaus-Peter Konig and Martin Hugo, 978-08874-0342-2

Designed by Molly Shields
Cover design by Justin Watkinson
Type set in City Medium/Times New Roman

ISBN: 978-0-7643-5049-8
Printed in The United States of America

Published by Schiffer Publishing, Ltd.
4880 Lower Valley Road
Atglen, PA 19310
Phone: (610) 593-1777; Fax: (610) 593-2002
E-mail: Info@schifferbooks.com

For our complete selection of fine books on this and related subjects, please visit our website at www.schifferbooks.com. You may also write for a free catalog.

Schiffer Publishing's titles are available at special discounts for bulk purchases for sales promotions or premiums. Special editions, including personalized covers, corporate imprints, and excerpts, can be created in large quantities for special needs. For more information, contact the publisher.

We are always looking for people to write books on new and related subjects. If you have an idea for a book, please contact us at proposals@schifferbooks.com.

Contents

Preface and Acknowledgments

This reference guide is based heavily on an array of previously published sources. Retrieving those resources involved the cooperation of numerous institutions and people, and this guide to mobile artillery would not have been possible without the active assistance of many others.

First and foremost, I would like to thank my cooperator, Tom Batha. Tom's contributions have been beyond supportive. While he joined my efforts after the project began and most of the research was already accomplished, he has been so helpful in the latter phases that I have listed him on the cover and title pages. Like me, he is an enthusiastic researcher of memorial guns and a collector and restorer of military equipment. Tom's knowledge of what still exists in the "field" proved invaluable in describing the status of various guns. His additions and corrections to the early draft have kept it both more accurate and more readable. As we approached publication, his help in selecting an appropriate scope and detail level usually proved to be the correct alternative. I appreciate Tom's assistance on all levels.

Alex Holder was indispensable in finding sources and esoteric fragments of information needed to fill gaps here and there. Perhaps more valuable is his understanding of the art and practice of being an "artilleryman." On many occasions he prevented me from running astray on the facts of the organization, deployment, and combat use of US Army artillery. His continuous coaching, prodding, and encouragement were always valued.

I also wish credit to David Kirchner for his assistance. A friend for many years, David is an indefatigable researcher of American breechloaders. He shared much of his insight about the location of holdings at the National Archives. He contributed his own findings about the acquisition of artillery during the First World War and the development of light infantry guns immediately following that conflict. Finally, his continuous urging that "someone should do a book" were in part responsible for motivating me to attempt just that.

The facts in this book originate from two distinct sources. Military (navy in addition to the obvious army sources) technical manuals, pamphlets, and other publications were originally produced to accompany the weapons themselves. As instructions for use and repair, most of the description of what the guns were, how they were constructed, their major parts, and service performance were routinely reported in these publications.

While today some are more commonly encountered than others, they are generally locatable at selective military libraries. As a whole, they provided the technical descriptions and performance characteristic tables.

Narrative about production orders and facilities, deployment and combat use, and the rationale for acquiring the weapons was more difficult to research. Most of this information has never been reported in secondary sources, and had to be extracted from the correspondence files of the army's ordnance department and the navy's bureau of ordnance. These files exist only as original paper files at two central National Archive facilities in downtown Washington, DC, and College Park, Maryland. I have enjoyed the professional cooperation of a long line of archivists at the military records divisions of these institutions. In particular, I am grateful to Mark Mollan at the Washington DC, NARA I facility for active assistance not just in pulling boxes of files but in suggesting more elusive holdings and help in locating them.

Most of the illustrations come from two sources. The gun plans are from official US Army or Navy ordnance technical publications. In later years these drawings were generally replaced by clear photographs in which the background clutter has been eliminated. In a few cases the drawings came from a publication produced by a private contractor or supplier. Those publications are listed in the bibliography. Photographs showing each gun during the time of its service are primarily from public domain holdings at the National Archives and Records Service (Still Photos Division, Archives II, College Park, Maryland). Thank you to the staff members of that department for endlessly indulging my requests. In particular, Holly Reed and Ruth Beamon were extremely helpful on numerous occasions. In a few cases, photographs were sourced from the National Park Service holdings. The collection of the Sandy Hook unit of the Gateway National Recreation Area was especially valuable. Thank you to the staff members for making available their collection of photos dating from Sandy Hook's years as the army's proving ground.

I am pleased to say that I am part of a small group of enthusiasts who track down and validate the existence of memorial guns in the United States. We give thanks to Richard Pope for starting the great "WW1 Memorial Survey." His tireless efforts to enlist partners in finding, photographing, and otherwise documenting older breechloading artillery have certainly made things easier for the rest of us. I shot all of the photographs of surviving guns while visiting the collections. However, I received invaluable advice on collections and locations from fellow explorers Charles Bugajsky, Roger Davis, C. B. Drennon, Mike Fiorini, Alan Hardey, and Ivan Hlavacek.

American military museums are notably generous in allowing photography in their establishments and granting use of those images in publications. I have tried to identify each establishment in the photo captions. I would like to thank two organizations in particular for allowing me to photograph their outstanding collections: Rock Island Arsenal Museum in Rock Island, Illinois, and the US Army Artillery Museum at Fort Sill, Oklahoma. A third outstanding collection of American artillery ordnance was formerly at the US Army Ordnance Museum at Aberdeen, Maryland. Unfortunately, that museum closed in 2010 before moving the ordnance school to Fort Lee, Virginia. Parts of the collection have been moved to Fort Sill and other depots, but much remains in storage, anticipating a new facility at Fort Lee. The hope is that some of the unique items in the collection will be put on public display in the near future.

Thanks also to Lynden Couvillion at the Fort Sill Artillery Museum for use of his photograph of the newly restored 3.2-inch converted rifle; Constance Beninghove of the National Museum of the United States Navy for the photograph of the 6-pounder naval field gun; the Dahlgren Heritage Museum at Dahlgren, Virginia, for its photo of the 7-inch tracked MkII gun; and Donald Lutz for allowing me to use the photograph of his collection's 3-inch naval 500-pound breechloading howitzer. In a few cases, period postcards represent the only remaining photographic images of certain guns. I wish to thank Karl W. Schmidt for making his thorough collection available and granting permission to reproduce it here.

Despite our best efforts, occasional errors of interpretation or its transfer to the written page may occur. Any such mistakes are entirely of my own making.

Introduction

The technical aspects of American mobile artillery have received relatively little historical coverage. While descriptions of combat usage in various campaigns have been adequately reported, the story of the weapons themselves has largely been overlooked. Questions arise: what guns were acquired? How many and from which producers? How did they perform? How long did they serve? What did they look like? Do any survive today? It also seems that virtually nothing has been published about the early generations of modern breechloading field guns of both the US Army and Navy. This book aims to address these deficiencies.

It is certainly not a definitive history of US artillery. Even for individual guns, technical manuals and sometimes secondary histories exist that are much more detailed than what is presented here. This should be viewed as a sort of illustrated directory or quick-reference identification guide to the various types of American mobile field artillery used in the modern era.

Scope

The most difficult challenge in compiling this work was the issue of scope. There is an obligation to make the choices logical and apply some sense of systematic coverage. In this volume, the intent was to provide coverage of a temporal span (modern breechloading artillery from 1875 to the Korean War, about 1953) and on a subject span. For the latter, I chose to cover artillery used by US military services in accompanying or supporting field operations. Essentially that has meant army field and siege artillery, anti-tank artillery, and naval landing guns. Not included are more fixed weapons used by coast artillery and anti-aircraft artillery. Mode of transport was also considered. The work basically covers wheeled guns (and those transported with wheels to their field emplacement), and not those that were on self-propelled mounts. Finally, portable weapons meant to support infantry, particularly in the two world wars, are not covered. While weapons like smoothbore mortars, rifle grenades, bazookas, and recoilless rifles certainly project explosive charges and have other attributes of artillery, they are best treated in other types of works and not covered here.

A case can be made for making exceptions to these seemingly arbitrary decisions about what to include and exclude. However, at some point in a work like this, a decision needs to be made—often influenced by a need to keep the work a manageable size.

Format

In general the work is organized into chapters in approximately chronological order by category or generation of guns. Each section has an introductory page, generally followed by three pages on each gun type. For each type, there is a summary containing a brief history of the gun's development and use, following by a technical description with particular attention to innovative or distinguishing characteristics, and information on how many were produced and by which arsenal or firm. Finally, there is brief commentary on service use, combat experience, and when they were discarded, along with surviving examples. Interspersed with the text is a sketch or diagram of the gun (scale varies) and a table of major gun characteristics. Sometimes it was necessary to select a specific mark or model of the gun as the source for technical data. In those cases, the model is designated in the table heading, though production quantities and builders always apply to the entire type. Also, there is usually a photo of the gun from its period of active service and an illustration of a good surviving example.

In some cases, existing documentation does not allow this format to be precisely followed. In those cases, additional or substitute illustrations were frequently used. Where technical details were lacking for gun characteristics, the entry line is omitted. At times production quantity, or quantity made by the producing firm, was not available or the numbers seemed inadequate. Many guns acquired right after the First World War, particularly where contracts were extended into 1919 and 1920, have published production quantities that seem too low. Perhaps surprisingly, that is also true for guns after the Second World War, where many continued in sporadic production up through the 1950s. Some accounts report only numbers made for field artillery and not for self-propelled mounts or other types of mounting. Another confusing statistic for this period is the number of guns made for, or actually transferred to, allies under lend-lease or direct sale. In most cases, they represent the best number available, but undoubtedly there are some inaccuracies. The "number aquired" was an attempt to characterize the number actually obtained by the US Army, versus the number of guns ordered by other countries. However, when the army issued a contract to build a gun, I listed the total made, even if some went to lend-lease partners.

Sources

A technical compilation such as this does not lend itself to the usual liberal referencing with footnotes. So many technical facts and statements are made that referencing even just the most important ones would be impractical. Because many of the statistical facts are taken from a few official service publications, and information about production sources and numbers comes from succinct archival files, it seemed better to simply include a descriptive "sources consulted" in the bibliography. Information about the number of surviving guns and some of their location references had been compiled by the various authors and does not exist in a verifiable source.

Likewise, the photos and plans are not individually cited. Plans are taken from service technical manuals and drawings. For clarity, most have been cleaned of identifying detail labels, which would not be readable on such small reproductions. All the period photos are from public domain archival sources. Most are from the holdings of the National Archives, Still Photos Branch, College Park, Maryland. Additional sources are the Naval History and Heritage Command in Washington, DC, and the US Army Heritage and Education Center at Carlisle Barracks, Pennsylvania. All current photographs of surviving examples were taken by the authors.

Designations

Rigorous discipline was exercised in utilizing the actual designation for marks, models, and descriptive sizes of guns. During the First World War, the US Army changed most (though not all) of its gun bore sizes to metric measurement. No attempt was made to express the designations in both systems—what the service used at the time of that particular weapon is what is quoted here. Likewise, the US system for range (yards) and weight (pounds) is adhered to. For some earlier guns, particularly those sourced from British firms and early naval types, the designation "pound" for bore size was sometimes retained. In those cases, the physical measurement is provided in the text or in the table of gun characteristics included in each section. The army and navy used their own systems to designate guns by size and model or make. Later, types were usually given a "modifications" designator to indicate significant changes in the design. This guide is not intended to give full descriptions to each modification, or even to mention them unless they resulted in a significant change in performance or appearance.

The First New Breechloaders

Production of field artillery during the Civil War had been nothing less than prodigious. In quantity at least, no more guns were needed immediately following the end of war in 1865. Moreover, the nature of the conflict masked the requirement for technical performance improvements. The relatively wooded terrain of the major operating theaters negated the need for longer-range guns. In most battles, the effective range was limited by the ability to physically see the enemy, and thus in the major encounters the older (and more reliable) bronze muzzleloading smoothbores performed as well as the limited numbers of more modern pieces available. The few samples of modern field artillery acquired from Armstrong and Whitworth did not prove decisive, particularly considering the state of technological development.

While the US Army was initially content with its considerable inventory (over 4,000 cannons) following the conflict, things soon changed. In Europe, the 1860s saw the continued rapid development of technological innovation for field artillery. There were plenty of campaigns to demonstrate the advantages of steel for ordnance production, and the operational superiority of rifled breechloading soon became apparent. The obvious excellence of Prussian steel breechloading artillery over the conventional French artillery during the Franco-Prussian War in 1870–71 sent shock waves through armies around the world. America was no exception.

The postwar American army had just five regiments of artillery, each consisting of a battery of 12-pounder muzzleloaders and one of 3-inch, rifled, but still muzzleloading ordnance rifles. An ordnance board created in 1868 urged the army to test and recommend breechloading field guns. Under the leadership of ordnance chief Stephen V. Benét, the army's ordnance department soon began to improve its field and mountain artillery weapons. Faced with the huge inventory of existing guns and little prospect of new appropriations, the service attempted to develop a new gun using existing resources. The result was the conversion of the Model 1861 3-inch ordnance rifle into a breechloading field gun. This new and relatively successful gun was indeed designed, but only a few were ever produced. Technology was moving too fast, and the gun lacked the full set of characteristics to be competitive.

Curiously, the conversion of this older gun to a serviceable piece found utility some twenty years later. Looking to affordably acquire a number of post saluting guns, the ordnance department remembered the efforts of the 1880s. In the early 1900s, quite a few "new" breechloading saluting guns were constructed using the still-numerous Civil War ordnance rifles. While this gun is not strictly mobile artillery, it is covered here for completeness and to assist in distinguishing it from the similar field piece.

The US Navy was the real groundbreaker of steel breechloading artillery. As early as 1874 it began to produce competitive designs of bronze versus forged steel rifled breechloading guns to replace its old Dahlgren boat howitzers. The first domestic "new generation" mobile breechloaders in America came from this effort (see chapter on Navy Field and Landing Guns).

3.2-Inch Converted Rifle

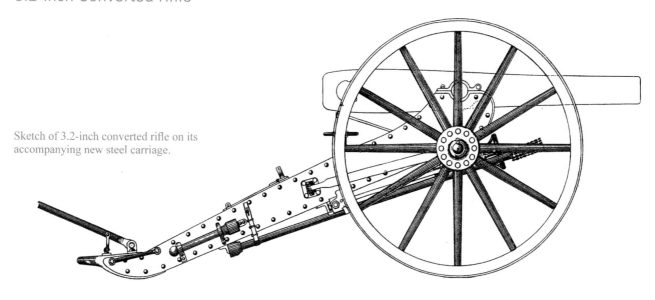

Sketch of 3.2-inch converted rifle on its accompanying new steel carriage.

In the late 1870s, the US Army began to realize that its substantial inventory of Civil War-era field guns was becoming obsolete in light of foreign developments. Clearly, rifled guns made of steel were being proven on European battlefields. Subjected to inadequate congressional appropriations, the ordnance department tried to come up with an economical solution that offered at least marginal improvement in gun performance. This led to efforts to turn the 3-inch Model 1861 ordnance rifle produced during the war into a breechloader. Almost 1,000 of these highly successful, wrought-iron, rifled muzzle-loading guns had been produced during the Civil War and most were still in active army service or stored by the ordnance department.

The prototype conversion was constructed in 1879. Ordnance rifle No. 914 had its breech end cut off and replaced with a new steel breech receiver holding a sliding breechblock, which was screwed into a recess bored into the old tube. The new 25-inch steel insert was made by Midvale Steel, with the assembly work done at West Point Foundry. The gun kept its 3-inch bore with seven grooves and lands. After evaluation, a second gun was fabricated in 1880. Rifle No. 774 was also converted at West Point Foundry. Changes involved using a new breechblock shape (cylindrical-prismatic), reaming to 3.18 inches, and cutting twenty-two new grooves with a uniform twist of one in seven. As it turned out, the bore dimensions were inexact, and later it was ground out to a bore of 3.2 inches. A new carriage and limber were also constructed for

this gun. The carriage was simple, composed of two spaced cheek plates (made by Nashua Steel Works) made of 3/16-inch-thick steel. Other parts were made of cast iron (lunette and axle supports), and it had wooden wheels and steel tires with Archibald wheel hubs.

Successful firing trials of this prototype led to orders for six more guns. This time they were inscribed on the muzzle face with new dates and serial numbers, running from No. 1 through No. 6. Incorporating the design features of their immediate predecessor, they were converted at the West Point Foundry in 1881–1882. Bore was standardized at 3.2 inches, and the piece used a Hotchkiss-type, banded projectile of just over 15 pounds. Quantities of ammunition were also procured.

Despite the ordnance department's initial enthusiasm, further orders for conversions were not forthcoming. In fact, the project was soon overtaken by the development of the all-steel 3.2-inch General Service Model gun fabricated in 1884. The guns were proof-fired and then released to the service in fiscal year 1884 (July 1883 through June 1884). However, they spent their limited lives in storage at various ordnance facilities, most notably Fort Monroe. They never saw active use after their trials and were eliminated from the army's inventory by 1900. Thus, while it was a dead-end development, the rather peculiar choice of the 3.2-inch bore size and resultant ammunition led directly to the army's selection of this size for the first true generation of new breechloading field artillery guns.

A surviving 3.2-inch Model 1861 rifle conversion has been restored at the US Army Artillery Museum at Fort Sill. The breechblock is in the open position.

3.2-Inch Converted Rifle

Gun Characteristics

Bore size: 3.2 inches

Construction: Wrought-iron tube, steel breech insert

Tube length overall: 72.65 inches

Nominal caliber: 20.2 calibers

Tube and breech weight: 826 pounds

Usual carriage: 3.2-inch BLR field carriage

Weight of gun and carriage: 2,015 pounds w/o implements

Maximum elevation: 20 degrees

Loading: Separate

Shell weight: 15.4 pounds

Maximum muzzle velocity: 1,460 fps

Maximum range: 5,800 yards

Builders: Original iron tube by Phoenix Iron Co., steel breech insert by Midvale Steel, asssembly by West Point Foundry

Number built: 1 3-inch prototype, 1 3.18-inch prototype, 6 3.2-inch production

3-Inch Saluting Gun

Around 1900, the need arose for a safe saluting gun for use at army posts for ceremonial duties and morning and evening salutes. A variety of old muzzleloading guns (usually the familiar 3-inch Model 1861 ordnance rifle and 12-pounder bronze smoothbore gun) were being used. They were deemed unsafe; serious accidents were occurring at an increasing rate. Existing orders prescribed a breechloading gun for this purpose, but there were not enough available, at least in excess of active unit armament. Consequently the ordnance department proposed to convert old 3-inch Model 1861 rifled guns to serviceable breechloaders.

The conversions were in some ways similar to those for the first 3.2-inch field guns made in the 1880s, but much simpler. No large steel insert was necessary; the conversions simply involved cutting off the old breech end and inserting a small steel sleeve into the chamber sized to hold a standard 6-pounder cartridge case. For simplicity and economy, a sliding block was devised based on the Hotchkiss mountain gun design. A squared-off slot (though examples of cylindrical variety also exist) was cut into the side of the breech to accommodate the steel sliding breechblock. Firing was done with a friction primer to avoid the $30 unit cost of a percussion firing mechanism. The carriage adopted was a cast iron pedestal cage-stand reminiscent of navy shipboard stands, allowing limited elevation and traverse.

Production of the necessary parts was undertaken with the American and British Manufacturing Company of Bridgeport, Connecticut, and a lesser number with the nearby United States Rapid-Fire Gun and Powder Company. Actual modification of the gun was simple enough to be accomplished at the forts where the gun was to be used—often the site where a 3-inch ordnance rifle already was located and where it could subsequently stay. Army cards recorded the forts as the gun production site.

Designs were finalized in late 1902. Exact numbers vary by source, but well over 200 saluting gun conversions were built. In fiscal year 1903, twenty sets of parts were completed and distributed, and 120 more were under contract. Additional orders followed from 1904 through 1907. The conversion did not entail any re-numbering of the guns; they retained their

A 3-inch saluting gun on display at Fort Warren, Boston Harbor. Many examples of this gun on its relatively simple cage stand still exist.

The 3-inch saluting gun on post at Fort Mills, Philippine Islands, in the 1930s.

original 1861–1865 manufacturing data, inspector marks, and serial numbers on their muzzle faces.

In their saluting role, many of these conversions lasted until the early 1930s. In 1932, the army moved to replace these obsolete converted pieces due to the dwindling stock of 6-pounder cartridge cases. The guns then were made available for ornamental or donation purposes.

The abundance of these converted guns and wide-spread distribution to various posts has meant that a considerable number survive. Generally not reported in historical texts as American field pieces, more than once they have been misidentified, and even mistakenly sold as one of the relatively rare 3.2-inch conversions from twenty years earlier—which they certainly resemble from the exterior. However, a close examination reveals that they have the 3-inch bore (not 3.2 inches), and the cut-out for the (often missing) breech mechanism is rectangular, rather than partially curved or cylindrical-prismatic. In some cases, Civil War re-enactors have changed the saluting gun conversions back to their original Model 1861 appearance.

3-Inch Saluting Gun

Gun Characteristics

Bore size: 3 inches

Construction: Wrought iron, steel breechblock

Tube length overall: 72 inches

Nominal caliber: Not applicable

Tube and breech weight: 725 pounds

Usual carriage: Cast iron saluting cage stand

Weight of gun and carriage: 1,340 pounds

Maximum elevation: Not applicable

Loading: Fixed

Shell weight: Not applicable

Maximum muzzle velocity: Not applicable

Maximum range: Not applicable

Builders: Original gun by Phoenix Iron Co., conversions done by American and British Manufacturing and United States Rapid-Fire Gun and Power Co.

Number built: Approximately 200+

Close-up ordnance department photograph of the breech mechanism for the 3-inch saluting gun.

3.2-Inch Field Guns

In 1882, the army began designing its first all-steel breechloading rifled gun. Even though it was a significantly different development, much had been learned from converting the ordnance rifle to a breechloader. The department worked up its own design, and Midvale Steel approached to supply the annealed steel forgings. The prototype gun was begun in 1883 and delivered for successful trials beginning in March 1884. An all-steel carriage was designed simultaneously.

Multiple batches of guns were ordered from 1885 to 1899, and three primary types were made—Models 1885, 1890, and 1897. All were bag guns with the powder contained in a separate cloth bag. The first two models used black powder, while the final model had a smaller chamber and used smokeless powder. Altogether, 372 were made. As the army's designation system hadn't quite settled down, there are at least four different serial number sequences for these guns. A supplier might be authorized to start a new sequence dedicated to its particular run (such as for Watertown Arsenal, and the American Ordnance Company), or the guns were assigned serial numbers from a longer sequence. Forgings came mostly from Midvale Steel and Bethlehem Steel, but finished guns came from Watertown Arsenal, Watervliet Arsenal, West Point Foundry, and the American Ordnance Company.

There was no perceived need for a large field artillery force. The quantity of guns funded by Congress was tiny compared to European standards. At the start of the Spanish-American War, the US army had a small complement of 3.2-inch guns, including a reasonable quantity of spares. It was also in the middle of converting from black powder to smokeless powder as a propellant—and was moving from the older Model 1890 gun to the smokeless-capable Model 1897. When the war started, two unsettling shortages developed: There were no spare carriages to use with the stock of extra gun tubes, and additional harness was also scarce. The other shortage stemmed from problems in ramping up smokeless powder production. This was so severe that the army had to send its older Model 1885 and 1890 guns into the field simply because they used the only readily available powder. Fortunately, the war was not much of a land contest, and while the army learned some tough lessons, victory was never in question.

After the new 3-inch guns appeared, the existing 3.2s began transferring to militia, training, and reserve stocks. In 1903, the militia reported seventy-three 3.2-inch guns being used. At the start of the First World War there were still 362 3.2-inch guns on hand, though few were in active regiments. Many were used as training guns in stateside posts; quite a few others were issued to coastal defenses as auxiliary land-defense guns (including, with some controversy, Hawaiian and Philippine defenses). Finally on June 16, 1919, the chief of ordnance declared the guns obsolete and authorized their disposal as donations to the Grand Army of the Republic (GAR) posts and municipalities. Fortunately that has meant that more than a few still exist on display—and numerous others are in private hands.

In the late nineteenth century, it was the ordnance department's practice to fabricate new guns to test innovations, in addition to converting existing guns. Consequently, at least four new 3.2-inch guns with improvements were made, all at Watervliet. In 1892, that arsenal produced one with a Driggs-Schroeder breech and another with a Gerdom breech. In 1896 and 1903, it built new 3.2-inch guns fitted with experimental breeches for fixed ammunition. A couple of these conversions also still exist.

3.2-Inch Gun Model 1885

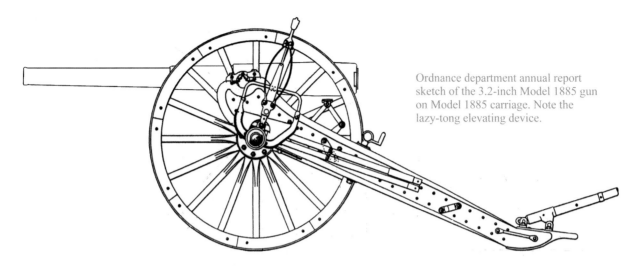

Ordnance department annual report sketch of the 3.2-inch Model 1885 gun on Model 1885 carriage. Note the lazy-tong elevating device.

This first modern field gun was made of gun steel and composed of a tube, jacket, and jacket sleeve in front of a trunnion hoop. The tube had twenty-four grooves and was rifled at ⅟₃₀ (rifling is defined as one complete turn or twist in "x" inches of bore length—in this case one complete twist in 30 inches). Designed for separate, bagged charges, the powder chamber was ellipsoid rather than cylindrical. It had a carrier ring holding the breechblock and DeBange-type obturator pad. The first twenty-five guns had the Freye-type closure, but they were soon changed to the DeBange style. The block had just three threaded sections. The vent was placed radially. The gun was supplied with 13.5-pound cast iron shells, shrapnel, or canister. These Model 1885 guns were marked on the muzzle face with manufacturer, year, serial number, inspector initials, and weight. The model number and gun size appeared on the face of the left trunnion. Carriage serial number and date were inscribed on a carriage plate, and the rear trail upper surface also contained the year and serial number. The initials US appeared on the upper tube surface between the trunnions. This gun used a bronze front sight seated on the rim base and a removable rear transom sight near the breech.

The carriage was entirely metal (except the wheel spokes). It was simply constructed with steel side flasks and five connecting transoms. Initially, the axle was hollow and was later made solid. It used Archibald wheels 57.75 inches in diameter. There was no system to check the recoil. However,

Army photograph of an early 3.2-inch gun with ammunition limber in traveling mode. This unit lacks the obvious brake mechanism.

it had distinctive brakes. When not in use, they were raised over the top of the wheel; when shifted and applied, they could be used either as a recoil or traveling brake. Elevation was made initially with a lazy-tong apparatus, though in later models a simple screw was used. A new type of limber, caisson (carrying a spare wheel), and battery wagon completed the suite of new vehicles. Models 1885 and 1892 were two of the carriages used with this gun. Originally, the gun was simply referred to (and marked as such on the guns) as the General Service Model, with no model year designation. The term Model 1885 wasn't used until a few years later. The same situation applied to carriage. First production orders were issued in 1885 for five guns made at Watertown Arsenal (Nos. 1–5) delivered in 1888–1889, followed by twenty from the West Point Foundry (Nos. 6–25 delivered in 1889). Seventy-five more were ordered from Watervliet Arsenal in batches in 1887, 1889, and 1891. These were designated as Model 1885 and carried serial numbers 1–75. The characteristics of these 100 guns were the same.

The gun did see service, though accounts of activities from 1898–1902 usually just mention the bore size of the weapons involved, not the precise model type. Sent with the expedition to Cuba were four light batteries from the 1st and 2nd Artillery Regiments, each with four 3.2-inch guns. A number of 3.2-inch guns were also sent to the Philippines, and subsequently augmented as the war turned into the Philippine insurrection from 1899–1902. Finally, 3.2s saw action with the relief column sent to Peking in 1900 during the Boxer Rebellion. Model 1885s were on hand with active batteries as late as 1906–07, but were soon shifted to instructional roles. They were classified obsolete in 1919 and subsequently scrapped or donated as memorial pieces.

3.2-Inch Gun Model 1885

Gun Characteristics

Bore size: 3.2 inches

Construction: Built-up steel

Tube length overall: 90.72 inches

Nominal caliber: 26 calibers

Tube and breech weight: 829 pounds

Usual carriage: 3.2-inch gun carriage Model 1885 and 1892

Weight of gun and carriage: 2,129 pounds

Maximum elevation: 20 degrees

Loading: Separate

Shell weight: 13.5 pounds

Maximum muzzle velocity: 1,685 fps

Maximum range: 6,531 yards

Builders: Gun: Watertown Arsenal (5), West Point Foundry (20), Watervliet Arsenal (75); carriage: Springfield Arsenal, Rock Island Arsenal

Number built: 100

A nicely restored early Model 1885 3.2-inch gun on display at the Rock Island Arsenal Museum. Note the two distinct barrel hoops and the brakes in their upright repose.

3.2-Inch Field Gun Model 1890 and 1897

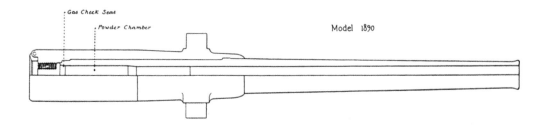

Comparison of the Model 1890 (and similar Model 1897) gun tube with the Model 1885 tube for the 3.2-inch guns.

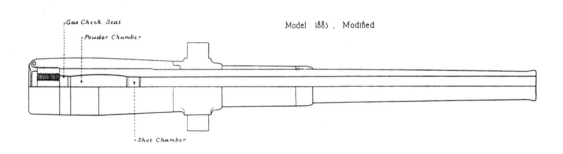

The subsequent order for additional 3.2-inch guns was filled using the Model 1890. There were two primary changes. The tube construction was simplified and consisted of just the tube and jacket, the latter holding the trunnions. From an appearance standpoint, the M1890 appears to have a single additional hoop on the tube versus two hoops for the M1885. Also, this gun had a cylindrical powder chamber. The vent was placed on the axial position versus radial. Other small changes were made in weight and length. A change was also made in rifling, increasing from $\frac{1}{50}$ to $\frac{1}{25}$. Still, the muzzle velocity, range, and performance were the same. Incremental improvements were

also made in the carriage and vehicles. New carriages in this series were labeled Model 1892.

Orders were placed for 160 M1890 guns starting in late 1891 and running through 1897. Deliveries were made from 1893 to 1898. They were numbered No. 1–160. Later a new series was produced, known as the Model 1897. These were similar but had a smaller chamber to accommodate the new smokeless powder. Plans were made to upgrade the recently completed Model 1890 guns to the Model 1897 standard. All 3.2-inch guns fired separate ammunition—the shell was inserted, followed by a pre-measured bag of powder. The chamber size

Photograph taken in Cuba during the Spanish-American War of an army 3.2-inch gun from directly behind.

needed for smokeless powder was roughly half that needed for black powder. Modification of Model 1890 involved inserting a lining into the chamber, reducing the size. Virtually all M1890s (but not the older Model 1885) were so converted. In fact, they were reclassified as Model 1897s. Some authors have missed the fact that 160 M1890s were made and served before being modified and reclassified as M1897s. The conversion was completed between 1898 and 1899. The final Model 1897s (and a number of M1890s still being fabricated when the change was ordered) had chambers originally configured for smokeless powder.

New orders for seventy-five guns were issued (all from Watervliet, Nos. 161–236) and delivered from 1898 to 1900. Finally, a run of thirty-six Model 1897 guns were ordered from the American Ordnance Company. They were numbered separately from No. 1 to No. 36 and delivered from 1899 to 1902. Altogether, 272 guns were made to either the Model 1890 or 1897 standard, though a couple were diverted or lost in trials along the way. All but the last twenty-two guns were made from Midvale forgings.

The early-production Model 1890 guns served along with Model 1885s in the Spanish-American War battlefields of Cuba and the Philippines, as well as the Boxer Rebellion. The gun was widely used by the regular army and state militias in the early 1900s. Twelve were even sold to Massachusetts. However, without a mechanism to check the recoil and unable to use fixed ammunition, their usefulness quickly diminished when the Model 1902 3-inch series began to appear. Like their earlier cousins, the later 3.2-inch field guns were relegated to training and institutional roles during the First World War. They, too, were declared obsolete in 1919, and in 1920 began being collected from dispersed posts and arsenals. From there, they were scrapped or distributed as memorial guns—although there are some reports that a few persisted in neglected depots for many more years.

3.2-Inch Gun Model 1897

Gun Characteristics

Bore size: 3.2 inches

Construction: Built-up steel

Tube length overall: 87.72 inches

Nominal caliber: 26 calibers

Tube and breech weight: 830 pounds

Usual carriage: 3.2-inch gun carriage model 1892

Weight of gun and carriage: 2,130 pounds

Maximum elevation: 20 degrees

Loading: Separate

Shell weight: 13.5 pounds

Maximum muzzle velocity: 1,685 fps

Maximum range: 6,531 yards

Builders: Gun: Watervliet Arsenal (Nos. 1–236), American Ordnance (Nos. 1–36); carriage: Rock Island Arsenal

Number built: 272 built new (M1897) or converted from M1890 and M1890M.

A surviving 3.2-inch Model 1897 gun on Model 1898 carriage in Abilene, Texas. At least thirty-two guns of the Model 1897 standard still exist on display, and at least six others are in private hands.

Developing a New Artillery System 1900–1917

At the end of the nineteenth century US Army thought turned toward a progressive system of gun sizes based on doubling shell weight. The new standard field gun would hurl a 15-pound projectile, and a 3-inch bore size best fit this requirement. A doubled, 30-pound shell could be delivered by either a 3.8-inch gun or howitzer. The shell size for 4.7-inch gun or howitzer was 60 pounds, and 120 pounds was the approximate projectile weight for a 6-inch howitzer. All of these sizes were subsequently developed for American field and siege artillery.

These years saw the rapid technical development of artillery. Throughout the world, smokeless powder came into widespread use and nations adopted cased or "fixed" ammunition, at least for lighter guns to increase the rate of fire. To withstand the increase in power, guns were made of high-quality alloy (at this stage mostly nickel) steel. Finally, guns were stabilized with hydraulic pistons instead of simple ground spades to moderate the severe recoil. Guns like the French 75 mm became famous for breaking new ground and giving its operators a substantial battlefield advantage.

By 1900, efforts were underway to develop a replacement for the 3.2-inch gun. It had become quite obvious that the new gun would need to have a long-recoil mechanism to minimize displacement between firing. In July 1900, bids were requested for 200 steel forgings for what would become the Model 1900 3-inch gun, though without a modern recoil system. Before any bids were accepted, the ordnance department changed its mind and cancelled the Model 1900 project. A subsequent design incorporated two additional requirements—one able to fire metallic, fixed ammunition, and the other to use stronger nickel-steel alloy in the tube and breech mechanism. This redesign, heavily influenced by a recently acquired Rheinische evaluation piece, led to the successful Model 1902 3-inch gun series. Without being innovative, the guns could compete with most foreign counterparts.

Three very similar models of standard regimental field guns were produced between 1900 and the First World War. For convenience, the US Army often referred to all three types as the Model 1902. While generally equipping separate regiments, the 3-inch guns had identical performance characteristics and experienced the same historical employment.

One of the main differences between the 1902 and later 3-inch models is the breech design. On the left is the Model 1902 breech, and on the right the Model 1904 and 1905 breech.

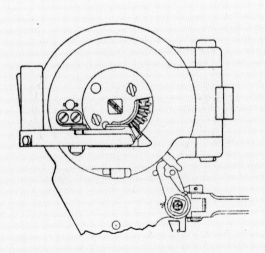
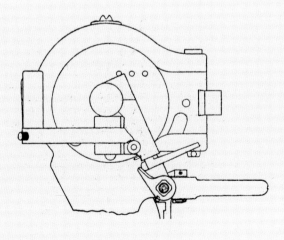

3-Inch Field Gun Models 1902, 1904, and 1905

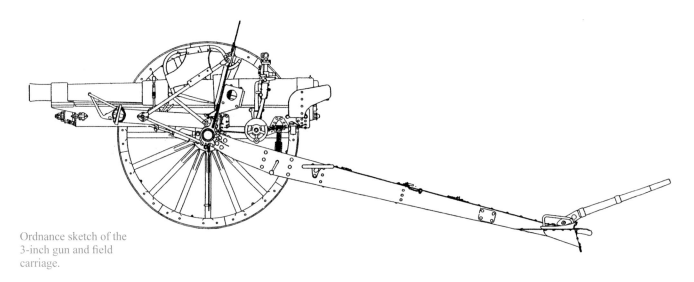

Ordnance sketch of the 3-inch gun and field carriage.

The Model 1902 gun was built with nickel steel, the first army use of this superior metal alloy. The tube was encased with a rear jacket and locking hoop. It had twenty-four lands and grooves, and rifling increased from $\frac{1}{50}$ to $\frac{1}{25}$. The gun had a Gerdom interrupted-screw breech mechanism with two slotted and two threaded sections. It opened to the right from a hinged block carrier. The guns fired fixed ammunition. Steel shell, common shrapnel, and an Ehrhardt high-explosive round were made available. For the first time, a long-recoil system was used to provide better stability during firing. Recoil was checked by a hydrospring within an oil-filled cylinder. Counterrecoil was provided with three nests of springs, and a spade was attached to the carriage trail. A double-screw elevating system provided elevation. Line sights were on the gun, and a Model 1904 panoramic sight accompanied each carriage for indirect fire.

The US Army had problems getting production started on this gun. In October 1902, it placed an order for forgings and produced fifty guns (Nos. 1–50) at Watervliet and carriages at Rock Island Arsenal. The next thirty-four (Nos. 51–84) were placed in May 1903 with American and British Manufacturing. Despite being sent to over twenty-five firms, the request for fifty guns did not receive an acceptable bid. It seems the production capacity of American cannon companies was simply inadequate for an order of this size. Consequently, the army received special permission to place the order with Rheinische Metalwaaren und Machinenfabrik of Dusseldorf, Germany. This firm had sold the army a prototype trials gun in 1901. Its offer was several thousand dollars less and had a shorter delivery time than any American bidder. The offer was accepted. The US Army was concerned that it had copied some of the Rheinische's patented features, and secured a release in return for its generous order. The guns (Nos. 85–134) were ordered

on June 1, 1903, and included carriages, limbers, accessories, and spare parts.

Additional quantities were ordered between 1904 and 1907. In 1911, Congress approved an appropriation to allow manufacture of spare guns on the basis of one per existing regiment. Even though the Model 1905 3-inch gun was in full production, to comply with the authorization, another seven model 1902 guns had to be ordered. In all, 181 guns Model 1902 (Nos. 1–181 inclusive) were produced between 1903 and 1912.

In late 1904 the army placed into production a slightly improved model. Model 1904 incorporated a superior Tasker breech. It had four sets of grooves/slots versus only two on the Model 1902. This meant a smoother operation for opening and closing. Also, the beveled gears on the breech face featured a metal cover to protect them from dirt. Performance was exactly the same as the Model 1902, and it used the same Model 1902 carriage and other artillery vehicles. Forty guns were produced from Bethlehem Steel forgings at the Watervliet Arsenal and delivered from June to October 1905. Curiously, all forty were procured using congressional funding for militia equipment. The army assigned them all to National Guard formations, and none were used in the regular army during their active service.

A year later, the Model 1905 entered production. While using the same improved Tasker breech as the 1904 type, it had two differences. The twist in rifling was increased from zero to $\frac{1}{25}$ until it was ten inches from the muzzle and then was uniform. Also, to counter-balance an increase in carriage weight, the gun weight was reduced by fifty pounds. This was accomplished by slightly reducing the overall tube thickness. The Model 1905 became the standard version of the 3-inch field gun.

Despite clear signs of European war preparation, appropriations for new artillery for both the regular army and militia remained small. Twenty orders for the Model 1905 gun were filled between 1905 and 1917, resulting in 441 guns. Lots were numbered sequentially, assigned serial numbers running from Nos. 1–441. Most forgings were provided by the well-known firms Bethlehem Steel and Midvale Steel. Guns were marked on the muzzle face with serial number, year of completion, weight, and inspector's initials. They were finished by the army's Watervliet Arsenal, American and British Manufacturing Company, and Bethlehem Steel.

All three models were carried on the same carriage. The ordnance department's Captain Charles B. Wheeler designed the Model 1902 field gun carriage. It was a straightforward, fixed trail carriage offering rugged simplicity as its best attribute. It had two standard 56-inch-diameter wheels with a 60-inch track. The carriage could provide 15-degree elevation and 5-degree depression. On-carriage traverse was limited to 8 degrees. A three-part shield, the top piece foldable and conspicuously notched for the gun barrel, was a first for American field guns. Two metal seats were attached on the left and right sides for gunner and cannoneer. Riding seats for these two crew members were attached to the shield facing forward. The seats were supported by two tubes fitted to carry a fixed round. These four rounds were immediately available for urgent firing. Accompanying vehicles were the Model 1902 limber, caisson, and store and forge wagons. A battery would be four guns and carriages; sixteen limbers; twelve caissons; forge, battery, and store wagons; and a store limber.

Production of the Model 1902 carriage generally kept pace with the guns. Most were made by the army's Rock Island Arsenal, though Rheinische, American and British Manufacturing,

3-Inch Gun Model 1902

Gun Characteristics

Bore size: 3 inches

Construction: Built-up nickel steel

Tube length overall: 87.8 inches

Nominal caliber: 28 calibers

Tube and breech weight: 835 pounds

Usual carriage: 3-inch gun carriage model 1902

Weight of gun and carriage: 2,520 pounds

Maximum elevation: 15 degrees

Loading: Fixed

Shell weight: 15 pounds

Maximum muzzle velocity: 1,700 fps

Maximum range: 6,500 yards at 15 degrees

Builders: Watervliet Arsenal (77), Rheinische (1 type gun + 50 production guns), American and British Manufacturing (34)

Number built: 181 + 1 type gun

A 3-inch Model 1905 gun of "B" Battery, Iowa Artillery, with the Mexican Punitive Expedition of 1916.

Surviving 3-inch gun Model 1902 in Columbia, Pennsylvania. Of the 181 guns fabricated, a surprising number still exist—over fifty have been located.

Model 1904 gun No. 2 in South Portland, Maine. Ten guns of this model are documented survivors.

A 3-inch Model 1905 gun (No. 174) in Newington, New Hampshire. Many guns of this model survive; over eighty-five are on display and several others are privately owned.

and Bethlehem Steel also produced carriages and limbers with their large gun orders. A plate on the carriage trail contained serial and manufacturing data. Most of these were sequentially assigned serial numbers, but a final series carried an appended "A." In the mid-1930s, a few carriages used by the New York Military Academy were modified with rubber tires and high-speed axles using Martin-Parry rigs purchased by the state in order to allow their use for training as truck-drawn artillery pieces. Four of these modified guns still exist.

As accepted, 3-inch guns replaced 3.2-inch weapons in both regular and National Guard regiments. All three types stayed in service simultaneously. However, the years before the First World War were unusually quiet. After the Philippine insurrection ended, the army was not involved in conflict. The Mexican Expedition of 1916–17 was the only place where 3-inch guns were deployed. Numerous batteries were dispatched to the border, but no American artillery was engaged. At the end of March 1917, there were 574 3-inch guns in service—96 with the regular army, 368 with the National Guard, 91 at depots and arsenals, and 19 at schools. However, in the First World War, the decision was made to use 75 mm guns of American or European types. The older-pattern 3-inch guns were not sent to France but retained at home for the training program.

After the war, the guns were maintained but not given extensive repairs. In 1925, they were removed from ROTC assignments. All remaining guns were declared obsolete in 1931 but kept as war reserve. Later they were issued as saluting guns to posts to replace the aging wrought-iron 3-inch saluting guns. This use saved many from immediate scrap and ensured numerous survivors beyond the Second World War.

3-Inch Gun Models 1904 and 1905

Gun Characteristics

Bore size: 3 inches

Construction: Built-up nickel steel

Tube length overall: 87.8 inches

Nominal caliber: 28 calibers

Tube and breech weight: M1904: 835 pounds; M1905: 788 pounds

Usual carriage: 3-inch gun carriage Model 1902

Weight of gun and carriage: M1904: 2,520 pounds, M1905: 2,475 pounds

Maximum elevation: 15 degrees

Loading: Fixed

Shell weight: 15 pounds

Maximum muzzle velocity: 1,700 fps

Maximum range: 6,500 yards at 15 degrees

Builders: Watervliet Arsenal, Bethlehem Steel, American and British Manufacturing

Number built: Model 1904: 40; Model 1905: 441

A 3-inch Model 1905 in army service. Note fixed rounds on either seat and opened tubes for the four rounds carried by the Model 1902 carriage.

Mountain Guns

In the nineteenth century, mountain guns proved to be a valuable weapon given the rough western terrain and the nature of frontier combat with Native Americans. The smoothbore army pattern 1841 mountain howitzer had seen considerable success in campaigns against the Indians, given its mobility in roadless countryside. After the Civil War, this type of weapon became a priority. Colonel Nelson Miles advocated a light field gun to replace the old mountain howitzers; the US Army purchased a Hotchkiss 1.65-inch gun in 1876. Intended to be a lightweight system for animal or human portage, the small bore made possible a lightweight shell so that a relatively large number of rounds could be carried. It was so simple that infantrymen and cavalry soldiers could use it without special training. The design helped set expectations for many projects to come.

Over the next thirty years, the US Army progressed through four mountain artillery designs. The first two types of guns were purchased examples of commercially offered guns—the 1.65-inch Hotchkiss mountain gun of the 1870s, followed by an improved model with a larger shell, the 3-inch Hotchkiss mountain gun. Driven by the sudden need to support operations in the Philippines, the army purchased yet another foreign-designed gun. In 1898, anticipating service in mountainous terrain with poor road infrastructure, the army accepted a new, small mountain gun from a British private concern—the 2.95-inch Vickers-Maxim mountain gun. Put into American production via license, some 120 guns of this type were acquired in 1898–1904. Attempts to perfect a domestic design never reached fruition. While five examples of the relatively advanced, long-recoil 3-inch Model 1911 (this time a true howitzer) were made, the type did not enter quantity production.

A considerable amount of testing and evaluation around the concept of mountain guns occurred in 1908–1912. A special mountain artillery board concluded that the type was useful to accompany infantry or cavalry where wheeled artillery couldn't go, or where rapid deployment was desirable in rough, hilly, or broken terrain. Certainly portability by animal or man was what distinguished the category. In fact, for the first time the board recommended the term "pack" instead of "mountain" as more appropriate to its envisioned use. There was also considerable debate about the advantages and disadvantages of howitzers versus guns. At least at this point guns were favored because of their longer range, faster muzzle velocity, and simplicity of service with fixed ammunition.

With the evaluation of the 3-inch mountain guns Model 1911, mostly accomplished in 1913–14, development of new designs ceased. As the country geared up for the First World War, mountain guns were low priority. When new projects were begun in the early 1920s–1930s, they were less focused on mountain operations than on a broader concept of easily transportable pack artillery.

1.65-Inch Hotchkiss Mountain Gun

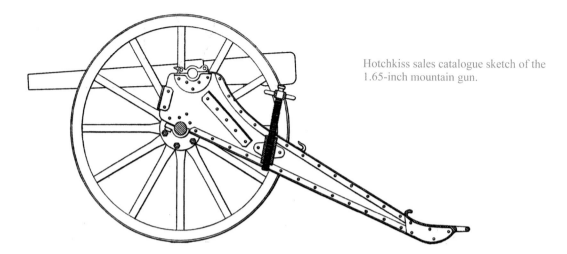

Hotchkiss sales catalogue sketch of the 1.65-inch mountain gun.

The little 1.65-inch Hotchkiss mountain gun was the first modern breechloader acquired by the US Army in the post-Civil War era. Made in Europe, the rather strange 1.65-inch size was the closest inch measurement to the 42 mm actual size. A trial gun was secured in 1876 and was soon subjected to field evaluation.

The tube was a single forging of oil-tempered, annealed steel. It was rifled with ten lands and grooves. The trunnion ring was screwed onto the tube. The breech housing was conical, with the sliding-wedge "Krupp-type" block withdrawing to the side. The steel carriage was simply made from two cheeks joined by transoms with a trail. The axle was carried in brackets riveted to the frame. It had 37.4-inch wheels. The carriage could give -5 to +15-degree elevation by way of an elevating screw directly under the breech. The gun used a simple fore sight at the trunnion and tangent sight on the breech.

The lightweight, simple construction met the requirements for ease of load. It took just two pack animals to carry—one for gun and one for carriage, plus a suggested two animals for ammunition. Typical battery size was six guns, but the limited deployment in the West usually meant that they were supplied in any number. The army purchased fifty-seven 1.65-inch guns, but one was lost overboard in transit to the United States. They were bought from Hotchkiss et Cie. (initially in Paris, but later guns were assembled at the Bridgeport factory of American Ordnance Company) over a prolonged period—from 1877 to May 1897—and cost $450. Along the way, there were a few incremental improvements, particularly with the ammunition. Fixed common shells with a brass cartridge case were supplied, along with a canister containing thirty lead balls. Serial number and date were marked on the top of the breechblock.

One of the 1.65-inch Hotchkiss mountain guns displayed as an ornamental piece in Honolulu in the 1930s. Supposedly it was used as a convenient prop for a publicity photo of visiting superstar Shirley Temple.

Despite the army's limited combat exposure after the Civil War, this gun did see combat. The trial gun acquired in 1876 was carried by Colonel Nelson Miles to the Battle of Bear Paw Mountain in October 1877. It was also used on several other occasions during the Indian Wars, such as in quelling the Crow uprising in Montana in 1887. Its most famous encounter was probably the battery of four 1.65-inch guns used at the Battle of Wounded Knee on December 29, 1890. At ranges as close as 50 yards, the effects were predictable. Small improvements were made in the 1890s, including adding a telescopic scope and improving the shell's bursting charge. While none were sent to Cuba in 1898, Bridgman's Battery (Light Battery G, 6th Artillery) carried four of the guns to the Philippines in August 1898. Others were brought by the 1st Artillery Regiment. These guns were involved in numerous engagements between 1899 and 1901. While they were certainly maneuverable, they were plagued with faulty ammunition and friction primers.

After being replaced with the 2.95-inch Vickers mountain gun, the old 1.65s still had a role to play as a reserve gun. Some were transferred to state militia units. In 1903, nine of the 1.65-inch guns were reportedly in reserve inventories (along with 3.2-inch field guns, one Hotchkiss revolving cannon, two naval landing guns, and numerous old 3-inch ordnance rifles and 12-pounder Napoleon smoothbore cannon). A handful were sold to the Treasury Department for use in the Pribilof Islands, safeguarding the sealing regulations. Several were still used as instructional pieces in 1908, but most were sold by auction or donated prior to the First World War. Eight were sold in 1908 to the commercial dealer Francis Bannerman. Additionally, Hotchkiss sold the gun to a number of European and Latin American countries, and collectors have imported some of those back into the US.

1.65-Inch Hotchkiss Mountain Gun

Gun Characteristics
Bore size: 1.65 inches (42 mm)
Construction: Steel
Tube length overall: 46.1 inches
Nominal caliber: 25 calibers
Tube and breech weight: 121 pounds
Usual carriage: Hotchkiss 1.65-inch carriage
Weight of gun and carriage: 341 pounds
Maximum elevation: 15 degrees
Loading: Fixed
Shell weight: 1 pound, 15 ounces
Maximum muzzle velocity: 1,345 fps (black powder)
Maximum range: 4,000 yards

Builders: Hotchkiss Ordnance Co.
Number acquired: 57

Many 1.65s survive, particularly in army museums and with private collectors. This example is at the Frontier Army Museum at Fort Leavenworth, Kansas.

3-Inch Hotchkiss Mountain Gun

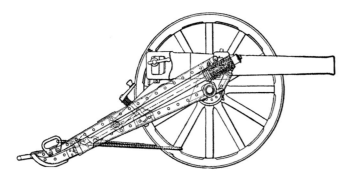

Ordnance textbook cut-away sketch of the 3-inch Hotchkiss mountain gun; note rope tied between spokes and trail to assist in braking the recoil.

In July 1889, Hotchkiss offered its newly developed 3-inch mountain gun. Building on the success of its 1.65-inch gun, the weapon was presented as a more powerful replacement—more in line with the capabilities of mountain guns used in Europe, but still lightweight and mobile. There was some discussion about whether this should be a 3.2-inch bore weapon like the new field guns, but because it wouldn't be able to fire the same ammunition anyway, the lighter 3-inch was acceptable. The army agreed with the need for increased performance and moved in 1890 to acquire a trials gun for $500. After the trial,

an order for a full battery was placed, soon followed by an additional order that brought the total acquisition to ten guns, carriages, limbers, and ammunition. All the guns were ordered between 1891 and 1892, but delivery from Hotchkiss took until 1894 to complete.

Its major components were similar to the army's previous gun, with a 3-inch bore and a short 14-caliber length. There were twenty-four grooves and lands; rifling was $\frac{1}{25}$.59. There was no compensation for recoil, which was checked simply with ropes running through the spokes of the wheels to the trail. The breech housing was square, unlike the cylindrical housing of the 1.65-inch gun, though it still used a sliding wedge closure. The carriage and trail had a simple steel plate assembly with iron rivets. It had 36-inch-diameter wheels and just a 24-inch-wide track. The gun fired cannon, shrapnel, or case canister as fixed rounds—ammunition unique to this gun. A friction primer was used to fire, though later the guns were modified for percussion firing.

Guns were marked with a serial number on the left trunnion face; carriage serial was on a plate on the trail. The one imported for trial carried Hotchkiss serial No. 168. Production guns had Nos. 403–412 made by American Ordnance Company. Usual pack loading was three mules—one each for gun, carriage, and wheels and accessories. A limber held four ammunition cases, each with eight shells, or thirty-two complete rounds.

An example of the operation of the 3-inch Hotchkiss mountain gun's elevating gear.

Some of the 3-inch Hotchkiss guns were issued in the Spanish-American War in 1898. The wealthy New Yorker John Jacob Astor IV financed the formation of a volunteer artillery unit. The "Astor Battery" was trained on six 3-inch Hotchkiss mountain guns on Long Island and then dispatched to the Philippines. Too late for the campaign against the Spanish, the guns were used during the subsequent Philippine insurrection. However, like their cousin, the 1.65-inch mountain gun, poor ammunition severely impacted their success in combat. The 47th Infantry couldn't get a single shrapnel shell to explode.

By 1904, these mountain guns were to be issued in emergency only. In 1908, several were still assigned as training guns at military schools. Apparently though, the army had already begun disposing them—two were sold in 1902 to Francis Bannerman for $18.88 apiece, and another pair was sold to the same dealer in 1908. It appears that at least four survive, all privately owned.

3-Inch Hotchkiss Mountain Gun

Gun Characteristics

Bore size: 3 inches

Construction: Steel

Tube length overall: 46.7 inches

Nominal caliber: 14 calibers

Tube and breech weight: 216 pounds

Usual carriage: Hotchkiss 3-inch mountain gun carriage

Weight of gun and carriage: 535 pounds

Maximum elevation: 20 degrees

Loading: Fixed

Shell weight: 12 pounds

Maximum muzzle velocity: 885 fps

Maximum range: 3,475 yards

Builders: Hotchkiss Ordnance Co.

Number acquired: 10

Only two surviving 3-inch Hotchkiss mountain guns are on display, both at Disneyland's Town Square in Anaheim, California. Several others are in private ownership.

2.95-Inch Vickers Mountain Gun

Originally designed by the Maxim-Nordenfelt Co. in England in 1896, this handy little mountain gun was taken over when Maxim merged with Vickers. The company designated it the 75 mm quick-firing mountain gun. It had a relatively short, 3-foot-long steel tube chambered for 75 mm ammunition. The tube had thirty lands and grooves and a uniform rifling of ¹⁄₂₅. A cylindrical cradle held the gun, with two hydraulic buffers, one on each side. The recuperators were two springs wrapped around each piston rod. It had only a 14-inch recoil length. The gun had a vicious recoil, and photographs show it jumping wildly into the air upon firing. The carriage used a simple screw to obtain a 27-degree elevation. There was no traversing possible, other than physically lifting and shifting the entire carriage. The guns were marked on the muzzle face (American manufacture) or on the upper tube casing (British manufacture); carriage data was on a plate affixed to the trail.

Three types of fixed rounds were supplied: common shot, shrapnel, and canister. The equipment could be transported as four pack loads: gun and breech, cradle and recoil mechanism, trails, and axle and wheels. Ammunition came in packs of twelve rounds each. However, the 2.95-inch round for this gun was not the same as that used in the later 75 mm American field guns. These mountain guns were usually organized into batteries of four guns each. In the early 1900s, there were generally a couple of batteries of 2.95s with regular artillery regiments.

In late 1897, the US Army began an inquiry to purchase a single sample for evaluation. The Philippines insurgency from 1898–1902 spurred an urgency for further acquisition. Thirty complete guns were bought from Vickers-Maxim (though carrying VM serial numbers in the 4500s, they were also given US Army numbers Nos. 1–30). Subsequently a license agreement was signed with Vickers, and three lots for a total of ninety more guns were produced in the US. While some of the forgings came from Crucible Steel of Harrison, New York, all the guns were completed at Watervliet and numbered 31–120. Deliveries were made from June 1903 until November 1904. Most of the guns experienced

Postcard showing the assembly of a 2.95-inch mountain gun from pack transport.

Several 2.95-inch mountain guns were used by the US Marine Corps. A monument on post at Parris Island, South Carolina, displays a US-made howitzer (closest) and its British-made mate.

a long life with the army, though several were transferred to the Marine Corps in China and spent many years with the Marines.

After its acquisition, the VM 2.95-inch mountain gun was never really replaced. No funding for series production of the 3-inch Model 1911 was approved, and unlike field and heavy guns, during the war no European mountain gun was needed. In fact, even with its limitations, the 2.95 soldiered on much longer than any other gun of this period. At the start of the First World War, 107 were reported on hand—seventy-two with the regular army, thirty-one at depots, and four at educational facilities. Of the seventy-two active guns, thirty-nine were with the 4th Artillery in the Southwest US and Panama, nineteen were with the 2nd Artillery in the Philippines, and fourteen were at the San Antonio Arsenal. In 1914, two batteries were sent to Veracruz, and in 1918 four 2.95s were supplied to the Czechs in Siberia.

In the 1920s, these guns were concentrated with the 4th Artillery at Camp Stanley, Texas, or in the Philippines. In 1934, the guns were reclassified as "Limited Standard, for Philippine Department only." While Ft. Huachuca and the San Antonio Arsenal continued to maintain up to sixteen mountain guns for Mexican border patrols, eventually almost all the remaining 2.95s, except a handful at schools and museums, were concentrated in the Philippines. They were used by both the regular US Artillery of the Philippine Department and units of the Philippine army organized in 1940–41. During the American defense of the Philippines in 1942, all sixty-eight mountain guns were lost, though they had exhausted their ammunition by mid-February.

2.95-Inch Vickers Mountain Gun

Gun Characteristics

Bore size: 2.95 inches (75 mm)

Construction: Nickel steel

Tube length overall: 38.1 inches

Nominal caliber: 11 calibers

Tube and breech weight: 236 pounds

Usual carriage: 2.95-inch mountain gun carriage

Weight of gun and carriage: 830 pounds

Maximum elevation: 27 degrees

Loading: Fixed

Shell weight: 12.5 pounds

Maximum muzzle velocity: 920 fps

Maximum range: 4,803 yards

Builders: Vickers-Maxim Ltd. (30), Watervliet Arsenal (90)

Number built: 120 + 1 type gun

Early army illustration of the 2.95-inch mountain gun.

3-Inch Mountain Howitzer Model 1911

Continuing military interventions and "small wars" spurred the ordnance department to take up a project for a new mountain howitzer before the First World War. The department constructed the Model 1908 howitzer, producing a single prototype. One of the problems revealed in 1909 firings was its excess weight, and attempts were made to reduce it. The 3-inch Model 1911 mountain howitzer was a direct attempt to address the faults of this previous experimental type. The howitzer was 14.5 calibers long, made of nickel steel, and used twenty-four grooves with a $\frac{1}{25}$ rifling. It fired 15-pound projectiles using separate powder charges calculated for three zones. Steel shell, high-explosive, and shrapnel rounds were available, and it achieved a maximum range of 5,570 yards.

While the tube was about the same as the Model 1908, the new carriage had a simple (and lightweight) upper chassis with box trail. While it could be elevated up to 40 degrees, the design could only achieve a traverse of 6 degrees total. The width of the tread was narrowed, and the hollow frame trail was substituted for the tubular section trail. A large protective shield was introduced, cut out to accommodate the barrel, its underslung hydropneumatic recoil cylinder, and two wheels.

The equipment could be broken down into five approximately equal loads for pack transport. There is no surviving example to inspect, but presumably they were marked in usual army convention with serial, date, inspector initials on the muzzle face, and similar information about the carriage on a plate on one of the trails.

Orders for five sets of forgings, under urgent priority, were granted to Watertown Arsenal on May 18, 1911. Carriages were procured from Rock Island and the gun assembly done at Watervliet Arsenal. This was a good example of using the capabilities of all three of the principal US Army arsenals for a priority fabrication project. In a relatively short time—between April and June 1912—the five mountain guns were completed and accepted. One unit was tested at the proving grounds; the other four were service-tested as an actual battery. These four service test units were subjected to considerable evaluation in 1913–14. The four-gun battery was dispatched to Mexico with the army's contingent for the Veracruz incursion in 1914, but there is no evidence that they saw combat.

With the approach of the First World War, army interest in new mountain guns appears to have lagged. No further developments of the type occurred until the 1920s when the pack howitzer project was started. There is little additional reporting on the use or fate of the five Model 1911 guns. They were never issued to an active unit and were likely stored

Photographs of the Model 1911 mountain howitzer are rare. This front view was taken at the army's trial report from December 1913. Note the unique shield extending well beyond the wheel base.

after trials and eventually disposed. The navy's production of four new mountain guns right after the war has led to speculation that the army guns were transferred to the navy, but that is not true. These were entirely different efforts and weapons (for one thing, these were howitzers and the navy weapons were guns). Sometime in the 1930s, four of the mountain howitzers were discarded. One was at the Ordnance Museum in 1938 but does not appear to have survived the Second World War. There are no known survivors of this last American mountain howitzer.

One of the Model 1911 mountain howitzers dispatched to Veracruz, Mexico, by the army in 1914. The howitzer is being ferried ashore on the prow of a light boat, reminiscent of the navy's tactical use of boat howitzers.

3-Inch Mountain Howitzer Model 1911

Gun Characteristics
Bore size: 3 inches
Construction: Nickel steel
Tube length overall: 46.5 inches
Nominal caliber: 14.5 calibers
Tube and breech weight: 210 pounds
Usual carriage: 3-inch Howitzer carriage model 1911
Weight of gun and carriage: 1,124 pounds
Maximum elevation: 40 degrees
Loading: Semi-fixed
Shell weight: 15 pounds
Maximum muzzle velocity: 900 fps
Maximum range: 5,570 yards

Builders: Forgings: Watertown Arsenal
    Howitzer: Watervliet Arsenal; carriage: Rock Island
    Arsenal
Number built: 5

Army photograph of how the barrel for the 3-inch Model 1911 mountain howitzer would be carried by mule pack.

MM. GUN —
...A   Mod. I
Bethlehem
(1-48)

3847

Light Field Artillery and Infantry Guns

A generation of light guns emerged in the late nineteenth century that fit awkwardly into the army's perception of field artillery. The first was the revolving cannon marketed by the Hotchkiss Ordnance Co. of Paris. This popular weapon was sold to nations around the world, particularly as a close-in weapon fired from warships to clear the decks of opposing vessels. For armies it was positioned as a gun to reinforce the light artillery zone of action—in other words, to fill in at close range. The US military purchased about 100 guns of this type. The army never knew quite what to do with them or how to organize them, though they were used with various detachments during some of the small conflicts of the late nineteenth century.

Similarly, the army purchased a handful of Vickers-Maxim 1-pounder (37 mm) quick fire automatic guns. Gaining popularity from use in South Africa, it offered the same advantage of rapidly delivering a volume of fire at close battlefield ranges. Made by Vickers in England, it was equipped with a water-cooled jacket that hampered its mobility in remote areas. Never adopted by the army, the guns were mostly kept stored until finally disposed of after the First World War.

The Sims dynamite gun was even less successful. Based on the concept of using compressed gas to launch a dynamite charge at an enemy, it originally found favor for coast defense. The army bought and deployed several large 8-inch and 15-inch guns for the defense of New York and San Francisco. Enthusiasm for the concept led to the acquisition of the Sims-Dudley 2.5-inch infantry gun. Sixteen of these guns were purchased during the initial, hurried preparations for the Spanish-American War, and several actually made it to the combat theater. They did not live up to their promise, however, and were soon gone from the inventory.

The US Army's Coast Artillery branch required a highly mobile light gun to provide flank defense, coverage of minefields, and land defense to augment its heavy fixed batteries. It adopted a 2.24-inch (6-pounder) size and purchased several examples of three slightly different commercial types to fill this role in 1898–1901. Some were taken from forts for use (off their wheeled carriages) on ship transports in the Spanish-American War, and others wound up in land defense programs in Hawaii and the Philippines, but none saw combat.

At the start of the First World War, the US Army again investigated using infantry guns. The state of trench warfare had persuasively argued for low-profile, man-portable light guns for use against an opponent's machine guns and outposts. By the closing years of the war, the specter of tank attacks also loomed. The United States acquired two new models of infantry guns. The French had developed a successful 37 mm gun, quantities were purchased for the American Expeditionary Forces (AEF), and the gun was put into production in the United States as the Model 1916. This was just about the only success the United States had in this category. The rapid production priority meant that some of the new guns made it to the combat theater in time for use. The gun persisted into the army's postwar armament. Through an error, a number of Bethlehem Steel-designed and produced 37 mm guns were also acquired. Some were bought from the French, and a contract with Bethlehem Steel was signed before the army discovered that they were very dissimilar to Model 1916. These guns were never issued to units and had a very short life helping to promote recruiting and bond sales.

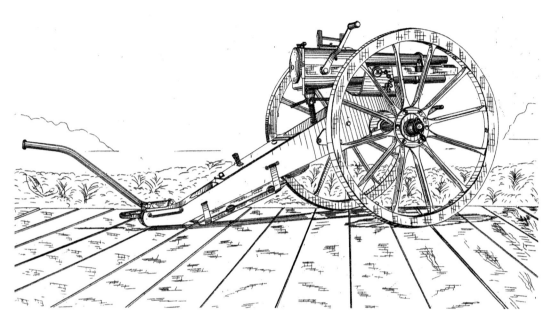

Army sketch of a 1-pounder (37 mm) Hotchkiss revolving cannon without shield.

Benjamin Hotchkiss was an innovative American designer of early breechloading guns. He found a better reception in Europe and established his office and factory in Paris. Later, with pressure from the American military, he invested in and licensed the American Ordnance Company of Bridgeport, Connecticut, to make and sell his cannons. One of his most successful early designs was a multi-barrel, rotating light cannon capable of rapidly firing fixed rounds. With its relatively low velocity and range, it was thought to be an effective infantry support weapon, in some ways more like an enlarged machine gun than a cannon.

The 37 mm gun was composed of five rotating barrels made of Whitworth compressed steel encased with a cast iron breech piece. The barrels were rifled with twelve lands and grooves and spaced by two large bronze disks. Rotation was mechanical and achieved with a hand crank shaft. The navy made and used similar 47 mm and 53 mm guns.

The mobile gun was supported on a carriage with two side brackets and two transoms. It could offer 4 degrees deflection left and right and an 18-degree elevation. A detachable, three-piece, 5mm-thick shield could be mounted. An ammunition limber with 300 rounds normally accompanied the rig. Ammunition was either common shell or case shot. Effective range was generally quoted at just 1,500 yards. The navy revolving cannon was usually mounted shipboard but could also be used as a boat gun or fitted to a wheeled carriage as a landing gun. This carriage was similar to the army's variety, though it had a pivot socket rather than a trunnion saddle to better accept the standard ship mounting.

After purchasing a single trial gun in 1876, the army went on to acquire eighteen additional 1-pounder revolving guns between 1879 and 1887. They were evaluated but not regularly issued, and were kept at arsenals pending need. The army also purchased a 40 mm revolving cannon to evaluate as a fortress flank defense gun, and a single larger 53 mm for testing. The navy acquired seventy-seven 1-pounder Hotchkiss revolving cannons (and eighteen 47 mm), using most of them shipboard. However, starting in 1886 when the navy first

Hotchkiss supplied more revolving cannon to the US Navy than the US Army. Most were used on simple deck pedestal or rail mountings, such as this piece.

purchased five examples, it also acquired a number of landing gun carriages for use in sending guns ashore to accompany naval landing parties.

On just a few occasions did the army revolving cannon see action. One cannon is reported to have accompanied Colonel Nelson Miles on the Milk River campaign in 1879. In fact, this was likely the trial gun purchased two years earlier. Its fire impressed observers on both sides. Four 1-pounders accompanied the expedition to Cuba in 1898, manned by members of the 10th Cavalry. Some were also sent to the Philippines; on one occasion a gun was mounted on an armed railway car patrolling the Manila Railroad. Opportunities for the navy to deploy its revolving cannon on landing carriage also were rare. Only in one instance (Panama, 1885) is employment mentioned in official reports.

The guns did not persist in inventory long into the twentieth century. By the First World War they were gone; there was no equivalent weapon even for training. Most were sold for scrap or to weapons dealers like Bannerman. While a number of navy guns survive today (and one on field carriage still exists at the National Museum of the Marine Corps), there is only one complete army-purchased gun with carriage on public display, at the US Army Artillery Museum.

1-Pounder Hotchkiss Revolving Cannon

Gun Characteristics

Bore size: 1-pounder (37 mm)

Construction: Tubes of compressed steel

Tube length overall: 46.4 inches overall, bore 29.5 inches

Nominal caliber: 20 calibers

Tube and breech weight: 495 pounds

Usual carriage: Hotchkiss revolving gun carriage

Weight of gun and carriage: 1,045 pounds

Maximum elevation: 18 degrees

Loading: Fixed

Shell weight: 1 pound

Maximum muzzle velocity: 1,395 fps

Maximum range: 1,500 yards

Builders: Hotchkiss in Paris or Bridgeport, Connecticut

Number acquired: 19 by US Army, 77 by US Navy
(less than 12 field carriages acquired)

The US Army Artillery Museum's Hotchkiss revolving cannon on its carriage.

2.5-Inch Sims-Dudley Dynamite Gun

The ordnance department had been intrigued with the concept of dynamite guns for some time. Guns firing exploding charges using compressed air or gas had been developed and deployed, albeit in limited numbers, for American coast defenses in New York and San Francisco. A smaller, field-gun-sized weapon was commercially developed by the Sims-Dudley Defense Company in the late 1890s. A 2.5-inch gun on light wheeled carriage was sold to Cuban revolutionaries and saw limited service against Spanish troops. At least two other countries also purchased small quantities of this weapon. In 1898, the War Department purchased sixteen guns in time to deploy them with the expeditionary forces heading to the Caribbean.

The gun consisted of two superimposed tubes. The hinged breech opened both tubes simultaneously. The upper tube, 14 feet long and 2.5 inches in bore, was loaded with the projectile. That was a 36-inch-long, finned shot weighing 11.5 pounds. It was tipped with a warhead containing 3.5 pounds of explosive gelatin and detonated by contact with water or a hard surface. The lower tube was 7 feet long and 4.5 inches in bore. It was fitted to receive a 1.65-inch (42 mm) blank, smokeless powder cartridge. The two tubes were connected—the firing of the cartridge in the lower tube generated gas pressure to launch the projectile from the upper tube. An effective range of 1,500 yards was achieved.

The gun had practically no recoil, so the carriage could be a light, simple frame with trail and 42-inch wheels. The whole gun and carriage could be drawn by a single horse, packed on just two mules, or carried by three or four men. The most awkward issue was the length of the tubes, not the weight. The large projectiles were heavy, and the guns were procured with just 100 rounds per gun.

It is not clear just how the army envisioned using the guns. They were classified as field artillery light guns and issued to service troops in 1898. A battery of four went to Cuba and saw action in the San Juan Hill assault, and nine were sent to Puerto Rico, where at least one was fired in combat. They had a poor reputation due to inadequate range and accuracy, at least compared

Sims-Dudley 2.5-inch light field gun illustration from the Annual Report of the Chief of Ordnance for 1898.

One of the Sims-Dudley dynamite guns in firing configuration in Cuba during 1898.

to conventional field pieces. All but one was recalled to the United States. Three were sent to the Sandy Hook Proving Ground, while twelve were prepared for issue to the Philippines—though it is doubtful they ever made it there. After the war, the guns were declared excess and quietly sold or discarded. Starting in 1904, the army began auctioning off the guns several at a time.

When enthusiasm was higher in 1898, the ordnance department acquired an enlarged, 3-inch dynamite gun from the Crescent Shipyard Co. It failed its test evaluation and was not ordered. In a few years the larger coast defense dynamite guns were removed, ending the army's exposure to this innovative, but less than satisfactory, branch of ordnance. The 2.5-inch guns were soon discarded. Several found their way to private collectors through Bannerman, and at least one heavily damaged example survives. Additionally, at least two of the Cuban-acquired guns are on display in Cuba.

2.5-Inch Sims-Dudley Dynamite Gun

Gun Characteristics

Bore size: 2.5 inches

Construction: Steel

Tube length overall: 168 inches

Nominal caliber: 67.2 calibers

Tube and breech weight: 356 pounds

Usual carriage: Dynamite gun carriage

Weight of gun and carriage: 1,217 pounds

Maximum elevation: 30 degrees, 15 minutes

Loading: Separate

Shell weight: 11.5 pounds

Maximum muzzle velocity: 600 fps

Maximum range: 1,950 yards extreme range, 1,500 yards effective range

Builders: Sims-Dudley Defense

Number acquired: 16

An 1898 ordnance department photograph of a dynamite gun. Only a single, heavily damaged example is known in the US, in private ownership. However, a pair of similar Cuban guns are on display in that country.

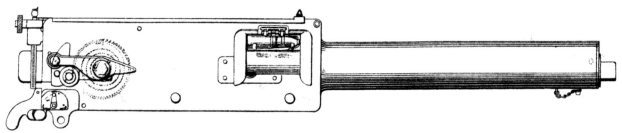

Sketch of the barrel and water jacket of the Vickers-Maxim 1-pounder quick-firing gun.

The British 1-pound automatic quick-firing gun made by Maxim had gained considerable popular publicity during its service in the Boer War. The Transvaal Republic had begun purchasing the weapon in 1899, and success against the British led to their own purchases beginning in 1900. Basically a fully automatic machine-cannon, the gun was responsible for the term "Pom Pom." A relatively heavy weapon consuming large quantities of ammunition with usually less than outstanding results, the gun had more of a psychological than real effect. In British service it was designated the "Ordnance Quick-Fire One Pounder, Mk I, Land Service." It was manufactured by Vickers Sons & Maxim.

The gun featured a recoiling barrel assembly surrounded by a water jacket. Recoil was checked with a hydraulic buffer and counterrecoil with two springs. Full, fixed cartridges were fed from a twenty-five-round belt into a feed block atop the gun. The gun was capable of full automatic firing with continual pressing of the trigger, though it could also be fired semi-automatically with separate trigger pressings. The tube had twelve grooves, rifled at 1/30 uniform twist. Cartridges were available as common shell with a nose fuse or a steel-pointed shell with a base fuse. Continual problems with the fuse and its tendency to bury before detonating plagued the earlier experiences with the gun. The simple carriage had a train, elevation and traversing gear, axle, and wheels. The most common carriage type could achieve a 16-degree elevation and a 30-degree traverse. With wheels, the carriage weighed over

One-pound QF Maxim Automatic Gun illustration from an ordnance department publication.

PLATE VIII.

800 pounds. An associated limber had twelve boxes of ammunition. This was either cast iron or steel rounds; propellant was cordite rather than the more usual nitrocellulose. Usually the gun was supplied with 300 rounds for service. A front and rear peep sight was calibrated to 3,000 yards. The typical crew was expected to be one non-commissioned officer (NCO) and four men.

In 1900, the army's ordnance department purchased one MkII for evaluation direct from the manufacturer. Soon three more complete batteries, of six guns each, were also purchased—two in 1901 and one in 1902. Eventually another two guns of differing carriage types were bought, in 1903 and 1905. Thus, the army acquired twenty-one guns. The guns were marked for the US Army by Vickers and carried serial Nos. 2452–2471. It appears that the twelve guns bought in 1901 were shipped directly to the Philippines for the campaign there (not unlike another Vickers product, the 2.95-inch mountain gun). The army simply reproduced the British ordnance manual for issue to gun crews, though it is not known if the gun ever saw combat. The US Navy used small numbers of this gun, primarily as a shipboard mount.

Both the ordnance department and field personnel disliked this gun because of its great weight and limited use. The chief of ordnance report in 1900 admitted that without the Philippine deployment, "the Department would not know what to do with these," and they were never adopted for regular field use. Between 1905 and 1918 the guns mostly languished in storage. Several were allocated for land defense of coast artillery forts, five at Fort Taylor in Key West in 1909. The guns were not used in the First World War. They were declared obsolete on June 15, 1919, and disposed of after the war was over.

1-Pounder Vickers-Maxim Automatic Gun

Gun Characteristics

Bore size: 1.457 inches (37 mm)

Construction: Steel, copper-covered barrel

Tube length overall: 43.5 inches

Nominal caliber: 30 calibers

Tube and breech weight: 410 pounds

Usual carriage: 1-pounder Mk II field carriage

Weight of gun and carriage: About 1,200 pounds

Maximum elevation: 20 degrees

Loading: Fixed round, 25 rounds/belt

Shell weight: 1 pound

Maximum muzzle velocity: 1,800 fps

Maximum range: 5,040 yards

Builders: Vickers Sons & Maxim

Number acquired: 21

No example of the army's 1-pounder Vickers-Maxim Automatic Gun is known to be on display in the United States, but a good example of the similar British version on early land carriage is at the Royal Canadian Artillery Museum in Shilo, Manitoba.

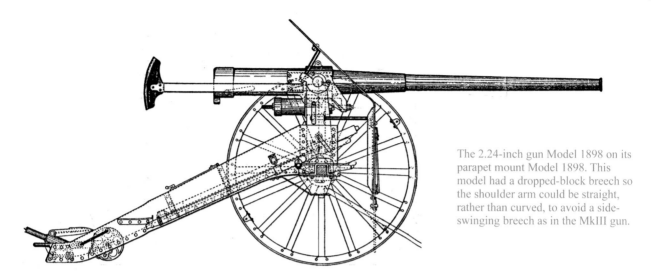

The 2.24-inch gun Model 1898 on its parapet mount Model 1898. This model had a dropped-block breech so the shoulder arm could be straight, rather than curved, to avoid a side-swinging breech as in the MkIII gun.

Coast Defense was an important branch of the US Army for almost all of the period this book covers. From 1888 to 1916, extensive permanent fortifications were built and garrisoned at multiple US and territorial seacoast harbors. Typically they were armed with a mix of heavy disappearing or barbette mount guns, large rifled mortars, and lighter rapid-fire guns. The service requested acquisition of at least one type of mobile, light gun. It was to provide additional coverage to minefields, supplement flanking fields of fire, and be available for land defense. They were to be issued a few at a time to each major post rather than organized into distinct, separate units.

To meet this need, the ordnance department acquired commercially available 2.24-inch (57 mm or 6-pounder) guns being made for the US Navy. Simple wheeled carriages were

also available. The start of the Spanish-American War spurred the acquisition. Between 1898 and 1901, ninety-four 2.24-inch guns and carriages were purchased from American suppliers.

The three types of guns shared ammunition and performance characteristics. There were twenty Model 1898 guns, forty Model 1900 guns (both from the Driggs-Seabury Co.), and thirty-four Mk III guns made by the American Ordnance Company. As some of the guns were deployed as army transport armament during the Spanish-American War, they were replaced with others. Carriages were a Model 1898 Parapet Mount or the 1898 Parapet Mount (Modified).

The tubes were 50-caliber forged steel. Breechblock was either a drop block (the twenty M1898 guns) or conical screw type. Most had eighteen grooves and a $\frac{1}{28}$.8 twist. They all fired

A pair pf coast defense 2.24-inch guns deployed during the Long Island maneuvers of 1905.

the same fixed common or steel shell rounds. The barrel had a shoulder bar for the gunner. It used an open tangent sight. The carriage was wheeled and of steel construction. The gun was held by a pivot socket in a Y-shaped pivot yoke. Carriage elevation was only -5 to +12 degrees. They were the first army guns with on-carriage recoil mechanisms. A small under-slung recoil cylinder filled with water and glycerin helped check the recoil, and counterrecoil was achieved with springs. The gun had a large, 0.25-inch-thick shield with an angled upper surface and hinged lower surface. It had a small trail wheel reminiscent of a navy landing gun. Ammunition could be carried by two boxes of nine rounds each, riding on each axle.

They served as intended, generally assigned two per major post. As they had no permanent position, most of the time they were kept in garage storage; in later years they were conveniently used as saluting guns around the headquarters flag. As these guns were never issued to the field artillery and no American coastal fort was attacked until 1941, they did not see combat. A fair number were sent to defenses in the Philippines and Hawaii as part of their land defense projects in 1915–1917. In some cases they were assigned permanent positions with concrete firing platforms and magazines (though still on mobile carriages). At the end of the First World War, their age was showing and they were eliminated. The 2.24-inch guns and carriages were declared obsolete on June 16, 1919, and authorized for scrap. Fortunately, a number were acquired for memorials and private collectors—about a half-dozen still survive.

2.24-Inch Gun Model 1900 on Parapet Mount Model 1898 Modified

Gun Characteristics

Bore size: 2.24 inches (57 mm)

Construction: Steel

Tube length overall: 116.12 inches

Nominal caliber: 50 calibers

Tube and breech weight: 850 pounds

Usual carriage: 6-pounder rampart mount Model 1898

Maximum elevation: 12 degrees

Loading: Fixed

Shell weight: 6 pounds

Maximum muzzle velocity: 2,400 fps

Maximum range: 6,241 yards

Builders: Driggs-Seabury, American Ordnance Co.

Number built: 94

A surviving 2.24-inch gun at the Plymouth, Michigan, Veterans' Memorial Park. Note the complete shield coverage.

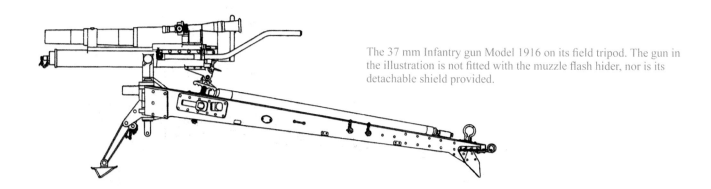

The 37 mm Infantry gun Model 1916 on its field tripod. The gun in the illustration is not fitted with the muzzle flash hider, nor is its detachable shield provided.

This French-designed light infantry gun originated from a Puteaux arsenal in 1885. As design improved, it entered quantity French production about 1914. It was meant as a weapon for infantry battalions and regiments to use against enemy machine guns and strongpoints—and was successful and popular in this role.

The gun had a relatively short steel alloy barrel. The breechblock housing was screwed into the tube. The breech itself was a Nordenfelt eccentric breech—similar in shape to that used on the French 75 mm gun. The block rotated to open and close the breech. The recoil cylinder piston was below the gun and used hydraulic oil and a counterrecoil buffer to brake the recoil and return the gun to firing position. The tube was marked on its upper surface with manufacturer, serial number, year, and inspector; similar carriage information was on a plate on the left trail.

The gun was usually mounted and fired from a tripod with longer rear legs. Between the rear legs was a transom that was also a seat for the gunner. It had a screw elevating mechanism. A detachable shield was also supplied. It could be set on wheels and axle for both firing and transporting. The wheels were 37.85 inches in diameter and had simple steel-rim tires. A separate ammo cart could accompany the gun and hold fourteen boxes of ammunition, sixteen rounds each. The gun fired fixed 37 mm rounds of either low or high-explosive type. Often with French-produced guns, a conical sheet metal flash hider was attached to the muzzle. The gun required only a two-man crew, along with any additional ammunition handlers.

The US began producing the design in October 1917. Work was divided among Poole Engineering (barrels), Krasberg Manufacturing (breech assemblies), and C. H. Cowdrey Machine

A poor-quality photograph of an interesting deployment. It shows a 37 mm Model 1916 with its shield on tripod with the American expedition to Siberia from 1918–20.

Works (recoil mechanism). Assembly was done at Maryland Press Steel Co. (recently acquired by Poole Engineering). Original orders were for 1,200 units, and 1,397 additional guns were ordered in September 1918. Initial deliveries began in June 1918; 884 were completed and 122 were shipped abroad by the war's end. Additionally, 620 fully assembled guns were acquired from the French in Europe directly for the AEF. The French produced 1,500 of these Canon de 37 mm Mle 1916 TR guns for their own use. Total American production was 1,155, though similar gun barrels were also made for tanks.

These guns were issued to howitzer companies attached to infantry regiments, three 37 mm (and three 3-inch Stokes mortars) per company. They saw combat in the First World War, though there were problems getting an adequate supply of ammunition from the French.

After the war, American production continued, but the army's reduced size meant that most of the guns went to storage depots. They were still actively used with remaining units and at overseas departments. The Marine Corps also adopted the gun, and it was standard issue right up until the Second World War. Additionally, many of the tubes were used as sub-caliber guns for larger field and coast artillery weapons in the 1920s and 1930s. In 1939, the guns were reclassified as limited standard. While not yet declared obsolete, new tables of organization for infantry units did not include infantry guns—their American Second World War combat exposure was limited to the 1941–1942 Philippine campaign.

37 mm Infantry Gun Model 1916

Gun Characteristics

Bore size: 37mm

Construction: Steel alloy

Tube length overall: 31.6 inches

Nominal caliber: 20 calibers

Tube and breech weight: 56 pounds

Usual carriage: 37 mm gun carriage Model 1916 (wheeled)

Weight of gun and carriage: 169 pounds

Maximum elevation: 21 degrees

Loading: Fixed

Shell weight: 1,234 pounds

Maximum muzzle velocity: 1,276 fps

Maximum range: 4,200 yards

Builders: Puteaux (France), Maryland Press Steel Co.

Number built and acquired: 1,778

Despite the large numbers acquired and their compact size, few 37 mm Model 1916 infantry guns survive on display. This sample is on its wheeled carriage at a military museum in Vincennes, Indiana.

37 mm Infantry Gun Model 1917
(Bethlehem Steel Type A)

Illustration of the 37 mm infantry gun Model 1917 from a Bethlehem Steel brochure.

Information on the origin of this gun is lacking. The design was privately developed by Bethlehem Steel and it was offered for sale around 1916 under the company designation of One-pounder 37 mm Semi-Automatic Gun, Mark C on Carriage Mark A. It was intended for naval landing operations or as a light infantry weapon. France contracted to purchase 200 units in 1916; one source states an order of 100 in the summer of 1917, and another 1,000 in early 1918. It appears that a few were delivered to the French army and may have seen limited combat service.

It was a handsome, small cannon. The gun tube was nickel steel, forged with the breechblock in one piece. The breech mechanism was a Bethlehem semi-automatic type. The tube was mounted on a cradle with pivot yoke, trail, and wheels. The long-recoil mechanism was mounted above the gun and consisted of a hydraulic cylinder and counterrecoil springs. The gun had no elevating or traversing gear and was handy enough to be pointed with shoulder guard and grip. The carriage did allow -5 to +15-degrees elevation and a traverse of 45 degrees. It had open sights and an armored plate shield. The gun fired its own fixed ammunition packed in boxes of sixty rounds. Four ammo boxes could be transported on a separate ammunition hand cart. Gun serial number is marked on the upper surface of the barrel

A 1918 three-quarter rear view of what would become the 37 mm Model 1917 infantry gun.

and on the left side of the breech housing; carriage information is on an attached plate on the left-hand trail.

Bethlehem Steel solicited an offer from the US Army in February 1916. The ordnance department expressed interest in May 1917, but no immediate orders were placed. Then in July 1918, the French offered to sell the Americans 200 37 mm guns (fifty were complete and the rest were still being produced by Bethlehem Steel) and up to 4 million rounds of ammunition. The army accepted the offer for the guns and take-over of the contract, thinking these were the adopted 37 mm Model 1916. When the error was discovered in November, it was too late. France had supplied seventy-five guns to the AEF, and 110 more were in the United States or in fabrication. The Bethlehem Steel guns, heavier and less maneuverable than the Model 1916 and firing an entirely different type of ammunition, were not needed. The AEF was ordered to return the guns and keep the newly produced ones at home. All told, 185 guns had been acquired through an error.

In American hands, the gun never saw combat; in fact most had only a two- or three-year life of service. While there was nothing technically wrong with them, they did not fill a military need, and there were too few to justify keeping in inventory. They were not issued to service units, but almost fifty were sent to recruiting offices. Middleton General Ordnance Depot had 109 such guns in storage in October 1919. On March 16, 1921, the gun was declared obsolete. It small size and handsome appearance has made it a popular item for distribution as a memorial gun, particularly in nearby Pennsylvania and New York. Consequently, many examples still exist in public and private collections.

37 mm Infantry Gun Model 1917

Gun Characteristics

Bore size: 37mm
Construction: Nickel steel
Tube length overall: 68.2 inches
Nominal caliber: 40 calibers
Tube and breech weight: 173 pounds
Usual carriage: 37 mm gun carriage Model 1917
Weight of gun and carriage: 973 pounds
Maximum elevation: 15 degrees
Loading: Fixed
Shell weight: 1.07 pounds
Maximum muzzle velocity: 2,100 fps
Maximum range: 4,100 yards

Builder: Bethlehem Steel
Number acquired: 185

Due to the rather peculiar circumstances of the gun's acquisition and use, a fairly large number of the 37 mm Model 1917 guns still exist—both in public and private hands. Over twenty-five are on public display. This shows a typical memorial display of this piece in South Connellsville, Pennsylvania.

Early Heavy Field and Siege Guns and Mortars

The concept of heavy, positioned siege artillery was not new. American experience during the Civil War had certainly reinforced the need for heavy pieces that could be used for besieging fortifications. While not normally fired from mobile carriages, they had to be transportable to the theater of need. There was little need for use in the frontier campaigns of the late nineteenth century, but prudence dictated that a range of weapons be developed. Not long after the development of the army's first modern 3.2-inch steel gun, developmental programs were started for a range of heavier weapons.

First came a heavier version of the 3.2-inch gun. The 3.6-inch gun was still obviously a piece of field artillery, though assigned to "heavy" as opposed to "light" batteries. A scaled-up version of the smaller gun, it used virtually the same carriage, simply cut out to accommodate the larger tube. The gun was evaluated in 1890 and production orders were issued in 1892. Only twenty-five guns were produced. They were never used in combat and saw limited deployment.

In 1885, the ordnance board completed a study for a new steel siege gun, recommending a gun of 5-inch size, 30-caliber length, and weighing approximately 3,500 pounds. It was joined by a similar, though larger 7-inch howitzer recommended by the same board in 1887. A prototype of each gun was produced and extensively evaluated in the late 1880s. The first ten of each type were ordered in 1891. Additional orders followed. Versions with new breech mechanisms and improved carriages were ordered during the Spanish-American War. Eventually, seventy production versions of each of the 5- and 7-inch guns were acquired. These weapons were mounted on wheeled carriages, but for best performance they needed to be fired from platforms with anchoring mechanisms to control the mount's recoil.

Finally, two different mortar sizes were also acquired in the 1890s: a small, 3.6-inch field mortar and a substantial 7-inch siege mortar. While called mortars, these were modern weapons—breechloading, rifled, made of steel. Mortars needed to be placed on fixed platforms. The weapons (and their platforms) did not have wheels and were transported on wagons. An important consideration for all this material was that its weight and transportation mode be compatible with existing roads, particularly with military pontoon bridges.

Initially, these heavy weapons were not organized into regular units. Most were spread in small numbers to posts and training establishments or even kept in storage. A full siege train was never organized, nor all the ancillary equipment supplied. Finally, during the Spanish-American War, many of these guns (sixteen 5-inch siege guns, eighteen 7-inch siege howitzers, six 7-inch siege mortars, and twenty 3.6-inch field guns) were moved to temporary seacoast defenses or added to coast artillery posts for land defense. Toward the end of the campaign, a few were prepared for shipment to Cuba or Puerto Rico but never reached their assignments in time to see action. After the war, some were sent to Hawaii and the Philippines to serve in land defense. This entire generation was obsolete by the start of the First World War, even for training.

3.6-Inch Gun Model 1891

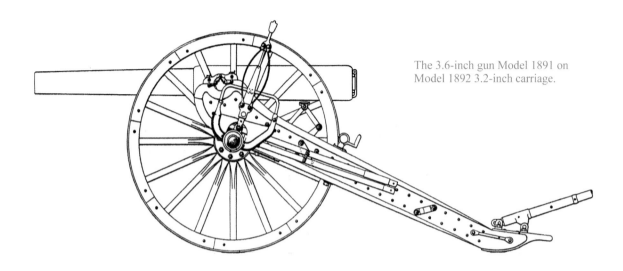

The 3.6-inch gun Model 1891 on Model 1892 3.2-inch carriage.

This piece was intended to be a heavier, longer-range complement to the new 3.2-inch field gun developed in the mid-1880s. It was basically a scaled-up version of that field gun, using the same type of barrel construction and breech mechanism. Like its slighter companion, it was built with a gun-steel tube and built-up jacket carrying 3-inch trunnions. The breech mechanism was a conventional cylindrical interrupted-screw block (three threaded and three blank sections). The carrier ring was hinged on the left side. It featured progressive rifling with twenty-six grooves and a twist rate of ⅟₅₀, increasing to ⅟₂₅ near the muzzle.

The carriage was also similar to the one developed for the 3.2-inch gun. In fact, the 3.6-inch gun carriage was based on the initial 1885 order of fifty heavy 3.2-inch field carriages. They required slight alterations; the most significant was cutting out the front of the upper transom under the trunnion bed to accommodate the elevating mechanism of the slightly longer tube. Most of the other battery components were the same—the caisson for the 3.2-inch gun was modified to carry thirty-six (instead of forty-two) rounds of ammunition. Other implements were identical, except where an obvious dimensional change was needed. The

The 3.6-inch gun at Sandy Hook Proving Ground.

gun was equipped with the same telescopic sight. A 20-pound cast iron shell and a shrapnel round were standardized.

The initial model was ordered on May 29, 1889. The forging came from Midvale Steel, and Watervliet Arsenal completed the gun on March 11, 1890. On January 22, 1892, the Board of Ordnance and Fortification requested an allocation of funds for the manufacture of twenty-four additional 3.6-inch guns ($24,000 for both open hearth steel forgings and $19,000 for completion work). Subsequently, forging and completion work was contracted to the army's Watervliet Arsenal in upstate New York. The guns were numbered 1 through 25. They were marked on the muzzle face with model, year of acceptance, arsenal, weight, and the inspector's initials. Carriage information appeared on a bronze disk bolted to the carriage side.

While the gun encountered no difficulties in production, proofing, or performance, it was not held in favor by the artillery branch. No additional orders were issued. While photographs show it being used in training at Fort D. A. Russell in Wyoming, there is no evidence of combat use. This type of gun was authorized for deployment to coast artillery posts for the Spanish-American War. At least eight guns made their way to Puerto Rico late in the Spanish-American War but did not see combat. By 1904, they had been relegated to colleges for instruction and to some seacoast forts for saluting. There is no record of the gun's use during the First World War, even for training. Eventually they were dispersed to schools, arsenals, and posts, and were recommended for disposal on June 15, 1919. Between 1920 and 1921, most were either scrapped or donated as decorative pieces to municipalities of GAR posts prescribed by federal law. Three 3.6-inch guns survive, though one is missing a carriage.

3.6-Inch Gun Model 1891

Gun Characteristics

Bore size: 3.6 inches

Construction: Built-up steel

Tube length overall: 93.45 inches

Nominal caliber: 23.5 calibers

Tube and breech weight: 1,200 pounds

Usual carriage: 3.2-inch gun carriage Model 1892

Weight of gun and carriage: 2,500 pounds

Maximum elevation: 20 degrees

Loading: Separate

Shell weight: 20 pounds

Maximum muzzle velocity: 1,550 fps

Maximum range: 6,783 yards

Builder: Gun: Watervliet Arsenal; carriage: Watertown Arsenal

Number built: 25

Only three surviving examples are known of the 3.6-inch gun. One has been recently restored, illustrated here with the Missouri National Guard in Jefferson City, Missouri.

3.6-Inch Field Mortar Model 1890

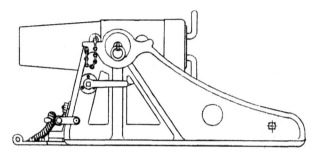

Sketch of 3.6-inch mortar Model 1890 on mortar carriage Model 1895.

The first modern breechloading mortar developed for the US Army, this model was intended for field use in siege operations and the land defense of coastal batteries from prepared positions. It was constructed of a single-piece gun steel (including trunnions). It was relatively short and light but otherwise demonstrated no major innovations. The rifling was of twenty grooves. It had a simple Freyre obturating pad of metal components. The carriage was cast steel and consisted of two side pieces and two transoms. A 3-inch diameter circular hole in each side piece allowed the use of handspikes to carry the gun. It was intended to be fired from a wooden platform, anchored by stakes through leather straps attached to it. The platform accompanied the carriage and was made of yellow pine or oak. A cast iron shell and a shrapnel shell was supplied as ammunition.

Only simple metal directional sights were provided on the mortar tube itself. Instructions called for a pointing scale to be used and placed on the platform. The assembled mortar (tube, breech, and carriage) weighed only 543 pounds. It was intended to be transported on a cart or wagon drawn by two horses or four mules. The elevation achievable was +14 degrees to 65 degrees, giving it a maximum range of 4,000 yards.

The first "type" 3.6-inch mortar (later assigned serial No. 1) was ordered on March 26, 1889. Midvale provided the steel forging, and Watervliet Arsenal completed the mortar on June 12, 1890. With such a simple design, there were no complications. Sixteen additional mortars were ordered on July 10, 1891, this time with forgings provided by the army's own steel foundry at the Watertown Arsenal. They were delivered in 1895. Further batches ordered in mid-1895, 1898, and 1900 resulted in a production run of seventy-six 3.6-inch

The 3.6-inch Model 1890 mortar on its wooden platform during the Spanish-American War. The photograph was taken in Cuba.

Model 1890 mortars. They were numbered consecutively, along with the type gun from No. 1 to No. 76 inclusive. All were provided by early 1904, when production ceased. The mortars were marked on the muzzle face with serial number, year of delivery, arsenal, and the inspector's initials. The model number was stamped on the left trunnion face. Production of the mortar carriage model 1895 at Watertown Arsenal kept pace as required.

The mortar saw limited use. Mostly stored at ordnance depots and training centers, four mortars were sent via Tampa to Cuba for the Spanish-American War, and eventually on to Puerto Rico. Another pair (or possibly four) were sent to Manila and deployed by American forces in Bayan, Mindanao, during the Philippine insurrection. Reports praised their utility. For those operations they were packed using excess gear of the 2.95-inch mountain gun. No subsequent record remains of their use. The first type mortar and carriage were sold as scrap in 1902. Apparently they were too obsolete even to be considered useful as training weapons during the First World War. Like the other siege material, the ordnance department recommended their elimination on June 15, 1919. Quite a few were donated to local organizations as decorative or memorial pieces, and many survive in private collections.

3.6-Inch Mortar Model 1890 on Carriage Model 1895

Gun Characteristics

Bore size: 3.6 inches
Construction: Steel, single forging
Tube length overall: 24.6 inches
Nominal caliber: 5.25 calibers
Tube and breech weight: 245 pounds
Usual carriage: 3.6-inch mortar carriage Model 1895
Weight of gun and carriage: 520 pounds
Maximum elevation: 65 degrees
Loading: Separate
Shell weight: 20 pounds
Maximum muzzle velocity: 750 fps
Maximum range: 4,000 yards

Builders: Mortar: Watervliet Arsenal; carriage: Watertown Arsenal
Number built: 76

A surprising number of these mortars survive. At least eleven are on display, like this example in Youngstown, New York. Another six are in private hands.

5-Inch Siege Gun Model 1890

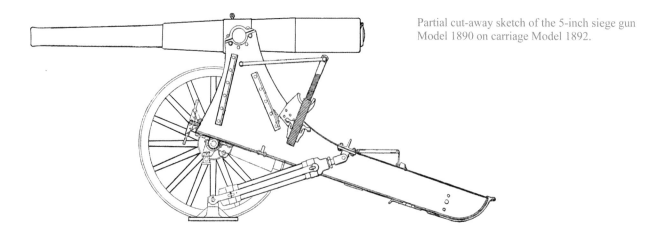

Partial cut-away sketch of the 5-inch siege gun Model 1890 on carriage Model 1892.

This gun was the result of an ordnance department study presented in 1885. The board proposed a modern siege gun of 5-inch bore, 30-caliber length, and weight of about 3,500 pounds. It was to be capable of being carried over ordinary roads and pontoon bridges. The development of a prototype was a prolonged process. The type gun forging was ordered from Midvale in 1886, the gun assembly was assigned to Watervliet, and the prototype carriage was fabricated at Springfield Armory. After completion, it was proofed at Sandy Hook, and forty-seven rounds were fired by June 30, 1888. In 1890, the type was recommended for service, and the board ordered ten forgings from Bethlehem Steel. By 1893, these were completed along with carriages constructed at Watertown, and ten more were ordered.

The gun was a built-up forged steel type with tube, jacket, trunnion hoop, and breech mechanism. A lifting eyebolt was screwed into the top of the trunnion hoop to facilitate hoisting the tube. It had an interrupted-screw breech type, with four threaded and four slotted sectors. The hinge for the breech carrier ring was on the left side of the breech recess. The gun carried the usual marks for number, place and year of manufacture, and initials of the inspector on the muzzle face. The model of the gun was stamped on the face of the left trunnion. The tube was rifled with thirty grooves and had a twist of $\frac{1}{50}$ increasing to 1 in 25. Thirty-three Model 1890 guns were manufactured, all at Watervliet Arsenal (Nos. 1–33).

The 5-inch Model 1890 gun, probably the first type gun displayed to the public at the Columbian Exposition in Chicago in 1893.

The first twenty carriages for the 5-inch siege gun were designated Model 1892. The gun trunnion was carried at a relatively high elevation. For traveling, another trunnion bracket was positioned below and behind the upper bracket, since it was necessary to lift the tube and reposition it on the lower bracket before moving it. Another obvious feature was a large hydraulic buffer cylinder mounted on the trail. When in firing position, this cylinder was connected to a pintle block and then to an anchor plate buried deeply in the earth below the firing platform.

A full 5-inch siege battery was to be composed of four guns on wheeled carriages and limbers, each drawn by eight horses; four ammunition wagons also drawn by eight horses; one forge and battery wagon drawn by six horses; one artillery store wagon and one implement wagon each drawn by eight horses. Ammunition was a cast iron round and a shrapnel round, each weighing 45 pounds. In addition to conventional sights on the barrel, each gun was supplied with a telescopic sight. Guns were fitted for 0.30-caliber subcaliber rifle barrels.

Like other heavy guns of this period, they were initially assigned to ordnance depots and not issued to units. But at the start of the Spanish-American War, the need for guns suddenly became urgent. In April 1898, sixteen of these guns were issued for new temporary coastal fortifications along the South Atlantic and Gulf Coasts. They had barely been issued (and few actually emplaced) when the orders were rescinded and the guns shipped to Tampa for the expeditionary force bound for Cuba. While records are incomplete, it appears the four 5-inch siege guns (and four 7-inch siege howitzers) were actually destined for Santiago at the time active operations ceased. Ten 5-inch guns were deployed to the Philippines in 1903. Emplacements of the Land Defense Project for Manila Bay were built at Fort Mills (Corregidor Island) and the guns were stored there in sheds from 1910–1916. Additionally, ten guns were deployed to Oahu as possible defensive material around 1914–1915. No use was made of the 5-inch siege gun during the First World War. The 5-inch siege gun was declared obsolete in 1919; both the Hawaiian and Philippine commands were authorized to use all remaining ammunition in 1920 prior to returning the guns for disposal.

5-Inch Siege Gun Model 1890 and 1898

Gun Characteristics

Bore size: 5 inches

Construction: Built-up steel

Tube length overall: 145.75 inches

Nominal caliber: 27 calibers

Tube and breech weight: 3,660 pounds

Usual carriage: 5-inch siege gun carriage Model 1892 and 1896

Weight of gun and carriage: 7,460 pounds

Maximum elevation: 20 degrees

Loading: Separate

Shell weight: 45 pounds

Maximum muzzle velocity: 1,830 fps

Maximum range: 8,000 yards

Builders: Gun: Watervliet Arsenal; carriage: Watertown Arsenal

Number built: 33 guns Model 1890, 37 guns Model 1898, 20 carriages Model 1892, 50 carriages Model 1896

Only a couple of the Model 1890 5-inch siege guns still exist. One (just the tube) is near New York City, and this example, though mounted on a later Model 1896 carriage, is a treasured mascot on the Caltech campus in Pasadena, California.

7-Inch Siege Howitzer Model 1890

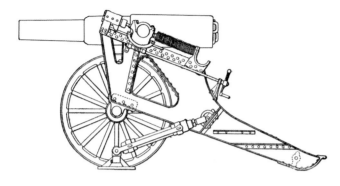

Left side, partially cut-out sketch of the 7-inch siege howitzer Model 1890 on carriage Model 1893.

Development of a heavy siege howitzer followed the 5-inch siege gun by about a year. Both were intended to be heavy field weapons for besieging enemy fortifications or field works. While they were mobile, they required prepared firing positions for effective use. The ordnance board completed the 7-inch siege howitzer design in 1886. Requirements included an ability to move over ordinary roads and bridges, and a range of 6,000 yards. The type gun was fabricated at Watertown Arsenal and was available for firing tests in 1888. By 1890, it was approved for production, and soon ten guns and carriages

were ordered. Watervliet Arsenal completed the guns from Midvale forgings, and Rock Island Arsenal made the required carriages. By 1893, these were completed (Model 1890 howitzer and carriage Model 1893), and another ten sets ordered. Forty 7-inch siege howitzers Model 1890 were delivered between 1895 and 1900, numbered from 1 through 40. Like other American pieces, the registry number, year and place of manufacture, and inspector's initials were stamped on the muzzle face. Soon after, thirty similar 7-inch siege howitzers Model 1898 were built at Watervliet Arsenal, for a total of seventy of this size howitzer. These later howitzers were numbered 1 through 30.

The howitzer was conventional steel, built up with a tube, jacket, trunnion hoop, and breech mechanism. It had an interrupted-screw breech with four slotted and four threaded sectors, opening to the left with hinge. It used a split ring obturator. The barrel was rifled with forty-two grooves starting with a twist of $\frac{1}{50}$ and ending with $\frac{1}{30}$. The model 1893 steel carriage was similar to the Model 1892 5-inch carriage. It had steel recoil springs fitted to a cylinder on either side of the carriage and a hydraulic buffer cylinder under the carriage that could be tied to a buried anchor plate for stability on a prepared platform. The howitzer was fitted with mechanical sights, though supplemental telescopic sights were later made available. The tube had accessories to fit a 0.30-caliber US magazine rifle Model 1898 as a sub-caliber device.

A few nice examples survive of the early 7-inch howitzer and carriage. About eight still exist. All are displayed outdoors; none are currently under museum care. The unit above is at a veterans facility in Yountville, California.

The army's proscribed heavy siege battery would have consisted of four howitzers and limbers drawn by eight horses each, four ammunition wagons (pulled by eight horses each), one battery and forge wagon (drawn by six horses), one implement wagon (with eight horses), and one artillery store wagon (four horses). Ammunition consisted of a cast iron shell, a common steel shell, and a shrapnel round, each 105 pounds.

The howitzers were not originally issued to regiments but stored at depots pending need. That occurred in 1898 with the outbreak of the Spanish-American War. In April 1898, eighteen howitzers were distributed to new temporary coastal batteries in the South. However, a month later they were ordered moved to Tampa for the Cuban campaign. While four appear to have been floated, none saw combat. In 1915, a number of 7-inch siege howitzers were in the Philippines at the Manila harbor defense forts as part of the land defense program. Concrete magazines and firing platforms were built, but the howitzers themselves stayed in artillery sheds pending need. Some of these howitzers were sent to Hawaii as part of the general defense scheme of that department, also prior to the First World War (ten howitzers were reported on hand on October 22, 1915). During that war these guns stayed at their stations and none saw combat. They were declared obsolete and approved for donation in June 1919. In 1920, the Philippine and Hawaii departments were authorized to fire all their remaining ammunition for these guns in practice prior to sending the units stateside.

7-Inch Siege Howitzer Model 1890 and 1898

Gun Characteristics

Bore size: 7 inches
Construction: Built-up steel
Tube length overall: 101.76 inches
Nominal caliber: 12.7 calibers
Tube and breech weight: 3,710 pounds
Usual carriage: 7-inch howitzer carriage Models 1893 and 1899
Weight of gun and carriage: 7,670-pounds
Maximum elevation: 40 degrees
Loading: Separate
Shell weight: 105 pounds
Maximum muzzle velocity: 1,100 fps
Maximum range: 8,062 yards

Builders: Howitzer: Watervliet Arsenal; carriage: Rock Island Arsenal
Number built: 40 howitzers Model 1890, 30 howitzers Model 1898, 40 carriages Model 1893, 30 carriages Model 1899

A photo of the early type of 7-inch siege howitzer and carriage taken at the army's proving ground. Note the hydraulic buffer in firing position under the trail attached to a ground-buried anchor plate.

Improved 5-Inch Siege Gun and 7-Inch Siege Howitzer Models 1898 with Carriages Models 1896 and 1899

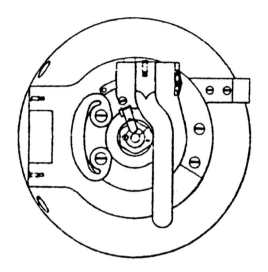
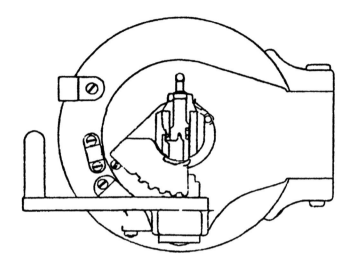

Differences in 5-inch breeches. Model 1890 on left, Model 1898 on right.

New models of the 5-inch and 7-inch siege weapons were developed and standardized for production in 1898. The new 5-inch siege gun and 7-inch siege howitzer differed from the Model 1890s in one major aspect. They used a new, improved Stockett breech mechanism. It swung out to the right rather than left, and thus had the hinge lugs on that side of the gun. Also, this mechanism had a comparatively shorter breechblock, permitting the gun to be shortened by several inches (142.95 inches versus 145.75 inches for the 5-inch, and 99.25 inches versus 101.76 inches for the 7-inch). The 5-inch was 21 pounds lighter (3,639 pounds versus 3,660 pounds) and the 7-inch was 60 pounds lighter (3,650 pounds versus 3,710 pounds). Otherwise, performance characteristics were unchanged and the data from the previous model tables apply.

The original 5-inch siege gun carriage Model 1892 (of which only twenty had been constructed) was succeeded by the Model 1896 carriage. Small improvements were made in this carriage. A tool box was added to the trail, and a road brake added, but its appearance remained close to the original model. Fifty Model 1896 and slightly altered Model 1896M 5-inch carriages were produced (Nos. 21–70 inclusive).

However, the new Model 1899 carriage for the 7-inch siege howitzer was a major revision. Only thirty Model 1893 and 1893M carriages had been built; the forty subsequent carriages were Model 1899 (Nos. 31–70 inclusive). To start with, it was possible to mount the howitzer in firing position a foot lower—60 inches above the ground versus 72 inches for the original Model 1893. The new carriage retained its lower trunnion bracket for traveling mode. Also, to reduce weight, the sides of the carriage cheeks and trail were cut out in circular patterns. The combination of lower profile and reduced steel in the side members resulted in a 1,000-pound weight reduction. The new carriage came in at only 2,960 pounds, compared to 3,960 in the 1893 model. With its distinctive cut-outs, the new carriage style is readily identifiable in period photographs.

Only two 7-inch howitzers Model 1898 tubes and just a single Model 1899 carriage are known to survive. This unit is in Eichelman Park overlooking Lake Michigan in Kenosha, Wisconsin.

Several nice examples of the later 5-inch siege gun (Model 1898 on Model 1896 carriage) survive. Four of these guns were discovered in a cemetery in Oregon in the 1980s, and subsequently were distributed to army museums. The best restored example is pictured above at the Oregon Military Museum at Camp Withycombe outside Portland. Others are at the Rock Island Arsenal Museum and the Watervliet Arsenal Museum. The fourth has recently been transferred to the Army Artillery Museum at Fort Sill. The Camp Withycombe sample is fitted with mahogany brake shoes, indicating that it may have served in the Philippines 100 years earlier.

The 7-inch siege howitzer model of 1898 on distinctive carriage model of 1899. This photo was taken at an army proving ground, probably Sandy Hook.

7-Inch Siege Mortar Model 1892

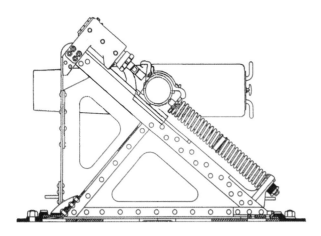

Sketch of the 7-inch mortar Model 1892 on carriage Model 1895.

This weapon was developed in conjunction with the other heavy siege material in the early 1890s. The intent was the same as for the smaller 3.6-inch mortar—to provide heavy fire against enemy entrenchments and fortifications. It was to be operated from a prepared platform, and while transportable, it was not really mobile. The initial type 7-inch mortar was ordered from Watervliet on March 23, 1893. Midvale provided the forging, and the unit was completed for shipping in December 1894. Subsequently, four batches of orders were issued for this type of weapon between April of 1895 and April of 1899. In all, sixty additional service mortars were made bearing serial numbers 2–61 (the type mortar was given serial No. 1). Bethlehem Steel and Midvale Steel shared the orders for forgings, but the mortars were completed at Watervliet Arsenal and the necessary Model 1895 carriages were made at Watertown Arsenal. Deliveries of service guns began in 1897 and were completed by mid-1901.

The mortar was a one-piece steel forging. It was rifled with twenty-eight grooves tapering from a twist of $\frac{1}{40}$ to $\frac{1}{15}$ calibers. It had an interrupted-screw breech with three threaded and three slotted sections. A conventional obturator spindle with split ring held a gas-check pad of asbestos and tallow. The carriage had two steel chassis sides connected with three transoms. On either side of the barrel were the recoil cylinders and two counterrecoil springs. The mortar was provided with a wooden platform of oak and yellow pine measuring 134 × 75 inches. The weapon used simple metal sights and separate

7-inch Model 1892 mortar on platform during evaluation firings at the Sandy Hook Proving Ground.

pointing scales and gunner's quadrant. It was provided with 125-pound cast iron steel, or shrapnel rounds.

The usual system of markings was applied where the muzzle face displays the mortar's serial number, year and place of manufacture, weight, and inspector's initials. A metal plate on the right side of the carriage chassis carried serial number, model, year, and place of completion.

Very little use was actually made of this mortar. It was not suitable for deployment either in the seacoast or mobile army operations of the Spanish-American War. Moreover, only six were reported serviceable in April 1898, with another twenty close to completion. Four mortars were eventually shipped to Puerto Rico, but no siege operations were undertaken. Unlike the 5-inch siege gun and 7-inch siege howitzer, it does not appear that any were stationed in Hawaii or the Philippines after the turn of the twentieth century. Maybe some training use was made of the mortars during the First World War, but even that is doubtful. No photographs have been found of the mortar deployed or firing except at proving ground evaluations. On June 15, 1919, they were declared obsolete along with all other old siege material. Several were contributed as memorial and display guns to municipalities. A surprisingly large number of the mortars and original carriages still exist.

7-Inch Mortar Model 1892 on Carriage Model 1895

Gun Characteristics

Bore size: 7 inches

Construction: Steel, single forging

Tube length overall: 58.3 inches

Nominal caliber: 7 calibers

Tube and breech weight: 1,715 pounds

Usual carriage: 7-inch mortar carriage Model 1895

Weight of gun and carriage: Approximately 8,000 pounds

Maximum elevation: 70 degrees

Loading: Separate

Shell weight: 125 pounds

Maximum muzzle velocity: 800 fps

Maximum range: 5,310 yards

Builders: Mortar: Watervliet Arsenal; carriage: Watertown Arsenal

Number built: 61

Several 7-inch siege mortars still survive. Nine have been identified on outdoor display and another is in storage. Unfortunately, none are under museum care and several show signs of weather-related deterioration. This example is at the courthouse in Phillips, Wisconsin.

Prewar Heavy Artillery

Although it had only a small regular army to equip, the US Army ordnance department developed a system of heavy pieces to complement its field and mountain artillery in the first decade of the twentieth century. A new generation of guns replaced the old 5-inch and 7-inch siege pieces of the Spanish-American War.

The smallest were the 3.8-inch guns and howitzers developed in 1907–08. In theory they could fire shells twice the weight of the 3-inch field gun (30 versus 15 pounds). However, the army found the shell too light to function as heavy artillery, and probably too expensive to use as just another piece of light artillery. At first just two batteries of each were procured, for service evaluation testing more than to realistically equip field units. While a few more howitzers were purchased just before the First World War, they never found favor within the army. Attempts were made to develop a new Model 1913 3.8-inch howitzer, and production orders for thirty-two forgings were awarded in December 1914. These were suspended in 1915 pending development of an improved version, and then cancelled altogether with the decision to adopt the 155 mm Schneider howitzer in 1917.

More success was achieved with the pair of 4.7-inch weapons. Again featuring a doubling of shell weight (60 pounds versus 30 for the 3.8), a new gun (Model 1906) and howitzer (Model 1907) were developed. It took other iterations (Model 1908 and then Model 1912) to get the howitzer right. Weapons of this size (both the gun and howitzer) were produced in greater numbers than the other models reviewed here. A total of 114 4.7-inch howitzers and fifty-two 4.7-inch guns were produced before America's entry into the war. These weapons were distributed to active regular and militia artillery regiments. The third and heaviest weapon developed was the 6-inch howitzer Model 1908. In fact, this howitzer and the 4.7-inch gun Model 1906 were known as the "new" siege artillery replacing the old 5-inch and 7-inch combination of guns.

The guns were satisfactory, though not particularly innovative designs. They were never given much of a chance for deployment. The Marine Corps acquired several 4.7-inch guns from the army and sent them to China. A couple of army batteries were dispatched with the Mexican Punitive Expedition in 1916 but never saw combat. When the First World War came, there were not enough of these guns, or anywhere near enough of the huge quantity of ammunition required, for the static warfare of the western front. With one exception, all the types remained stateside or in Hawaii.

The exception was the 4.7-inch gun. It was the one American gun thought appropriate for expanded production and deployment in significant numbers with the expeditionary force. Large production orders were issued, though as with all planned wartime production, delays dogged the program. Nevertheless, a limited number of guns were floated for overseas duty in 1918. Two regiments fired their 4.7s in combat before the end of the war. Plans to produce several hundred of the 4.7-inch gun and carriage were initiated in 1917–1918. Most of these orders were cancelled after the war, but a significant number were produced through 1919. Only this 4.7-inch gun stayed in the army's inventory, though only as strategic reserve material. All the other 3.8-inch, 4.7-inch, and 6-inch heavy artillery guns and howitzers were eliminated after 1920. Because of the need for memorial guns following the First World War, several representatives of these types survive.

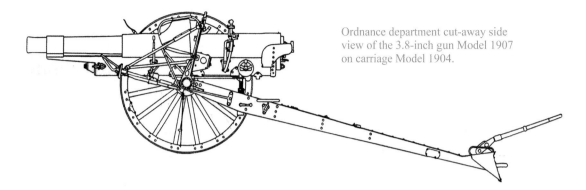

Ordnance department cut-away side view of the 3.8-inch gun Model 1907 on carriage Model 1904.

The 3.8-inch sized weapons were developed with the thought that they had a projectile weight double that of the standard 3-inch field gun. They were still light enough to accompany the field artillery on the same roads, but more useful when a heavier round was required. The gun and carriage were purposely designed to incorporate as many features as possible of the Model 1905 3-inch gun then being adopted. In fact, in many ways the gun was thought of as a "heavy" standard field artillery piece rather than a true siege or heavy gun. In truth, that was also the gun's problem. While the weapon worked as expected, it never really found a home in the artillery. Only two batteries for a total of eight guns (and one Model 1905-type piece) were produced. The US Army never requested that the type enter series production.

The tube was of conventional built-up nickel steel. It used thirty-four lands and grooves and rifling of $\frac{1}{50}$ increasing toward the muzzle to $\frac{1}{25}$. The Tasker breech mechanism was of conventional design and operation—opening with a lever mounted on the right with a hinge pin. The carriage was designed for a long recoil. The hydraulic recoil cylinder with counterrecoil springs was in a housing slung below the gun tube. The carriage could provide elevation from -5 to +15.5-degrees and had a traversing worm shaft to give 106 mils (6 degrees) of traverse.

The 3.8-inch gun Model 1907 rear-quarter view on the parade ground of Fort Riley in 1910.

There was no on-carriage ammunition storage (like the Model 1902 carriage for the 3-inch), but the gun did have a protective shield with hinged lower apron. The gun fired fixed ammunition, either the usual common shell or shrapnel, of 30-pound projectile weight.

Like other heavy batteries of the period, the 3.8-inch gun was to be organized into batteries of four guns each. Twelve caissons (with forty complete rounds each) and sixteen limbers (with eighteen complete rounds) were included in each battery to carry ammunition. New vehicles, similar in layout to those for the 3-inch but obviously fitted to carry the larger ammunition rounds, were developed and designated 3.8-inch Model 1904s appropriately.

The prototype gun was produced in early 1906. Four more forgings (all forgings for the 3.8-inch gun came from Midvale Steel) were ordered in October 1906 and the final four in August 1907. Guns were numbered 1–9, with the information stamped on the muzzle face. Model 1904 carriages were produced by Rock Island Arsenal in 1910. Presumably, carriages were marked with a separate information plate attached to the chassis or more likely the trail. Indecision over whether to fully commit to the 3.8-inch size and the success of the 3-inch gun discouraged further production, and no more were ordered. By 1911 the gun was no longer listed as an adopted type.

The type gun was evaluated at the Fort Riley firing test of 1909, and performance was judged satisfactory. With only two batteries' worth of guns manufactured, the guns did not see wide service. They were issued to the 83rd Field Artillery Regiment, but stayed stateside for training during the First World War. The guns in that regiment were replaced with Model 1917 75 mm field guns in late 1918. In June 1919, the 3.8-inch gun Model 1907 and carriage were declared obsolete and approved for disposal (along with the sister 3.8-inch howitzer Model 1908). It does not appear that any were donated as memorial guns. No 3.8-inch guns are known to exist.

3.8-Inch Gun Model 1907 on Carriage Model 1904

Gun Characteristics

Bore size: 3.8 inches

Construction: Built-up nickel steel

Tube length overall: 111.25 inches

Nominal caliber: 28 calibers

Tube and breech weight: 1,535 pounds

Usual carriage: 3.8-inch gun carriage model 1904

Weight of gun and carriage: 3,875 pounds

Maximum elevation: 15.5 degrees

Loading: Fixed

Shell weight: 30 pounds

Maximum muzzle velocity: 1,700 fps

Maximum range: 8,000 yards

Builders: Forgings: Midvale Steel; gun: Watervliet Arsenal; carriage: Rock Island Arsenal

Number built: 9 (1 Type Model 1905, 8 production)

Photographs of the 3.8-inch gun are rare. This image appears to have been take at Rock Island Arsenal, probably around 1910–12.

3.8-Inch Howitzer Model 1908

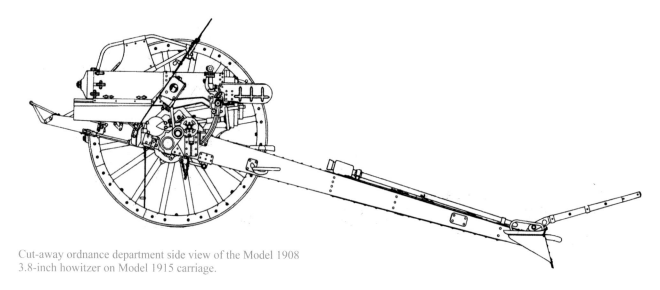

Cut-away ordnance department side view of the Model 1908
3.8-inch howitzer on Model 1915 carriage.

The 3.8-inch howitzer project started a little later than its companion gun. In 1906 it was described as a howitzer on a long-recoil carriage firing the same size shell as the 3.8-inch gun with a muzzle velocity of 900 fps. The design was sufficiently advanced to order the first forgings in mid-1908. Eight howitzers were delivered by the end of 1909—enough for two batteries for service testing. There then seems to have been a problem in designing an adequate carriage. In March 1908 the first carriage order was revoked to allow its complete redesign to reduce weight. Requisite recoil springs had to be imported from Rheinische of Germany in 1909. Eight Model 1908 carriages were finally produced for the eight production howitzers.

The tube was a simple built-up nickel steel body and breech hoop, the latter holding the breech mechanism. The breech was interrupted screw with four sections. The breech opening and operating handle was on the right side, secured with a hinge pin. Firing was by a firing pin fixed in the hub of the block carrier. The gun used semi-fixed ammunition, one of three zone powder charges being loaded in a brass cartridge case. Shells were either common steel or shrapnel. The carriage was a box-trail with sections removed to reduce weight. An innovative variable-recoil system was designed by ordnance officer Lawson M. Fuller. The large hydraulic recoil cylinder sat prominently atop the tube, similar to other American howitzers of the period. The two spring counterrecoil mechanisms were incorporated

The 3.8-inch howitzer Model 1908 on carriage Model 1908 being used in firing tests at Fort Riley in late 1909.

in the same housing. The box trail was made of flange steel. It could provide elevation from -5 to +40 degrees, and allowed 6 degrees traverse. Wheels were 58 inches in diameter and track width was 60 inches. A hardened-steel 0.15-inch-thick shield was included, with two axle seats attached facing forward. Despite its prolonged development, the carriage design does not appear innovative or otherwise remarkable.

After a hiatus, forty more slightly modified Model 1908M1 3.8-inch howitzers were authorized in October 1911. This gun had a modified traveling lock lug for the breech mechanism and a resulting 2-inch increase in overall length and extra 9 pounds in weight. Even then, the order was cut back to twenty in October. Rationale was that other projects were more urgent. In any event, the final twenty were not delivered until 1914. Once again the pursuit of a successful carriage took longer. In 1911 the army admitted that the new carriage was not advancing quickly due to the question of whether this caliber would finally be adopted for service. Eventually twenty new howitzer carriages Model 1915 were produced and issued to the service. Attempts were made in 1916–17 to develop a split-trail carriage for the howitzer along the lines of the Model 1916 3-inch gun. Besides a trials prototype, it was never ordered into production.

The call to employ the 3.8-inch howitzer never came. There was no opportunity for use of the small numbers in inventory. The twenty-eight units acquired stayed in the United States during the First World War as training substitutes for new 155 mm howitzers. Then in June 1919—for many of the howitzers, just five years after completion—they were declared obsolete and released for disposal. In 1920 several were provided for war memorials, but most fell victim to the Second World War scrap drives. There is only a single 3.8-inch howitzer surviving today, as a war memorial in a cemetery.

3.8-Inch Howitzer Model 1908 on Carriage Model 1915

Gun Characteristics

Bore size: 3.8 inches

Construction: Built-up nickel steel

Tube length overall: 48 inches

Nominal caliber: 12 calibers

Tube and breech weight: 423 pounds

Usual carriage: 3.8-inch howitzer carriage Model 1908 and 1915

Weight of gun and carriage: 2,040 pounds

Maximum elevation: 40 degrees

Loading: Semi-fixed

Shell weight: 30 pounds

Maximum muzzle velocity: 900 fps

Maximum range: 6,338 yards

Builders: Forgings: Bethlehem Steel and Midvale Steel; howitzer: Watervliet Arsenal; carriage: Rock Island Arsenal

Number built: 29 howitzers (1 type, 8 M1908, 20 M1908M1), 29 carriages (1 type, 8 M1908, 20 M1915)

The only surviving example of a 3.8-inch howitzer is Watervliet No. 6, currently displayed as a memorial in a cemetery in Lewistown, Illinois.

4.7-Inch Gun Model 1906

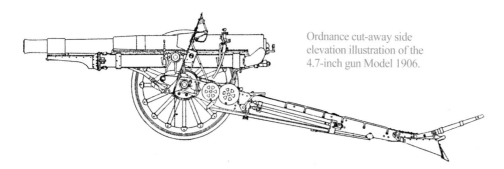

Ordnance cut-away side elevation illustration of the 4.7-inch gun Model 1906.

This was probably the most successful of the pre-war heavy guns. The 4.7-inch gun was produced in greater numbers and lasted the longest of this generation. It was a fairly conventional design, not too distant from the successful Model 1905 3-inch type. It followed the doubling rule where its 60-pound projectile was twice that of the next smaller 3.8-inch gun. The forging for the type gun (also known as the Model 1904) was ordered in September 1906.

The tube was built-up, with tube, jacket, and locking hoop. The transition to nickel steel alloy was just being made; in fact, the first twenty-one production guns were made of gun steel, but the rest were made of nickel alloy steel. The tube jacket extended to the rear to encompass the breechblock, which was a standard interrupted screw with four sectors. Projecting down from the tube was a lug to hold the center hydrospring recoil cylinder and prominent 7-inch-diameter steel tubes holding the counterrecoil spring on either side. The gun fired with a continuous-pull mechanism. It was supplied with fixed ammunition, most commonly shrapnel or HE common steel projectiles, each weighing 60 pounds. Later, in order to get greater range, a 45-pound shell was developed that, with a 2,050-fps muzzle velocity, could attain an 8,700-yard range.

The conventional solid, fixed trail carriage had a pintle bearing supporting a steel yoke that held the gun trunnions. A double-screw elevating mechanism could deliver -5 to +15 degrees of elevation, and on-carriage traverse was 8 degrees. The carriage had 60-inch wheels with a 60-inch track width. Initially the wheels had steel tires, but later were given solid rubber tires to permit better road towing. A range quadrant and panoramic sight were provided.

Small production orders were placed between 1907 and early 1917, totaling sixty-seven M1906 guns, all produced at Watervliet Arsenal. They went to units as completed; Battery C, 5th Artillery was the first recipient in 1911. They served throughout the army, including being stationed in the Hawaiian Department. The improved Model 1906M1 followed; serial

A 4.7-inch gun Model 1906 with Battery G, 5th Artillery in 1916 during deployment to support activities along the Mexican-US border. Note the early version of the wheels with steel tires.

numbers up through 226 were ordered and delivered through 1919. In January 1917, additional separate production orders were approved. These were placed at Watervliet (240 guns), Northwest Ordnance (500 guns), Walter Scott Co. (250 carriages), Studebaker (500 carriages), and Rock Island Arsenal (198 carriages). Results were disappointing. This was a gun type already in production, developed with no new recuperator or breech technology. The fact that production could not be rapidly ramped up, even in government arsenals, proved embarrassing to the ordnance department. It appears that a total of 470 were made. At one point the army considered converting the guns to 120 mm to take advantage of French ammunition supply, but the idea was scrapped because of the likely delay.

Sixty-four 4.7-inch guns were floated to Europe to equip part of three field artillery regiments. Two of these (302nd and 328th) used their guns in combat. After the war, the guns were returned and went into storage, along with most of the others. For several years they were retained as part of America's war reserve. In 1930 orders were given to stop manufacture of additional parts, and tools could be eliminated. In 1932 it was decided to donate all 453 guns and 467 carriages still on hand. They were gone from the army's inventory by mid-1938. The 4.7-inch gun proved to be a popular memorial piece. Some seventy are known to survive in museums and as civic memorial guns.

4.7-Inch Gun Model 1906 on Carriage Model 1906

Gun Characteristics

Bore size: 4.7 inches

Construction: Built-up, common or nickel steel

Tube length overall: 134.92 inches

Nominal caliber: 27.5 calibers

Tube and breech weight: 2,688 pounds

Usual carriage: 4.7-inch gun carriage Model 1906

Weight of gun and carriage: 7,393 pounds

Maximum elevation: 15 degrees

Loading: Fixed

Shell weight: 60 pounds (also 45 pounds)

Maximum muzzle velocity: 1,700 fps

Maximum range: 7,550 yards (8,700 with light shell)

Builders: Gun: Watervliet Arsenal, Northwest Ordnance Co.; carriage: Rock Island Arsenal, Walter Scott Co., Studebaker Corp.

Number built: 470 (No. 3 destroyed in firing and replaced with a new gun of same serial number)

Almost seventy 4.7-inch guns survive, most as public war memorials. This well-maintained sample is at a National Guard armory in Butner, North Carolina.

4.7-Inch Howitzer Model 1907

In the early 1900s, considerable effort was expended to develop a heavy howitzer for the US Army. Only the ungainly 7-inch siege howitzer had filled that niche and was considered too large for mobile use. After a tentative design had been developed, a first prototype forging was ordered in June 1907 from Driggs-Seabury Ordnance Co. of Derby, Connecticut. Watervliet Arsenal finished the gun. The carriage was designed at Rock Island, and the company was instructed to rush the project because of the serious lack of progress. While the gun was given Model 1907 serial No. 1, instructions were provided to label the carriage simply "pilot" with no serial number.

Its layout was unusual. The short nickel steel barrel (just 12.4 calibers in length) had forty-two grooves, and rifling was a uniform ⅟₂₀ twist. The hydropneumatic recoil cylinder was placed atop the barrel. The two cylinders holding the counterrecoil springs were attached on each side, left and right of the barrel. This "nest" of cylinders is unique to this American howitzer, and a clear differentiator in photo recognition. Otherwise the trail was a conventional fixed, box trail with an opening for the breech to recoil. The carriage could allow elevation from

The sole surviving 4.7-inch Model 1907 howitzer, with a shield, in Taylorville, Illinois.

The first 4.7-inch Model 1907 howitzer at Rock Island Arsenal just after completion.

-5 to +40 degrees. There were no on-carriage axle or riding seats for crew members. The projected muzzle velocity of 900 fps calculated to a maximum range of 6,640 yards with the 60-pound projectile The muzzle face was marked with the serial number, inspector, manufacturer, weight, and year of acceptance. Corresponding information was on a plate mounted on the trail, between the tool boxes. The army was in such a hurry to start service trials that a battery's worth of four howitzers and carriages was ordered even before the type gun was completed. Four new forgings were ordered from Midvale Steel in August 1907. The carriage order was issued to Rock Island Arsenal on May 15, 1907, numbered 1–4. The four guns were completed at Watervliet (Nos. 2–5) and shipped on September 24, 1908.

This initial order was never followed with series production. It is not clear if there was a problem with the design or manufacture, but in very short time the subsequent Model 1908 4.7-inch howitzer was developed, evaluated, and produced. Its characteristics do not seem to vary at all from the Model 1907; the only visible difference is the arrangement of the recoil mechanism atop the gun tube. In any event, the five Model 1907s were never used or issued to a service unit, and eventually were moved to arsenal storage. They were authorized for donation as memorial or ornamental guns in 1919–1920. Thankfully, one example survives at a local historical society in Taylorville, Illinois (often not the case with short-run, relatively unsuccessful types).

4.7-Inch Howitzer Model 1907 on Carriage Model 1907

Gun Characteristics

Bore size: 4.7 inches

Construction: Built-up nickel steel

Tube length overall: 63 inches

Nominal caliber: 12.4 calibers

Tube and breech weight: 950 pounds

Usual carriage: 4.7-inch howitzer carriage model 1907

Maximum elevation: 40 degrees

Loading: Separate with brass cartridge case

Shell weight: 60 pounds

Maximum muzzle velocity: 900 fps

Maximum range: 6,640 yards

Builders: Howitzer: Watervliet Arsenal; carriage: Rock Island Arsenal

Number built: 5 (1 type, 4 production)

No ordnance drawing has been located for the Model 1907 4.7-inch howitzer. This photograph of an assembled unit (without shield) at Rock Island Arsenal clearly shows the unique front appearance of the various recoil and counterrecoil cylinders.

4.7-Inch Howitzer Model 1908 and Model 1912

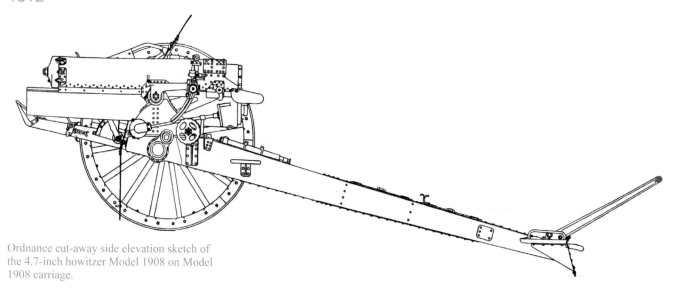

Ordnance cut-away side elevation sketch of the 4.7-inch howitzer Model 1908 on Model 1908 carriage.

On the heels of the Model 1907 4.7-inch howitzer, a new design with a different arrangement of the recoil mechanisms was produced. The initial type gun and carriage were ordered from Watervliet and Rock Island in January 1909. Subsequently, Model 1908 and the nearly identical Model 1912 became the army's standard howitzer prior to the First World War, over 100 issued.

The howitzer tube was built-up nickel steel consisting of a body and breech hoop. The tube had forty-two grooves and was given a uniform rifling of ½₀. The hoop extended beyond the tube to make the recess for the breech mechanism. It had an interrupted-screw breech mechanism with four sectors and a loading tray. The hinge pin for the carrier was on the right side. There were two clips along the length of the barrel to act as guide rails during the recoil. A continuous-pull firing mechanism was used.

The carriage was a fixed-trail box carriage configured to operate with a variable recoil. A prominent housing sat atop the barrel and contained the hydropneumatic recoil cylinder and spring counterrecoil cylinders. A quick-return mechanism could return the howitzer to firing settings after reloading. A heavy shield protected the crew, and two axle seats were attached to its front to carry crew members while traveling. Elevation

A 4.7-inch howitzer and carriage Model 1908 at Aberdeen Proving Ground.

was by rocker mechanism and could deliver elevations from -5 to +40-degrees. Carriage traverse was 3 degrees to either side. The howitzer fired projectiles (HE common steel or shrapnel) of 60 pounds using separately loaded brass cartridge cases with individual zone propellant charges. Wheels were 58 inches in diameter and had a 60-inch track width.

An initial order for twenty-four series production howitzers was placed in 1910. Additional orders followed at a few per year. By May of 1915, fifty-four Model 1908s had been ordered. All were delivered by the end of 1916 (serial numbers 1–54). The Model 1912 4.7-inch howitzer differed only in the new hoop for attaching the breech; its performance characteristics were the same. Also, a new Model 1908M1 carriage was introduced along the way; it had an improved type of steel axle. Carriages were made either at Rock Island Arsenal or the Detrick & Harvey Machinery Co. Model 1912 howitzers were ordered in small lots between 1912 and 1916. The final two were not delivered until September 6, 1918. Fifty-five Model 1912s were completed (serials 1–55) by Watervliet Arsenal from Midvale or Bethlehem forgings. Howitzers were marked on the muzzle face with serial and manufacturer, on the breech face above the breech opening with model number, and on a carriage plate on the fixed trail with carriage serial and manufacture information.

The howitzers went to heavy artillery units, training facilities, and militia units. None saw combat, but some were sent to the Mexican border in 1916. Others reached the garrison in Hawaii. In 1917–19 they stayed home, authorized as training substitutes for 155 mm howitzers yet to be supplied. On June 19, 1919, the army recommended that all three models of 4.7-inch howitzers be declared obsolete, and by 1922 they were scrapped, along with their carriages, or distributed as memorial pieces. Several nice examples still exist in cities today.

4.7-Inch Howitzer Model 1908 and 1912 on Carriage Model 1908

Gun Characteristics

Bore size: 4.7 inches
Construction: Built-up, nickel steel
Tube length overall: 69 inches
Nominal caliber: 13.6 calibers
Tube and breech weight: 1,056 pounds
Usual carriage: 4.7-inch howitzer carriage Model 1908
Weight of gun and carriage: 3,988 pounds
Maximum elevation: 40 degrees
Loading: Separate brass cartridge case
Shell weight: 60 pounds
Maximum muzzle velocity: 900 fps
Maximum range: 6,640 yards

Builders: Howitzer: Watervliet Arsenal; carriage: Rock Island Arsenal, Detrick & Harvey Machinery Co.
Number built: 54 Model 1908, 55 Model 1912

A 4.7-inch howitzer Model 1912 today in storage at the Rock Island Arsenal Museum.

6-Inch Howitzer Model 1908

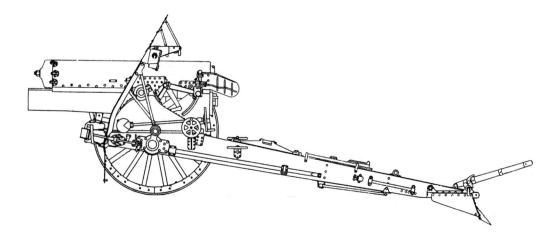

Ordnance drawing showing a cut-away, side elevation of the 6-inch howitzer Model 1908 on its Model 1908 carriage.

This was the largest of the new heavy siege guns developed between the Spanish American and First World Wars. Its design was consistent with the 3.8-inch and 4.7-inch howitzers introduced around the same time. Design documents of March 1906 projected that it could fire a 120-pound projectile at 900 fps with a range of over 6,500 yards and to use (for the first time in an American gun of this size) separate loading with brass cartridge cases. An initial type gun, known at the time as the Model 1906, was produced for trial in 1907. Because of changes necessary to accommodate a new carriage, an additional type gun was fabricated in 1909, known as Model 1908.

The nickel steel tube was a single forging, with a breech hoop that had a large, upright lug to attach to the recoil piston rod. The tube had projecting guide bars. It was rifled with fifty-four grooves of a uniform 1/18 twist. The interrupted breech had four sectors. The breechblock was held by a block carrier hinged on the right side, and the block was pierced with two vent holes. It was fired by a continuous-pull mechanism. The howitzer fired either common steel or shrapnel rounds of 120 pounds. Brass cartridge cases were prepared for three zones of powder charges in silk pouches.

The carriage was a box-trail type supporting the tube and recoil cylinder mounted on top of it, which delivered a variable recoil. The hydropneumatic cylinder had two counterrecoil spring cylinders mounted on either side. The howitzer had an effective quick-return mechanism allowing it to return quickly

One of the five surviving 6-inch Model 1908 howitzers. This is howitzer No. 20 (made at Watervliet) on carriage No. 29 (made at Bethlehem Steel), now on display near an American Legion in St. Paul, Minnesota.

to a setting after firing. The slightly changed Model 1908M1 carriage had an enlarged counterrecoil spring column, different gear for the quick return, and different axle construction. This added 228 pounds to the carriage weight. The carriage could give -5 to +40-degree elevation and total traverse of 6 degrees. The howitzer had 60-inch wheels and a similar 60-inch track width. All models had an open tangent sight and a Model 1904 or Model 1915 panoramic sight. The carriage had a 0.15-inch-thick protective shield. Initially, modified 4.7-inch caissons and limbers were used, but eventually dedicated Model 1909 artillery vehicles were adopted.

The initial production order of twenty-four howitzers and carriages was delivered in 1910–1911. Another eight followed in 1912–1913. Carriages were built by Rock Island, and for the first time, Bethlehem Steel (which was usually associated with steel forgings and gun tubes). Additional small numbers were ordered and built until April 1916, some of them finished by Bethlehem Steel. Forty-two 6-inch Model 1908 howitzers and carriages were completed.

Like the other pre-war howitzers, the 6-inch guns saw service only in the US and Hawaii. No thought of sending them to Europe for the First World War was entertained. In 1918 they were authorized as training substitutes for 155 mm howitzers. In June 1919, they were declared obsolete, and a year later at least fifteen were made available for donation as memorial guns. At least five are known to survive, one nicely restored and on display at the US Army Artillery Museum.

6-Inch Howitzer Model 1908 on Carriage Model 1908

Gun Characteristics

Bore size: 6 inches

Construction: Built-up nickel steel

Tube length overall: 87 inches

Nominal caliber: 13 calibers

Tube and breech weight: 1,925 pounds

Usual carriage: 6-inch howitzer carriage Model 1908 or 1908M1

Weight of gun and carriage: 7,354 pounds (Model 1908 carriage)

Maximum elevation: 40 degrees

Loading: Separate brass cartridge case

Shell weight: 120 pounds

Maximum muzzle velocity: 900 fps

Maximum range: 6,704 yards

Builders: Howitzer: Watervliet Arsenal; carriage: Rock Island Arsenal, Bethlehem Steel

Number built: 42

Taken at Fort Riley, Kansas, in 1910, this photograph shows a 6-inch howitzer Model 1908.

First World War 75 mm Field Artillery

Upon entry into the First World War, the US realized the difficulty of acquiring very large numbers of guns, carriages and vehicles, ammunition, and trained artillerymen. Almost immediately, orders were placed for more 3-inch guns of the older but proven Model 1905 type and the new Model 1916 gun. The latter was not yet perfected (and subsequent events were to prove that was indeed true), but confidence of success prompted production orders for several hundred. Also American domestic production capacity of cannons of all sizes would have to be drastically enhanced; new factories and producers would be required.

In June 1917, on the advice of European allies, the decision was made to standardize American guns to metric French sizes. One of the most persuasive arguments was the convenience of using ammunition already in production in France. American 3-inch guns Model 1916 and Model 1917 were redesigned to a 75 mm bore. However, even then these types were mostly reserved for training in the United States. Combat units were equipped with French-made 75 mm Model 1897 guns, to be supplemented by American-made versions license-produced during 1919.

While some accompanying vehicles for the First World War 75 mm artillery pieces were obtained with each gun type, a new generation was designed and produced in large numbers to serve all three types. These were primarily the 75 mm gun caisson Model 1918 (carrying seventy fixed rounds), the Model 1918 75 mm gun-caisson limber (with thirty rounds), and the Model 1917 battery and store wagon. These were made during the war in large numbers, most coming from the American Car & Foundry Co. Over 43,000 limbers and caissons were produced during the war and immediately thereafter. Designing the bore and chamber of the three guns almost simultaneously meant that they used the same ammunition—a 13-pound common steel high-explosive shell, a gas-filled shell of the same weight, and a 16-pound shrapnel round.

Production facilities erected in America, many by companies new to cannon manufacture, were impressive. Many provided elements for both the huge Model 1916 and Model 1897 programs. Gun forgings came from established firms like Midvale and Bethlehem Steel, but also from the Standard Forging Co. and Symington-Anderson. Gun tubes were supplied by Bethlehem Steel, Watervliet Arsenal, Symington-Anderson, and the Wisconsin Gun Company. Carriages were from Bethlehem Steel, Rock Island Arsenal, New York Air Brake Co. (M1916s), and Willys-Overland (M1897s).

While a few American-produced guns reached France, the war was primarily conducted by the AEF with French-supplied guns. However, in 1919 large numbers of each of the three types of 75 mm field guns were supplied domestically before the contracts were terminated. These guns became the staple of US forces for the next twenty years. When it was found that the Model 1897's recuperator could be serviced only at sophisticated arsenals, Model 1916 and Model 1917 75 mm guns were preferred for isolated overseas garrisons. Panama and Puerto Rico saw allocations of Model 1916 in the 1920s and 1930s. Model 1917s were the mainstays for the Hawaiian and Philippine departments. Otherwise, the regular army and National Guard relied on the French 75s. Modifications were made to all of these guns to allow for high-speed towing in the 1930s, and the Model 1897 underwent a complete modernization right before the Second World War.

75 mm Gun Model 1916

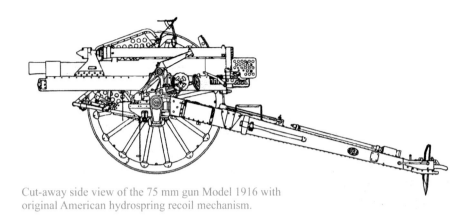

Cut-away side view of the 75 mm gun Model 1916 with original American hydrospring recoil mechanism.

Following the successful development and deployment of the 3-inch Model 1905, improvements were planned for the next generation of guns. In particular, the ordnance department began looking at split trails for its next gun carriage. A Deport 75 mm gun with this feature was imported and extensively studied in 1912. Many of its split trail features were incorporated in a prototype Model 1913 3-inch gun. Excited about the gun's potential performance, the army ordered thirty-nine in late 1914 but had to suspend production early the following year when carriage trials revealed serious problems. After redesign, it emerged again as the Model 1916 3-inch gun, and 262 were ordered in September 1916. Soon this order was increased to 603 guns, to be supplied by Watervliet and new producer Symington-Anderson of Rochester, New York. In June 1917, French artillery bore sizes were adopted to simplify ammunition supply. The Model 1916 was quickly reconfigured to this new bore size. Only thirty-four guns had been produced; they were bored out and relined to 75mm. All orders were changed to the new caliber.

An interesting picture taken in France in late 1918, showing all three types of 75 mm guns acquired by the Americans during the First World War. On the left is the 75 mm Model 1897 (French 75), in the center is a 75 mm Model 1917 (British 75) produced in America and shipped to France for training in 1918. On the right is a 75 mm Model 1916 (American 75), one of the few shipped to France for modification and potential adoption of the St. Chamond-type recuperator.

The gun had a conventional nickel built-up steel tube with jacket, locking, and breech hoop and a drop-block, semi-automatic breech mechanism. A short, visibly prominent hoop near the muzzle held two flanges on the underside of the jacket guiding the gun in recoil. A lug on top of the barrel connected to the piston of the oil recoil cylinder, which was mounted above the tube. It was the variable recoil length type. Under the tube were the two spring cylinders of the counterrecoil system. A hand wheel controlled an elevating worm with bevel gears mounted on the rocker. The full, split trails were equipped with driven spades. The carriage used standard American 56-inch wheels with 3-inch steel tires. Hand brakes were fitted, as was a standard protecting shield and apron. The guns had a Model 1916 panoramic sight. They were marked in usual fashion on the muzzle face and with a carriage plate on the trail.

Certainly with its split trail and high elevation, this was an innovative design, and there were high hopes that it would become the standard gun for America's war participation. Large orders were placed, eventually totaling almost 4,000 units. However, the gun's complexities soon demonstrated that it needed further design modifications, and manufacturing encountered other problems. By early 1918, emphasis shifted to the M1897 75 mm design, and the M1916 was relegated to a secondary role. In an attempt to solve problems with the hydrospring recoil system, French-built St. Chamond hydropneumatic recuperators were purchased. One was mounted on a test gun shipped to France for a special evaluation. Of 673 ordered, only sixty recuperators were eventually acquired during 1919; when used with the M1916 gun carriage, it was designated the M1916M1. The model didn't solve all the problems and remained in storage.

75 mm Gun Model 1916

Gun Characteristics

Bore size: 75mm

Construction: Built-up nickel steel

Tube length overall: 90.9 inches

Nominal caliber: 28.4 calibers

Tube and breech weight: 749 pounds

Usual carriage: 75 mm gun carriage Model 1916

Weight of gun and carriage: 3,045 pounds

Maximum elevation: 53 degrees

Loading: Fixed

Shell weight: 13 pounds

Maximum muzzle velocity: 1,900 fps

Maximum range: 12,490 yards

Builders: Gun: Watervliet Arsenal, Bethlehem Steel, Wisconsin Gun, Symington-Anderson; carriage: Bethlehem Steel, Rock Island Arsenal, New York Air Brake

Number built: 810 gun tubes, 362 carriages

Staggering numbers of artillery vehicles, most notably limbers and caissons, were built for the war effort. Here, shortly postwar, they sit in outdoor storage at Aberdeen Proving Ground.

Early production 75 mm Model 1916 with hydrospring recoil. Photograph dated September 6, 1918. Note the high elevation possible with the new split-trail carriage design.

Model 1916 75 mm gun equipped with the St. Chamond pneumatic recoil system. This mechanism was mounted under the gun tube rather than on top of the barrel, hence the large, open gap in the shield designed with the hydrospring equipment in mind.

One of the fifty-one Model 1916 75 mm guns mounted as an anti-aircraft gun on a truck as an expediency during the First World War.

There are only two 75 mm Model 1916 guns surviving in their original configuration. This example is in a cemetery near Shiloh, Ohio.

By the end of 1918, 251 guns were completed and thirty-four were floated to Europe but did not see combat. Most were retained at home for training. Guns were ordered from Bethlehem Steel, Watervliet Arsenal, Symington-Anderson, and the Wisconsin Gun Co. Carriages were obtained from Bethlehem, Rock Island, and the New York Air Brake Co. Ultimately 810 gun tubes and 362 carriages were delivered. Changes, mostly in the arrangement of jackets and clips, resulted in six different model guns, though with the same performance characteristics. As there were many more M1916 guns available than corresponding carriages, the tubes found other uses. Fifty-one guns were mounted on trucks as a transitional AA gun known as the Model 1916; others were mounted on pedestal coast defenses in Panama, and the coast artillery acquired 100 as ex-caliber and sub-caliber tubes for use with large-caliber guns. After the war, the remaining field gun served in secondary roles—either in overseas departments or in reserve storage.

75 mm Gun Model 1917

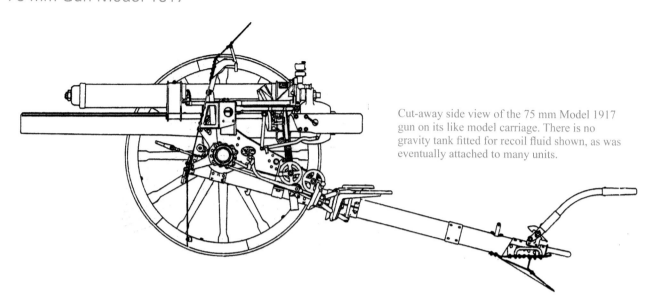

Cut-away side view of the 75 mm Model 1917 gun on its like model carriage. There is no gravity tank fitted for recoil fluid shown, as was eventually attached to many units.

The British contracted with Bethlehem Steel for a wide range of war materials at the start of the European conflict. Among the artillery pieces Bethlehem was to supply was a large number of 18-pounder (3.3-inch) standard divisional field guns designed in 1904. With its conventional hydrospring recoil and pole trail, it was a serviceable if not spectacular design. To take advantage of this existing tooling, the army sought to continue production to the standard US 3-inch size as a way to quickly obtain more field guns. On May 22, 1917, the US Army asked Bethlehem to produce 268 of this type of gun. Vickers granted royalty-free licenses. Later in the summer the change was made to a 75 mm bore, well before any deliveries had been made. Additional orders were forthcoming as frustration grew with production of other 75 mm types.

The tube was constructed in the same manner as its immediate British 18-pounder predecessor. It consisted of wire wound over an alloy steel tube. A jacket and prominent, bulbous breech ring covered the wire. The breech was an interrupted-screw type with four sections. It had an automatic extractor, and ammunition was fired with a continuous-pull firing

Rear-quarter ordnance department view of the 75 mm gun Model 1917. The pole trail, borrowed directly from the British 18-pounder design, is clearly evident.

mechanism. The tube had longitudinal projecting guides on each side of the jacket that were used to hold it in place during full recoil. The top, pneumatic recoil cylinder was surrounded by two cylinders containing the recoil springs. On the front end of the projecting hydraulic recoil cylinder, a gravity tank containing oil was often used to refill the cylinder. Due to the need to adjust the tube balance with the bore change, its length was shortened. This created several differences between the gun built for American service and the British one (both built at the same Bethlehem Steel facility). An obvious one is that the British 18-pounder has a noticeable muzzle swell, and the projecting recoil guides on the barrel end about 6 inches short of the muzzle face rather than near the end of the barrel. The American gun had shorter but more bulbous breech housing and was marked with data on the muzzle face.

The carriage was little altered from its British counterpart. It had a main tubular steel pole trail ending with a spade, lifting handles, and towing lunette. Elevation from -5 to +16 degrees was achieved with a double-headed screw mechanism. A total of 8 degrees of on-carriage traverse was possible. It had standard 56-inch wooden spoke wheels, with 3-inch steel-rim tires. A top and main shield offered crew protection. The gun was equipped with a rocking-bar sight and Model 1917 panoramic sight. A carriage plate contained information about the gun, manufacturer, serial number, and inspector.

Compared to the problems in starting manufacture of the M1916 and M1897 guns, the Model 1917 was simple. Of course, Bethlehem was already familiar with the design, and fully tooled. Only minor changes were required due to the change in caliber to 75mm. Production was regular through much of 1918,

75 mm Gun Model 1917

Gun Characteristics

Bore size: 75mm
Construction: Wire wound, alloy steel
Tube length overall: 88.21 inches
Nominal caliber: 28.4 calibers
Tube and breech weight: 995 pounds
Usual carriage: 75 mm gun carriage Model 1917
Weight of gun and carriage: 2,887 pounds
Maximum elevation: 16 degrees
Loading: Fixed
Shell weight: 13 pounds
Maximum muzzle velocity: 1,900 fps
Maximum range: 8,805 yards

Builder: Bethlehem Steel
Number built: 909 guns, 921 carriages

One of the two 75 mm gun Model 1917 and carriages until recently part of the US Army Ordnance Museum at Aberdeen Proving Ground.

providing anxiously anticipated guns for training centers. Most of the M1917s were kept stateside, but 124 had been shipped to France by the time of the armistice. None entered combat. After the end of the war, production contracts were adjusted. Bethlehem (the only producer) provided 909 guns and 921 carriages. Between the wars, the type was allocated for use by the divisions and beach defense in the Hawaiian and Philippine departments. The hydrospring was within the maintenance capabilities of these locations, as opposed to the M1897 types. All of the guns stayed in the army's inventory, even if in storage, until the needs of foreign transfer arose in 1940–1941. The type saw combat in the Philippines and Java in 1941–42.

The Model 1917 75 mm gun on its original carriage is quite rare; they were never contributed for war memorials. Three exist in US museums and two are in foreign museums.

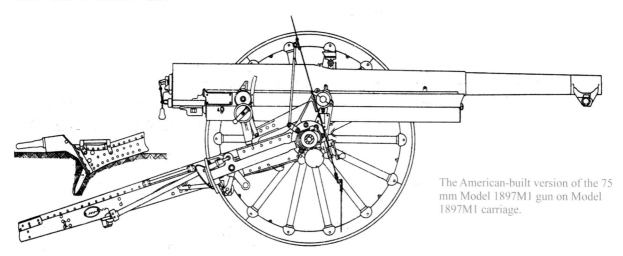

The American-built version of the 75 mm Model 1897M1 gun on Model 1897M1 carriage.

In May 1917, the French Military Mission offered to supply French-made 75 mm guns to the AEF starting in August. Given the critical shortage of field guns, the offer was gratefully accepted. While deliveries proved uneven, American forces were adequately provided with the M1897 75 mm by the time they entered combat. Altogether, the US purchased almost 2,800 such guns from the French—about 1,800 used during the war in France and 955 used after the armistice to allow the

French to finish work that the US had ordered. These guns came from three tube manufacturers and ten carriage manufacturers. French-made guns identified the manufacturer above the breech and on the front of the trail below the recoil mechanism. They were designated M1897.

The tube was built-up nickel steel, and consisted of the tube and reinforced breech hoop. It rested on a cradle with bronze slides. Distinctive rollers near the muzzle kept the tube

The first American-produced 75 mm M1897M1 at Aberdeen on November 1, 1918—just ten days before the armistice.

stable when it recoiled back to the cradle. A Nordenfelt eccentric breechblock was used. Its offset breech was opened by rotating it through a 120-degree axis. It was automatic—opening ejected the previous, empty cartridge case. A lug on the underside of the tube connected to a hydropneumatic, constant recoil mechanism. This "Puteaux recuperator" was the heart of the French 75's success. Its smooth functioning allowed the guns to fire rapidly and stay on target—the two obvious benefits of a long-recoil system. The mechanism itself consisted of a smaller liquid-filled recoil cylinder and larger counterrecoil cylinder with oil and nitrogen. The mechanism was well-designed but required fine machining by hand to tight tolerances. This meant they were hard to construct in standard US manufacturing plants.

The carriage was a single fixed trail with spade. Two nickel steel flasks had transoms and a closed top plate. The American-made carriage M1897M1 had slightly different wheel spokes, rims, and cases for sights and equipment. The two wooden wheels were slightly smaller than usual American pieces (52 versus 56 inches in diameter) with 3.5-inch-wide (versus 3-inch-wide) steel rims. The carriage was usually equipped with the French Model 1901 non-telescopic sight on the left side of the trunnions. It had a rather small steel shield and apron.

On February 8, 1918, the US formally adopted the M1897 for manufacture and encountered problems in receiving and modifying the plans to metric measurements. However, the biggest stumbling block was finding tools and skilled labor to produce the Puteaux recuperator. Only seventy-four American guns were completed before the armistice was signed. While orders were scaled back, over 1,000 guns were ultimately produced in American plants, bringing the total received to 3,994 guns and 4,154 carriages. American-made guns were

75 mm Gun Model 1897

Gun Characteristics

Bore size: 75 mm

Construction: Built-up nickel steel

Tube length overall: 107.126 inches

Nominal caliber: 36 calibers

Tube and breech weight: 1,015 pounds

Usual carriage: 75 mm gun carriage model 1897

Weight of gun and carriage: 2,657 pounds

Maximum elevation: 19 degrees

Loading: Fixed

Shell weight: 13 pounds

Maximum muzzle velocity: 1,805 fps

Maximum range: 9,200 yards

Builders: Guns: ABS, ATS (French arsenals), Symington-Anderson, Wisconsin Gun; carriages: several French firms; Willys-Overland, Rock Island Arsenal

Number built: 3,994 gun tubes, 4,154 carriages

Because large numbers of the Model 1897 75 mm guns were never modernized, many still exist at local and municipal memorials, like this one in Sherman, Texas.

A Model 1897 75 mm gun of the 16th Field Artillery Regiment and its limber at Fort Myers in April 1932.

marked on the muzzle face and on the side of the trail. They were designated M1897. Later modifications carried a plate on the right side of the carriage support

In France, the AEF's field artillery depended on the M1897. The gun fired its first American combat rounds on October 23, 1917, and was continuously used thereafter. After the war these guns were returned to the US. The army continued to use them and many were kept in storage. The Marine Corps received fifty guns and used them for many years. Large numbers were converted to an interim high-speed configuration in 1933–37. Other tubes were mounted on the entirely new M2 series of carriages in 1934–1941 and to self-propelled mounts. Others were transferred through lend-lease, mostly to Great Britain. As most were replaced by the time combat started, it is not surprising that large numbers still exist in museums and as memorial guns. Roughly 200 still exist, perhaps thirty-five to forty of them in the original First World War configuration.

The M1897 75 mm gun is a popular museum piece. This example is
at the National World War I Museum at the Liberty Memorial in
Kansas City, Missouri.

First World War Expedient Heavy Mobile Artillery

As the US entered the First World War, it was painfully apparent that heavy guns and howitzers were lacking, too, and the European allies' ability to fill this need was doubtful. As a stop-gap measure, the US Army and Navy took steps to free up excess gun tubes. The army's only readily available source was the armament deployed in coastal defense. By this stage of the war, it was obvious that the German surface navy would not be assailing American ports, and that guns could be selectively removed from coast defense batteries. They would be placed on railway or wheeled carriages (and a much smaller number used in arming transports) for use in Europe. This was intended to be a temporary fix, and the armament was to be re-emplaced after the war's end. Only American continental defenses were involved; no reduction to the more modern defenses of the Philippines, Hawaii, or Panama Canal was made. The army also obtained excess naval guns from that service and from a private dealer.

Intermediate 5-inch and 6-inch guns were selected for use on wheeled carriages. The Morgan Engineering Company of Alliance, Ohio, was quickly commissioned to design and produce a related family of wheeled carriages for these guns. The resulting design was a simple, robust, steel-frame box carriage holding a sleeve with recoil and counterrecoil mechanisms. A complicated 300-piece, 72-inch-diameter wheel was anticipated, but the contractor came up with a one-piece cast steel wheel and hub that simplified production. By early January 1918, the work was classified urgent and intensely underway. The US ordered 157 wheeled carriages for the guns, and there were additional orders for transport wagons and limbers, one per gun. All but thirty-six were reported completed by the war's end.

The intention was to organize the assembled guns into full batteries of similar types. Each would contain four guns, carriages, and limbers towed by four 120-hp tractors. Fourteen ammunition trucks, an artillery supply truck, a telephone truck, and four transport vehicles would complete the organic vehicle assignment. But the completed gun and carriage was too heavy for many bridges and roads. Morgan Engineering was asked to produce additional traveling carriages so the load could be split, with corresponding tractors.

In addition to the 5-inch and 6-inch guns, the army closely observed the navy's development of a tracked carriage for Marine use as a heavy 7-inch field gun. The army had already acquired twelve of these guns for use on railroad mounts, and followed up with its own order for thirty-six tracked carriages carrying surplus ex-naval 7-inch guns. Production was underway, but no units completed, when the war ended.

These expedient mounts did not persist long after the end of the war. On June 16, 1919, the ordnance technical committee declared the wheeled carriages obsolete. All but one of the carriages was scrapped. The guns were either donated (the 5-inch), returned to fortifications (6-inch Model 1900) or retained for future use (6-inch Models 1903 and 1905). The 7-inch tractor mounts suffered the same demise. Their carriages were soon scrapped and the tubes stored for future use. While some of the completed guns reached France, none of this expedient field artillery ever saw combat.

5-Inch Gun Model 1897 on Carriage Model 1917

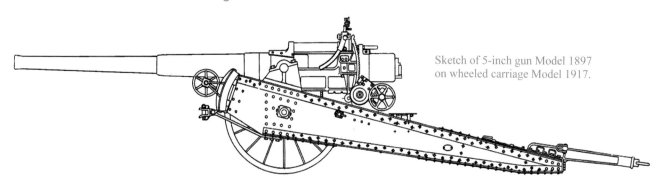

Sketch of 5-inch gun Model 1897 on wheeled carriage Model 1917.

In the late 1890s, thirty-five 5-inch Model 1897 seacoast guns were fabricated by Bethlehem Steel (Nos. 1–25) and Watervliet Arsenal (Nos. 1–10). They were all mounted on the Model 1896 Balanced Pillar mount, usually in paired emplacements at many coast defense forts. The gun was made of a forged steel tube, jacket, and Stockett breech mechanism hinged on the right side of the breech. The tube had thirty grooves and a twist of ¹⁄₅₀ gaining to ½₅. While certainly a serviceable weapon, it was heavy (a benefit in the fixed seacoast role) and fired separate ammunition from an awkward carriage type. Most important, it wasn't a "quick firing" gun preferred for use in light fort armament during the First World War, and thus the guns could be

released. In August 1917, twenty-eight mounted guns were selected for removal and subsequent remounting on new wheeled carriages for the AEF to use in Europe

Modifications to the existing tubes were not extensive. Trunnions of the original coast defense mount were incorporated on attached trunnion bands; these were removed and the tubes were given a new recoil band. A specially developed steel, 52-pound MkII common shell was supplied as standard field ammunition.

The field carriage was one of four similar variants. In fact, it appears to have used the same side members of the 6-inch types, though more closely spaced by the transoms due to the

Morgan Engineering photograph of one of the first 5-inch guns on its new Model 1917 wheeled carriage.

narrower dimensions of the tube width. From a photo identification standpoint, the two noticeably shorter recoil cylinders on top of the barrel are the most recognizable feature. The carriage used massive, solidly-cast, 72-inch-diameter wheels. A panoramic sight Model 1917 equipped each carriage. The wheeled carriages ordered from Morgan Engineering were the first batch of this new wheeled generation of guns procured.

The twenty-eight carriages were ordered from Morgan Engineering on September 28, 1917; the first example was completed by February 1918, and the other twenty-seven followed by the end of April. Additional orders for limbers were placed at Morgan on December 1, 1917, and transport wagons were ordered on February 15, 1918. They were held with other vehicles and equipment at army depots pending shipment to France. It appears that twenty-six completed units were shipped in August. The war ended before any were issued to combat units. Guns and carriages were returned to the United States in June 1919.

Despite the original intention, no effort was made to return the tubes to their abandoned emplacements. They were declared obsolete on June 16, 1919, and the ordnance department authorized the elimination of the gun tubes and wheeled carriages of the 5-inch program. Subsequently, the carriages were ordered scrapped, but a portion of the 5-inch gun tubes were donated for war memorials, though distribution dragged out until at least 1930. About eight tubes survive on display.

5-Inch Gun Model 1897 on Carriage Model 1917

Gun Characteristics

Bore size: 5 inches

Construction: Built-up steel

Tube length overall: 231.5 inches

Nominal caliber: 45 calibers

Tube and breech weight: 7,583 pounds

Usual carriage: 5-inch gun carriage Model 1917

Weight of gun and carriage: 23,543 pounds

Maximum elevation: 40 degrees

Loading: Separate

Shell weight: 52 pounds

Maximum muzzle velocity: 2,600 fps

Maximum range: 16,400 yards

Builders: Gun: Watervliet Arsenal & Bethlehem; carriage: Morgan Engineering

Number built: 28

There are no surviving 5-inch Model 1897 guns on Model 1917 carriages. However, a few of the original 5-inch gun tubes exist. They were once mounted as coast defense guns and then removed in the fall of 1917 for use on wheeled carriages, and finally dismounted from those carriages postwar. This tube, still retaining the collar to affix the dual recoil cylinders to the carriage, is in a park in Woodstown, New Jersey.

6-Inch Gun Model 1900A2 on Carriage Model 1917A

Morgan Engineering promotional sketch of its 6-inch carriage Model 1917A.

6-inch Improvised Field Mount
Model of 1917, Type A

The original Model 1900 50-caliber seacoast guns were produced through 1904, most of them mounted behind 4-inch-thick shields on Model 1900 barbette carriages. Forty-eight guns were originally produced by the Watervliet Arsenal, and all but one at the proving ground found their way into fixed emplacements. While capable of rapid traverse, the guns still used separate loading rather than fixed ammunition. Because their carriage type allowed for rapid traverse, they were considered an important part of the intermediate armament at American forts. Consequently, a smaller percentage of the emplaced guns were removed compared to the 5-inch and

6-inch disappearing types. At least twenty-five emplaced guns were removed starting in September 1917, though some were used for seaborne transport armament and not all were made available for wheeled mounts.

The gun tube was made of conventional built-up steel tube, two A hoops, and breech bushing. It was rifled with thirty-six grooves and lands, varying from a twist of $\frac{1}{50}$ to $\frac{1}{25}$. The breech mechanism was threaded directly into the breech bushing instead of the surrounding jacket. The breechblock was conically shaped. Modifications for the tubes were limited primarily to the removal of the trunnions and addition of a recoil band

An excellent photographic comparison of an army 6-inch gun on Model 1917 wheeled carriage (foreground) and a companion 6-inch gun on Model 1917A behind. A sharp eye can discern the presence of two small recoil cylinders atop the barrel of the rear carriage versus a single one on the closer unit.

intended to connect the tube with the recoil mechanism to be mounted on the sleeve of the new carriage. After modifications, the gun became Model 1900A2. It was to use the same new MkII 90.5-pound common steel shell developed for all 6-inch guns for field artillery use.

The development and fabrication of the type M1917A wheeled carriage lagged behind the other two 6-inch types. Like the others, it too was manufactured solely by Morgan Engineering. It closely resembled the other wheeled carriages of this generation of guns. Its distinctive difference was the presence of twin large recoil cylinders mounted above the barrel, unlike the single cylinder of the 6-inch Model 1917 carriage. Eighteen of these carriages were ordered on September 28, 1917. All were completed by mid-1918. Limbers and transport wagons were ordered from Morgan Engineering. When completed, most of these carriages were married to their tubes and stored at army depots on the East Coast before being shipped to Europe. An army report states that four of these mounts (6-inch Model 1900 gun on Model 1917A carriage) were floated for Europe. However, like the other types of expedient guns, these were not issued to a combat unit and did not see use during the conflict. The shipped guns were returned to the US.

The gun tubes were the most valuable of the borrowed coast artillery armament. Shortly after the war's end, most of them were removed from their wheeled carriages and re-mounted as coast defense guns on Model 1900 barbette carriages that had been in storage. In 1936, just two guns in storage retained their recoil bands for the wheeled mountings. The carriages were scrapped following the ordnance department's June 1919 declaration of obsolescence. There are no known surviving examples.

6-Inch Gun Model 1900A2 on Carriage Model 1917A

Gun Characteristics

Bore size: 6 inches

Construction: Built-up steel

Tube length overall: 310.4 inches

Nominal caliber: 50 calibers

Tube and breech weight: 19,968 pounds

Usual carriage: 6-inch gun carriage Model 1917A

Weight of gun and carriage: 39,202 pounds

Maximum elevation: 40 degrees

Loading: Separate

Shell weight: 90.5 pounds

Maximum muzzle velocity: 2,600 fps

Maximum range: 18,200 yards

Builders: Gun: Watervliet Arsenal; carriage: Morgan Engineering

Number built: 28 Model 1900A2 guns, 18 Model 1917A carriages

The wheeled carriages for large mobile guns were popular in bond drives and patriotic postwar celebrations. Pictured here is a 6-inch Model 1917A carriage.

6-Inch Gun Models 1903A1 and 1905A1 on Carriage Model 1917

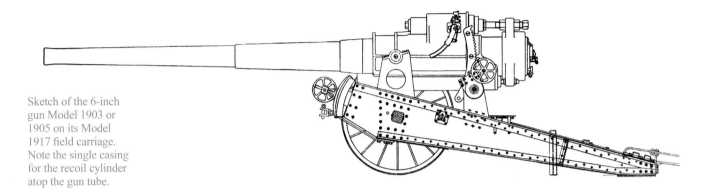

Sketch of the 6-inch gun Model 1903 or 1905 on its Model 1917 field carriage. Note the single casing for the recoil cylinder atop the gun tube.

In mid-1917, ninety-five seacoast 6-inch guns were selected for temporary removal from their mounts for emergency use as heavy field artillery with the expeditionary force preparing for service in France. Most of these were the seacoast guns Models 1903 and 1905 taken from similar Model 1903 and 1905 disappearing carriages. The original intent was to return and re-mount them when war was over, leaving their seacoast carriages in place. Modification to the guns involved removing the trunnions and applying a new recoil band, and they were re-designated Model 1903A1 and Model 1905A1.

The original gun type was among the best developed for American seacoast use. Differing only in minor aspects, these were sturdy, though somewhat heavy 50-caliber tubes. The earlier tubes had thirty-six grooves; the later ones had fifty-four. The Stockett breech mechanism was threaded directly into the jacket. The guns used a breechblock with a truncated ogival shape. On their new carriages, they could be fired from their mounts either by friction or electrically. The round to be fired was the Mark II steel common shell, weighing 90.5 pounds. The 50-caliber length and 45-degree elevation provided a useful 18,200-yard range. Seventy 6-inch guns Model 1903 and thirty-four Model 1905 guns had been produced by 1910 at the army's Watervliet Arsenal. They were exclusively used by the Coast Artillery Corps, mounted on disappearing type carriages. The new wheeled field carriage was similar to the other types produced at Morgan Engineering Co.

A pre-war survey had already suggested that there was a surplus of these guns for seacoast defense, and that they were suitable for mobile artillery. A letter to each local harbor defense authorized their removal in mid-August 1917. The seventy-four

A wheeled 6-inch mount Model 1917 at the proving ground.

carriages Model 1917 were ordered in September 1917 and completed between August and November 1918. Morgan Engineering was contracted to produce these carriages, along with limbers and transport wagons so the guns could be moved long distances in two loads. Like the other contemporary mounts, they were simply steel upper carriages with elevating gear and recoil mechanism mounted on solid cast-steel 72-inch-diameter wheels. The Model 1917 carriage can be distinguished in period photos by its large single recoil cylinder directly atop the gun tube sleeve.

Completed on schedule, apparently sixty-eight units were floated for France. However, they arrived too late to be assigned to units and deployed for combat. All were returned to the US after the war.

This relatively large number of guns on wheeled carriages and associated vehicles was put into storage following the armistice. In June 1919, the ordnance department declared them obsolete and authorized disposal. However, the tubes were retained for future disposition. In 1940, with the development of the new 6-inch coast defense emplacement and shielded barbette carriage, these tubes found a new home. Virtually all were modified and reused in the 200 Series 6-inch emplacements built by the United States in 1940–1945. The old wheeled carriages were scrapped in the early 1920s, though fortunately someone saw the value of preserving one complete unit for the US Army Ordnance Museum at Aberdeen Proving Ground. That gun and carriage still survive in the ordnance collection at Fort Lee, Virginia.

6-Inch Gun Models 1903A2 on Carriage Model 1917

Gun Characteristics

Bore size: 6 inches

Construction: Built-up steel

Tube length overall: 316.9 inches

Nominal caliber: 50 calibers

Tube and breech weight: 20,766 pounds

Usual carriage: 6-inch gun carriage M1917

Weight of gun and carriage: 43,455 pounds

Maximum elevation: 40 degrees

Loading: Separate

Shell weight: 90.5 pounds

Maximum muzzle velocity: 2,600 fps

Maximum range: 18,200 yards

Builders: Gun: Watervliet Arsenal; carriage: Morgan Engineering

Number built: 74 M1917 carriages and approximately 60 Model 1903A1 and 14 Model 1905A1 guns

The one surviving WWI expedient wheeled carriage, a Model 1903 6-inch gun on Model 1917 carriage as it appeared on display at the Aberdeen Ordnance Museum for many years.

6-Inch Mk II Mod 3 Gun on Carriage Model 1917B

Naval tubes were the final source of 6-inch guns for new mobile artillery. The navy had routinely kept a large reserve of spare guns. After taking what it needed for armament of transports, it offered excess guns to the army. Coming somewhat later than the army's own project, the guns weren't accepted until February 4, 1918, and a bewildering variety of calibers and types were selected. The 1918 Table of Cannon and Projectiles lists ten different Mark/Models of 6-inch guns, ranging from the early 30-caliber Mk II Mod 1 through 35-, 45- and 50-caliber types. The navy initially offered fifty-two guns but ultimately released forty-six, shipping them from the Naval Gun Factory and the Puget Sound and Norfolk Navy Yards to Watervliet Arsenal. Additionally, thirty older 30-caliber, 6-inch navy tubes were available for purchase from the commercial dealer Francis Bannerman, who had recently acquired them in an auction from the navy. After some discussion about allowing some to be sold to Cuba for harbor defense, the army bought all thirty guns in June 1918.

According to army records, the following navy gun models were part of the received inventory:

6-inch navy, 30-caliber MkII Models 1, 2, and 3
6-inch navy, 30-caliber MkIII Models 1, 3, and 4
6-inch navy, 40-caliber MkIV Models 4 and 8
6-inch navy, 50-caliber, MkV
6-inch navy, 45-caliber, MkVIE

To gain uniformity, all tubes were to be cut to a common 30-caliber length and mounted on a slightly modified wheeled carriage known as the Model 1917 Type B. While full performance details were not published, it was expected that the guns would be able to fire the standard 90.5-pound rounds at 1,950 fps. At a shorter 30-caliber length, range would be less than that for the army tubes but still acceptable under the circumstances.

The carriage appears only slightly modified from the Model 1917 and Model 1917 Type A. The most readily apparent

The incomplete project for navy 6-inch guns on Model 1917B wheeled carriages never got to the stage for production of technical manuals or published sketches. This photo taken at Aberdeen Proving Ground is one of the few visual records of the gun, showing it at maximum elevation.

difference is the elongated recoil cylinder and mechanism atop the gun barrel. The actual modification of the gun tubes and fabrication of the carriages were given less priority than the army 5-inch and 6-inch projects. Watervliet apparently got only partway through the project of uniformly cutting the tubes. The plan was to produce one carriage for two tubes, thus allowing for a 100 percent stock of spare tubes. Orders were placed with Morgan Engineering for thirty-seven M1917B wheeled carriages. It is not clear how many carriages were actually finished. Reports dated to the armistice (November 11, 1918) list only a single completed example. The only evidence of progress is a pair of photographs showing a single navy tube on its M1917 Type B carriage at the Aberdeen Proving Ground shortly after the war's end. This may well have been the only carriage for this gun type ever completed.

In any event, the war's end terminated any further need for these guns and mounts. It is likely that the contract for the carriages was immediately terminated and the gun tubes scrapped or sold to private firms. No surviving examples of the modified navy 6-inch or its army wheeled model 1917B carriage exist.

6-Inch Mk II Mod 3 Gun on Carriage Model 1917B

Gun Characteristics

Bore size: 6 inches

Construction: Built-up steel

Tube length overall: 196 inches

Nominal caliber: 30 calibers

Tube and breech weight: 12,566 pounds

Usual carriage: 6-inch gun carriage M1917B

Maximum elevation: 45 degress

Loading: Separate

Shell weight: 90.5 pounds

Maximum muzzle velocity: 1,950 fps

Maximum range: 15,000 yards

Builders: Original guns: Naval Gun Factory; carriages: Morgan Engineering

Number acquired: 76 ex-navy tubes, 37 carriages, M1917B contracted, 1 completed

The companion photograph of the navy 6-inch on Model 1917B carriage, this time at no elevation. Note the considerably shorter barrel reflective of the 30-caliber length of the tube compared to the army gun variants.

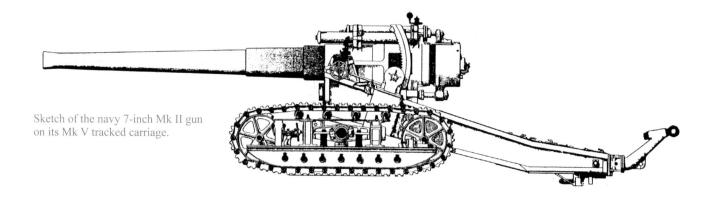

Sketch of the navy 7-inch Mk II gun on its Mk V tracked carriage.

The navy 7-inch 45-caliber Mark II gun was originally developed as an intermediate secondary gun for battleship casemates. Eight American battleships carried the weapon in the early twentieth entury. It was fabricated with conventional built-up steel. The guns were made by the Washington Naval Gun Factory, supplemented by contracts with the army's Watervliet Arsenal and private producer Bethlehem Steel. Never heavily used, the guns were still in good condition when the war started. In addition to a typical number of spares, additional quantities of this gun became available when they were removed from battleships to allow for better watertight integrity in case of mine or torpedo damage.

Early in the war, the navy began a project to provide heavy artillery for the prospective deployment of a Marine Corps division to Europe. The navy's Bureau of Ordnance designed a carriage for surplus 7-inch guns. The design was hurriedly completed between March and May 1918. Realizing that the new weapon would be too heavy for conventional wheeled transport, the navy adopted an innovative track-layer or caterpillar carriage. While still needing to be towed (it was not self-powered), the use of a rotating track allowed for a much better ground pressure solution. The upper steel carriage was a simple steel frame, the gun resting in a cylindrical slide with trunnions. The relatively high profile allowed by the caterpillar tracks readily facilitated a 40-degree elevation without requiring that a pit be dug for the recoil. The mount used an effective hydraulic recoil with pneumatic counterrecoil system. It was claimed to

Photograph of a tracked carriage 7-inch gun in the early 1920s.

be the heaviest mobile field mount deployed during the war (i.e., one that could be towed in a single load).

The gun would still use separate loading, and the 152.5-pound shells were common steel. The mount had a Schneider-type quadrant sight mounted on the left trunnion. Range at maximum elevation was an impressive 24,000 yards. Trials demonstrated that the design was well balanced, and the unit was easily moved with a single tractor.

An initial order for twenty units was placed with the Baldwin Locomotive Works on May 20, 1918. In one of the more impressive commercial performances of the war, the units were delivered in September. Though training was undertaken with the Marine's 10th Regiment and equipment gathered in Philadelphia, the armistice was signed before orders were issued for overseas shipment. The Marine's twenty guns stayed in Philadelphia for several years, and a plan to ship some to Guam for navy defenses was not implemented. Eventually the guns were removed from their tracked carriages and used as temporary fixed seacoast guns during the Second World War in places like Bora Bora and Oahu or provided to friendly foreign governments.

Simultaneous with the new carriage development, the navy offered excess tubes to the US Army. Twelve were taken and mounted on railway carriages. The army ordered thirty-six tractor mounts from Baldwin Locomotive as a follow-on to the navy order for the Marine Corps. At the time of the armistice, eighteen units were far enough along to warrant completion, and orders for the remaining eighteen were cancelled. The army took delivery of the eighteen units, but they were not issued. Soon the tubes were removed and went into storage for possible future use as either coast defense or additional railway material. Like their Marine counterparts, the tractor carriages were soon scrapped. They were never issued to units in either service.

7-Inch Gun Mk II on Tractor Mount Mk V

Gun Characteristics

Bore size: 7 inches

Construction: Built-up steel

Tube length overall: 323 inches

Nominal caliber: 45 calibers

Tube and breech weight: 28,700 pounds

Usual carriage: 7-inch gun carriage MkV

Weight of gun and carriage: 76,000 pounds

Maximum elevation: 40 degrees

Loading: Separate

Shell weight: 152.5 pounds

Maximum muzzle velocity: 2,700 fps

Maximum range: 24,000 yards

Builders: Gun: Naval Gun Factory, Watervliet Arsenal, and Bethlehem Steel; carriage: Baldwin Locomotive

Number acquired: 20 for US Marine Corps, 18 for US Army (of 36 contracted)

The sole surviving 7-inch tracked gun belongs to the US Navy's museum system. In recent years it has been transferred from Marine hands at Quantico to the Dahlgren Heritage Museum in Dahlgren, Virginia, and is currently undergoing restoration.

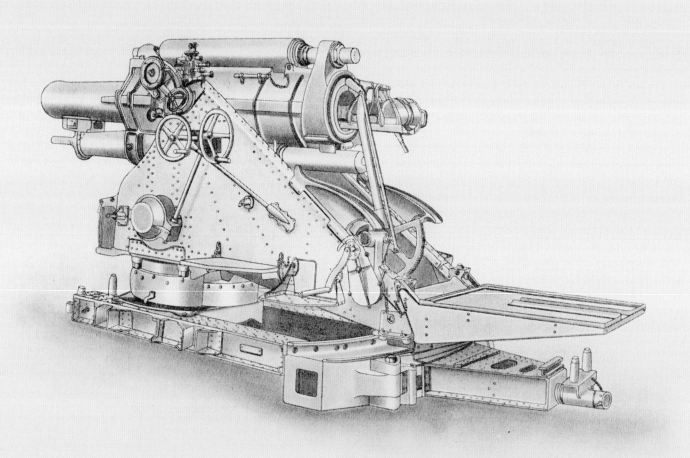

First World War British Heavy Artillery

In late 1917, the US acquired heavy British guns as another stop-gap measure to meet its artillery needs in the First World War. Though not necessarily of the most advanced design, and firing what would be non-standard ammunition, they were already in series production in England or with private ordnance producers in the United States. Many of the weapons were immediately available, and that's what mattered most that year.

Four gun types were selected. The lightest was the 5-inch gun, a type that had been produced at Elswick since 1904. Two hundred guns, carriages, limbers, and equipment sets were acquired, but not until after the war, in compensation for other outstanding contracts. A 6-inch gun was also under production at Vickers. One hundred were ordered, but the projected delivery date was not realistic, and they were not available until after the war's end. The 5-inch and 6-inch gun contracts were completed, though, and the guns moved directly into storage in the US. Eventually, the 5-inch guns were disposed of, many donated as memorial or decorative pieces. The 6-inch guns were kept as a strategic reserve of heavy artillery throughout the 1920s and 1930s and were transferred to an American ally right before the Second World War.

Two of Great Britain's heavier pieces were also selected— an 8-inch and 9.2-inch howitzer. The 8-inch howitzer was actually being produced at Midvale Steel in Pennsylvania under British contract. The US acquired some units directly from the British in Europe and then added production orders to the British runs at Midvale. In fact, both the army and Marine Corps participated in these orders. The heavy 9.2-inch howitzer was also a Vickers design, in limited production in England since 1916. The US acquired some guns directly from British production and sought to set up production with Bethlehem Steel. Due to their relatively quick transfer, both types were issued to American forces in France before the war ended. To support the British economy, the US allowed its contracts with English firms to complete the orders postwar. The more than 500 8-inch howitzers acquired served as war reserve with the army, and eventually most were transferred back to England as Second World War lend-lease. The 9.2-inch howitzers were issued to the American Coast Artillery for training but eventually were scrapped or used as ornamental items.

The supply and production history of these guns is not readily available. Final quantities were delivered after most of the ordnance department reports were published right after the war, and some numbers are incomplete. In some cases, British records seem more accurate; in any event, the production by type and manufacturer reported here should be considered best estimates.

5-Inch, 60-Pounder Gun Mk 1

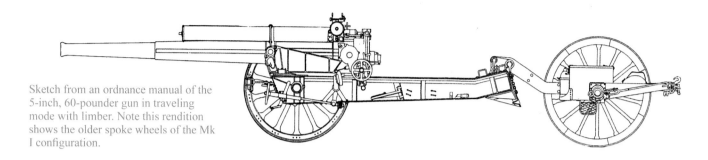

Sketch from an ordnance manual of the 5-inch, 60-pounder gun in traveling mode with limber. Note this rendition shows the older spoke wheels of the Mk I configuration.

This was the lightest of the four sizes of guns supplied by the British. Arrangements were made to acquire 200 5-inch guns produced by the Elswick Ordnance Company, a subsidiary of Sir W. G. Armstrong Whitworth & Co. It was a British-designed and produced gun; no consideration was given to producing the gun in the United States. Introduced in 1904, it was developed for use in divisional heavy batteries. Although it was first made in limited numbers, a larger quantity was produced during the war (some of which stayed on until the early campaigns of the Second World War). The gun was known as the 60-pounder Mk I, and the initial horse-drawn carriage was soon replaced with a Mk II carriage featuring large, 60-inch-diameter tractor wheels designed for motor transport. While the US Army did not originally request this gun—the British offered it to resolve their outstanding contractual obligations after the war ended—it proved to be a serviceable if not outstanding weapon. In January 1919, the ordnance department accepted 200 in lieu of remaining 9.2-inch howitzer deliveries. The latter were no longer desired in view of pending domestic orders for the superior 240 mm howitzer.

The gun was wire wound between an inner and outer tube, with an encasing jacket and breech bushing. Rifling was a uniform $\frac{1}{30}$. The conventional interrupted screw breechblock was hinged and opened to the right. The recoil mechanism was mounted by lugs atop the tube. It consisted of a hydraulic cylinder filled with glycerin and water. Two adjacent spring cylinders recoiled with the gun to a long, maximum 57-inch

A First World War 5-inch gun obtained from British production. All except a couple of evaluation pieces were delivered after the cessation of hostilities. This could be one of those pieces, as it has the older type of wheels.

distance. The gun sat on a top carriage that had the trunnion bearings. The trail was of the solid type, with a cut-out box for the breech recoil. It allowed for an elevation of -5 to +21.5 degrees and a 4-degree traverse left and right. The trail ended in a broad, fixed spade and large connector for the towing lug. Large, 60-inch-diameter tractor wheels (no tires, just steel ribs) were equipped with independent brakes.

The gun was equipped with a tangent sight and foresight on the right side and panoramic sight for indirect fire on the left side. It used separate loading ammunition and was generally supplied with an explosive and a shrapnel type shell. British reports indicate that 67,000 rounds of ammunition were supplied to the US by June 30, 1919. Usual vehicles included the MkII limber, MkII ammunition wagon, and MkII ammunition wagon limber. In most situations, the gun and carriage could be moved as a single unit when towed by tractor or motor vehicle. Gun manufacturing data and serial were engraved on the breech face, relining information on the muzzle face, and carriage and recoil data on the breech face and muzzle face, respectively.

As deliveries were not received until after the war's end, they saw no combat in American hands. For over ten years these guns sat in army arsenals and ordnance depots. In June 1931, the secretary of war suggested they be disposed of by donation—at that date there were twenty at Aberdeen Proving Ground and 177 at Rock Island. A year later, all 197 surplus guns and carriages were offered as ornamental and memorial pieces. The gun was popular in this role; it was an impressive-looking piece of relatively manageable proportions. While many were scrapped during the Second World War, numerous examples exist in municipal parks and cemeteries.

5-Inch, 60-Pounder Gun Mk 1 on Carriage Mk II

Gun Characteristics

Bore size: 5 inches

Construction: Wire-wound steel

Tube length overall: 168.05 inches

Nominal caliber: 30 calibers

Tube and breech weight: 4,858 pounds

Usual carriage: 60-pounder gun carriage Mark II

Weight of gun and carriage: 12,096 pounds

Maximum elevation: 21.5 degrees

Loading: Separate

Shell weight: 60 pounds

Maximum muzzle velocity: 2,080 fps

Maximum range: 12,280 yards

Builders: Elswick Ordnance (Armstrong)

Number acquired by US: 200

The 5-inch gun was widely accepted as a memorial gun. Over thirty still exist, many displayed at municipal monuments and cemeteries, like this nice example in Rittman, Ohio.

6-Inch Gun Model 1917

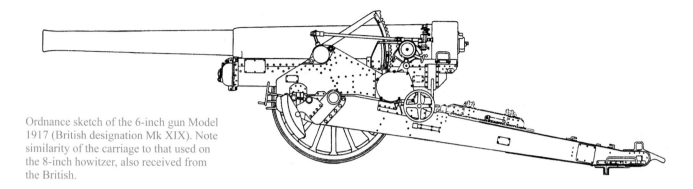

Ordnance sketch of the 6-inch gun Model 1917 (British designation Mk XIX). Note similarity of the carriage to that used on the 8-inch howitzer, also received from the British.

The US ordered 100 Vickers Mk XIX 6-inch guns in 1917. This weapon had first been produced in October 1916 as an incremental improvement in a long line of British 6-inch guns. It was normally placed on a slightly modified 8-inch howitzer carriage. A considerable number served with British Army siege batteries. The US Army ordered 100 sets of guns, carriages, and equipment. Another fifty gun bodies were acquired, presumably for spare barrels. In American service they were designated the Model 1917, but in many statements the Mk XIX designation seems to have stuck. The British designated the carriage Mk VII, as modified from the Mk VIIIA for 8-inch guns.

The gun was a fairly conventional design. The tube was wire wound around a steel tube and covered with a steel jacket.

A relatively short 35 calibers and capable of considerable elevation, it had some of the capabilities of a howitzer, though without the availability of different powder loads. The gun was equipped with a breech bushing and interrupted screw breech opening to the right. A single-motion opening and closing lever was similar to that made for the 5-inch, 60-pounder gun. A hydraulic buffer and spring recuperator cylinders were attached to a prominent lug on the underside of the tube. This gun had a unique percussion-type firing mechanism not interchangeable with other weapons. The carriage was sturdy box construction, cut out to allow full elevation and recoil. The carriage could allow 38-degree elevation and 8-degree traverse. It used separate-loading powder and shell and was supplied with high-

The 6-inch gun Model 1917 spent virtually all of its American career in storage; few photographs were taken. Here is one example of a gun being used for towing evaluation in 1941. Note that it has been modified with high-speed pneumatic tires.

explosive or shrapnel rounds of 90-pound weight. Guns were marked in the usual British fashion with data etched on the breech face.

Completed guns continued to be delivered long after the end of the war—one final battery's worth of four guns were still on order on March 26, 1920. The ordnance department stored 100 complete guns and fifty barrels. In 1933, records showed 150 tubes, 99 carriages, and 99 limbers in storage at Aberdeen. However, they lacked ammunition. The army considered starting ammunition production or reconfiguring the guns to use standard 155 mm rounds. No ammo solution was authorized, but the guns were kept for a possible military emergency.

Then in late 1939, discussions began about supplying the guns to Brazil. That nation was interested in rapidly expanding its military and was unable to get ordnance from a Europe already at war. The United States wanted access for airbases in northeast Brazil, and these guns figured into an important military assistance package. A supply agreement for the 99 complete units was finalized on May 8, 1940, and guns began arriving in Brazil by October 1. At the time they still had their old tractor wheels, but the US was to supply replacement pneumatic tires, along with helping the Brazilians with machine tools so they could manufacture their own ammunition. While virtually the entire stock of American-held guns was transferred and none exist today in the US, at least a dozen exist in museums in Brazil and other countries.

Late in the war, negotiations were begun to purchase British 6-inch howitzers, but the project was curtailed at the end of the war without any deliveries made.

6-Inch Gun Model 1917 (British Mk XIX)

Gun Characteristics

Bore size: 6 inches

Construction: Wire-wound steel

Tube length overall: 226.72 inches

Nominal caliber: 35 calibers

Tube and breech weight: 10,248 pounds

Usual carriage: 6-inch gun carriage Model 1917

Weight of gun and carriage: 22,512 pounds

Maximum elevation: 38 degrees

Loading: Separate

Shell weight: 90 pounds

Maximum muzzle velocity: 2,350 fps

Maximum range: 17,500 yards

Builder: Vickers

Number acquired: 100, plus 50 additional gun bodies

Ninety-nine of the 100 complete American 6-inch Model 1917 guns were transferred to Brazil in 1941. At least eleven still exist in that country—like this example on a fixed, 360-degree platform at a Brazilian ordnance museum in Rio de Janeiro.

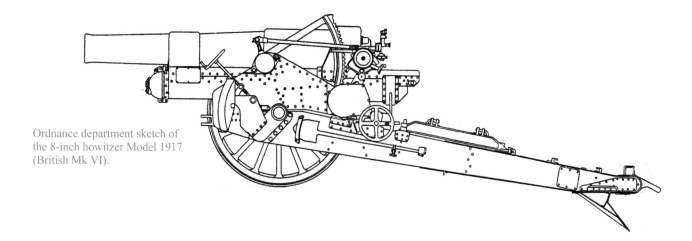

Ordnance department sketch of the 8-inch howitzer Model 1917 (British Mk VI).

Developed in 1915, this Vickers howitzer was a significant component of the British heavy artillery during the war. The original Mk VI weapon entered production in March 1916. It had a short 14.7 caliber and built-up tube mounted on a simple box trail. The Mk VII was a follow-on Vickers design of longer caliber (17.3), with a wire-wound tube of higher muzzle velocity for greater range. The final version was the Mk VIII½, again a built-up tube but with thicker powder chamber walls. Guns were marked with model and serial number on the face of the cover for the breech opening mechanism. In American service the shorter Mk VI was designated the Model 1917; the longer Mk VII and Mk VIII½ were the Model 1918. Their carriages bore the same model year.

The Americans used all three types, which featured in common a firing platform buried flush with the ground. The box trail was simply constructed but varied in the area cut out to allow for some models' longer tubes. The top carriage held the cradle, which in turn used guide clips to hold the tube with its interrupted-screw breech with single-motion opening. The howitzer used a hydropneumatic recoil cylinder

Aberdeen Proving Ground 8-inch howitzer. Even though the US Army obtained roughly 500 guns of this type, photographs of them are quite rare.

and two pneumatic counterrecoil cylinders. Elevation and traverse gears were on the side, as were a locking-bar sight and panoramic sight. The maximum carriage elevation varied between 38 degrees and 50 degrees depending on model, and total traverse was limited to 8 degrees. The carriage was equipped with large, 66-inch-diameter tractor wheels, 12 inches wide. The howitzer used separate-loading ammunition, with various charges for different zones. Only a high explosive shell was issued.

Before the war in 1916, Midvale was asked about supplying 8-inch howitzers as a substitute for the department's projected 7.6-inch design. In June 1917, rights to manufacture were negotiated and orders for eighty were placed. Attempts to acquire howitzers sooner led to a request to buy guns being made for Russia, but that failed. In January 1918, General John Pershing was authorized to buy howitzers directly from the British, and fifty-two were acquired. Additional howitzers were bought from the British as they were produced at Midvale. The US Navy ordered an additional sixteen for the Marine Corps. A definitive total by source and model has not been found. Howitzers continued to be delivered from both British and American orders for several years after the war (some as late as September 1920). The largest number reported in army inventory was 508 howitzers and 646 carriages in May 1926. Adding the sixteen Marine Corps guns and some wastage, perhaps 530 were acquired by the United States.

8-Inch Howitzer Model 1917 (British Mk VI)

Gun Characteristics

Bore size: 8 inches
Construction: Alloy built-up steel
Tube length overall: 133.6 inches
Nominal caliber: 15.9 calibers
Tube and breech weight: 6,552 pounds
Usual carriage: 8-inch Howitzer Carriage Model 1917
Weight of gun and carriage: 19,100 pounds
Maximum elevation: 50 degrees
Loading: Separate
Shell weight: 200 pounds
Maximum muzzle velocity: 1,300 fps
Maximum range: 10,760 yards

Builders: Vickers, Midvale Steel
Number built: At least 285 acquired by US Army

An American 8-inch howitzer of the 44th Artillery Regiment (CAC) originally published in *Liaison* magazine.

There are no known surviving 8-inch Model 1917 or 1918 howitzers in America. Fortunately, a few do exist in museums in other countries, such as Great Britain, Canada, Finland, and this fine example at the Museum of Artillery, Engineers and Signal Corp in St. Petersburg, Russia. It was likely made by Midvale Steel in Pennsylvania.

After the war these weapons were no longer issued to units, and in 1922 they were concentrated in war reserve status. In 1933, the army used some of the Asbury breech mechanisms to assemble new T-3 155 mm guns (eventually the M1 "Long Tom") undergoing service trials. The Marine Corps transferred their howitzers to the army in May 1934. Finally in March 1940, with 466 on hand, 200 were kept in reserve and 266 authorized for transfer to the British. Then in September, another 32 8-inch howitzer MkVI went to help Finland when the Soviet Union attacked. A year later all remaining 434 howitzers were released under lend-lease. The British reconfigured a number of their "gifts" to 7.2-inch bore howitzers and employed them in combat.

As these guns were never issued for donation, it is not surprising that none exist today in the US. Fortunately, a number of good examples are in foreign army museums, including in England, Canada, Finland, and Russia.

8-Inch Howitzer Model 1918 (British Mk VII & Mk VIIII½)

Gun Characteristics

Bore size: 8-inch

Construction: Wire-wound (Mk VII). Built-up alloy steel

Tube length overall: 154.676 inches

Nominal caliber: 18.5 calibers

Tube and breech weight: 7,730 pounds

Usual carriage: 8-inch howitzer carriage model 1918

Weight of gun and carriage: 20,050 pounds

Maximum elevation: 45 degrees

Loading: Separate

Shell weight: 200 pounds

Maximum muzzle velocity: 1,525 fps

Maximum range: 12,360 yards

Builders: Vickers, Midvale Steel

Number built: At least 116 Mk VII and 61 Mk VIII½

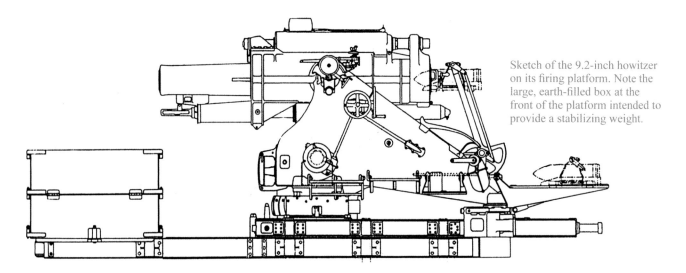

Sketch of the 9.2-inch howitzer on its firing platform. Note the large, earth-filled box at the front of the platform intended to provide a stabilizing weight.

The British Royal Gun foundry and Coventry Ordnance Works produced the Mk I 9.2-inch howitzer, first introduced in 1914. This was a heavy siege howitzer of short barrel (just 13.2 calibers) fired from a prepared platform. In 1916, Vickers introduced the Mk II howitzer with a longer barrel and range. Both guns actively served on the western front. The US Army was committed to developing and producing the Schneider-type 240 mm howitzer as its heavy siege gun, but it would be years before supply met needs. In the interim the army asked for and received a number of British 9.2-inch howitzers. It appears that forty-four were supplied to the AEF in France, either direct from British inventory or sold from units completed at Bethlehem Steel. The Mk I howitzer became the American Model 1917, of which twenty-seven were supplied. The Mk II became the Model 1918; seventeen of these ultimately transferred. A single Model 1918 was completed in 1919 from the American orders.

The 9.2-inch howitzer Mk I was a wire-wound tube with a jacket shrunk over the wire, while the Mk II used two tube sections. Gun data was etched on the rear breech face. A breech bushing held a screw-type breech with threads and slots. The weapon used a hydropneumatic variable recoil. The recoil cylinder was mounted above the tube, the recuperator cylinder (also pneumatic) below. Later models had a small gravity tank attached to constantly refill the cylinder with oil. The relatively simple top carriage was made of steel plates. The howitzer had no wheels, but was placed on a dedicated platform that had a large earth box to the front to help stabilize the rig during firing. To the rear was a swinging arm with a winch for loading the heavy shells at a loading angle of -3 degrees. A rocking-bar sight was included, as was a panoramic sight on the left side. The gun fired 290-pound HE shells with a point-detonating fuse using separate loading. The outfit was normally moved in three loads—howitzer tube, top carriage with cradle, and platform by special wheeled transport wagons.

The army issued orders for a number of howitzers from Bethlehem Steel, which was preparing to produce this gun for the British. Two hundred eighty-eight new howitzers were ordered from Bethlehem, but these were prioritized behind British orders. Consequently, only one completed howitzer was delivered—in February of 1919.

British units arrived in time for service. The 65th Artillery (CAC) regiment's 2nd Battalion had a battery of 9.2-inch Mk I and MkII 9.2-inch howitzers. Battery "D" emplaced near Toul fired the first American 9.2-inch rounds in September 1918. After the war the howitzers in France were sent home and placed into storage along with further deliveries from England and Bethlehem Steel. In April 1919, forty 9.2-inch howitzers were placed at coast artillery posts for supplemental training. As they had no fire control equipment, they could only be used to train crews in rapid loading of large-caliber guns.

The entire inventory of forty-five complete guns (MK I and II) and 45,000 shells were withdrawn from this use in 1923 and moved to war reserve storage. In 1926 the 9.2-inch howitzer was listed for disposal. In an ordnance department decision of December 1926, there is a curious remark: "Question of donating 9.2-in was given considerable thought. In view of the bulk and more or less unsightly appearance of the carriage it is not acceptable for donation. The tube in its sleeve would not be pleasing to the eye. Only the tube itself would be appropriate." Apparently thought too ugly to display on its firing platform, only a few tubes became memorial donations. Today the five survivors (including examples of the long and short type) are all bare tubes.

9.2-Inch Howitzer MkI on carriage Model 1917

Gun Characteristics

Bore size: 9.2 inches
Construction: Steel wire-wound
Tube length overall: 147.8 inches
Nominal caliber: 13.2 calibers
Tube and breech weight: 6,800 pounds
Usual carriage: 9.2-inch howitzer carriage model 1917
Weight of gun and carriage: 29,200 pounds
Maximum elevation: 50 degrees
Loading: Separate
Shell weight: 290 pounds
Maximum muzzle velocity: 1,187 fps
Maximum range: 10,061 yards

Builders: Vickers
Number built: 27 acquired by United States

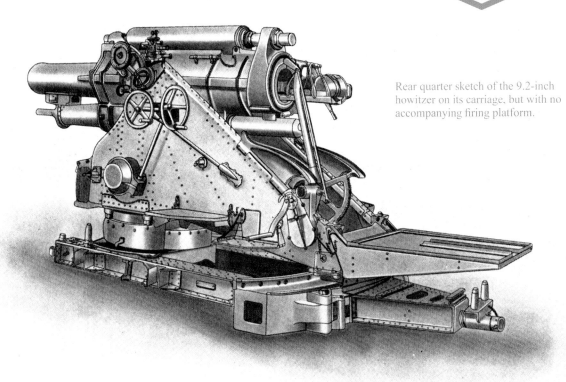

Rear quarter sketch of the 9.2-inch howitzer on its carriage, but with no accompanying firing platform.

An American short (Model 1917) 9.2-inch howitzer with shells, probably shown at an ordnance department facility.

9.2-Inch Howitzer MkII on Carriage Model 1918

Gun Characteristics

Bore size: 9.2 inches

Construction: Steel wire-wound

Tube length overall: 177.51 inches

Nominal caliber: 17.3 calibers

Tube and breech weight: 7,576 pounds

Usual carriage: 9.2-inch howitzer carriage model 1918

Weight of gun and carriage: 35,500 pounds

Maximum elevation: 50 degrees

Loading: Separate

Shell weight: 290 pounds

Maximum muzzle velocity: 1,510 fps

Maximum range: 13,084 yards

Builders: Bethlehem Steel

Number acquired: 18

Just five American-used 9.2-inch gun tubes still exist. This (longer) M1918 tube is in a cemetery in Selma, Alabama. The army thought the entire howitzer and carriage too ugly for display and allowed only the gun tubes to be donated.

New First World War Heavy Artillery

In the years leading up to the First World War, the United States had neglected the development of medium and heavy siege weapons. Experience on the western frontier and in colonial-type wars was useless in designing these guns, much less producing them in large quantities. A generous estimate is that only 200 guns and howitzers of 4.7-inch and 6-inch size built in the previous decade were usable. The designs were mediocre. Design development on a 9.5-inch howitzer soon commenced. There were also concerns about manufacturing capacity, as the government arsenals were not big enough and not likely to be expanded. The situation with forgings was somewhat better. Private American companies produced prodigious amounts of forged steel, but even that capacity was almost fully contracted by the British and French. Finishing complete guns and precision recoil parts proved to be the tightest bottleneck. Finally, supplying the huge amounts of ammunition needed for prolonged trench or siege warfare across a supply line of 3,000 miles of ocean would prove daunting.

The solution was two-part: in the short term, the US would acquire heavy pieces from the allies or use surplus coast artillery tubes to arm the 1918 campaign. The longer-term plan was to adopt four French designs. One of these projects, manufacturing the French Filloux 194 mm gun, never advanced beyond the production of two prototypes; however, the other three became major initiatives. The 155 mm gun, 155 mm howitzer, and 240 mm howitzer would be license-produced in the US, and ammunition supplied by the French. The 155 mm howitzer was the relatively modern French Schneider Model 1917. It was a compact, proven design capable of relatively good mobility. The 155 mm gun, known as the GPF, was also a capable weapon. Quantities of both were acquired directly from the French and issued to the expeditionary force, and contractors were also found for American production. Unfortunately, predictable delays, particularly in making the recoil mechanism's precision parts, pushed back deliveries until after the war was over. Of roughly 7,000 guns projected, only 146 were produced by the time of armistice in 1918. However, production continued, and these weapons provided the backbone of American heavy field artillery for another twenty years.

The 240 mm howitzer story is different. This was a new design, not one already in production. The French Schneider concern was asked to design the howitzer based on its recent heavy types and to use the 240 mm ammunition still available for older models. Production was to be done in the US. Again delays were encountered, and no howitzers were provided until 1919. Still, several hundred were made and issued to the US Army.

In the 1930s, these three guns were modified to high-speed towing capability. These changes involved mostly wheels and brakes rather than significant changes in major carriage parts. Eventually all were replaced with similar-sized modern models. Until production could meet demand, the 155 mm gun and 155 mm howitzer served in combat theaters well into 1943. Supplied in large quantities, numerous examples of these weapons still exist. However, only a single 240 mm howitzer is known to survive.

155 mm Howitzer Models 1917 and 1918

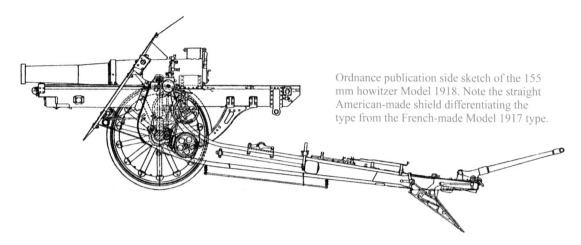

Ordnance publication side sketch of the 155 mm howitzer Model 1918. Note the straight American-made shield differentiating the type from the French-made Model 1917 type.

This howitzer was the result of lengthy development by its French producer during the early twentieth century. The guns were sold to Russia and adopted by the French Army, ultimately as the bagged-powder, separate load Model 1917. The French offered to sell fifty-nine batteries' worth of guns to the US on July 9, 1917, and the offer was accepted on August 17. Four days later orders were placed with the French Military Mission. It was intended for counter battery and interdiction missions, and to form the heavy pieces of each division's artillery brigade.

The howitzer had a built-up tube and jacket of a relatively short 13.4-caliber length. It had an interrupted-screw breech with one-motion operating lever. On top of the breech was a prominent, square counterweight. It fired 95-pound HE rounds. Fire control was provided by both quadrant and panoramic sights (type M1918

French). Firing was by either a French continuous-pull (M1917) or American firing lock mechanism (M1918). The recoil mechanism was a typically complicated, finely machined French hydropneumatic, constant-recoil type. While effective, it was difficult to manufacture. It had two cylinders and used compressed nitrogen gas for the counterrecoil force. The carriage was a simple fixed trail type, with two steel flasks and a fixed spade. It gave 42 degrees of elevation and 6 degrees of total traverse. It had two 53-inch spoke wheels on a 60-inch track. When towed, the trail was supported by a separate limber and the tube retracted and locked. A rectangular shield provided protection.

The US paid French firm Schneider et. Cie. for its plans to manufacture the howitzer. The government funded vast manufacturing plants at the American Brake Shoe & Foundry

A 155 mm howitzer on US-made Model 1918 carriage with its characteristic two-piece shield.

for tubes, Mosler Safe and Osgood-Bradley Car for carriages, and Dodge Bros. for recuperator mechanisms. Orders for 3,000 howitzers were issued in August 1917, but due to the perceived shortage of carriages, 1,361 were ordered from France. France also supplied 772 complete guns in Europe before the armistice. Altogether, the US acquired 3,008 complete 155 mm howitzers, though many were not delivered until after the war ended.

France produced and used this gun, along with many others transferred to allies or purchasers during and after the war. The French-made weapons were designated Model 1917; the American-made weapons were Model 1918. The American models had rubber tires rather than steel rims, a straight rather than curved shield, and a slightly different firing mechanism. Carriages and guns were interchangeable. French tubes were marked on the breech face and counterweight, American tubes on the counterweight with serial number on the muzzle face. Both types of carriages carried an information plate.

With American wartime production limited, French-supplied howitzers armed the divisional units in France. The weapons saw heavy service in the campaigns of 1918. After the war there were more than enough to supply the small peacetime army and provide a large war reserve. Some of the excess howitzers were transferred to allies under lend-lease. In March 1941, 300 excess (non high-speed) 155 mm howitzers were released to the British and sixty were released to Greece. The Marine Corps began acquiring howitzers in late 1941. Modified for high-speed towing, they continued to serve in 1942–44 pending replacement by the 155 mm howitzer M1. The army and Marine Corps used them extensively for combat in North Africa, Italy, and the South Pacific. Many still exist as war memorials and in military museums.

155 mm Howitzer Models 1917 and 1918

Gun Characteristics

Bore size: 155mm

Construction: Built-up nickel steel

Tube length overall: 91.81 inches

Nominal caliber: 13.4 calibers

Tube and breech weight: 2,690 pounds

Usual carriage: 155 mm carriage M1917 or M1918

Weight of gun and carriage: 7,600 pounds

Maximum elevation: 42 degrees, 20 minutes

Loading: Separate

Shell weight: 95 pounds

Maximum muzzle velocity: 1,480 fps

Maximum range: 12,300 yards

Builders: Tube: Schneider, St. Ouen, Tarbes, LeHavre, American Brake Shoe; carriage: Osgood-Bradley, Mosler Safe, various French firms

Number built: 3,008

While quite a few American-used 155 mm Models 1917–18 howitzers still exist, almost all are on high-speed conversion carriages from the Second World War. Only two remaining examples with the old spoke-wheel carriages are known—such as this one at the First Division Museum in Wheaton, Illinois.

155 mm Gun Models 1917 and 1918 (GPF)

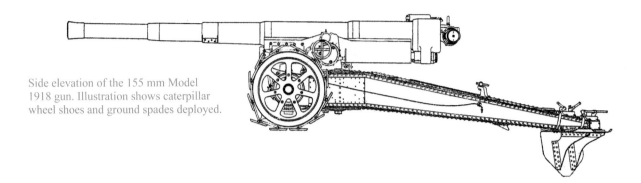

Side elevation of the 155 mm Model 1918 gun. Illustration shows caterpillar wheel shoes and ground spades deployed.

This was a modern 155 mm gun produced by Puteaux in France. It was known as the Grande Puissance Filloux, or GPF. In August 1917, the US ordered forty-eight guns from the French for direct delivery to the AEF in France; more followed.

The tube was built up with a shrunk-on jacket and moderate 38.2-caliber length. There were forty-eight grooves with a uniform rifling of 1/29.89. It had an interrupted-screw breech of four sectors. Under the rear part of the tube was a cradle holding the variable hydropneumatic recoil system. The gun recoiled in a slide on this cradle, and the barrel attached to the recoil piston with a lug. There was one main recoil cylinder and two counterrecoil cylinders, using compressed air for the return pressure. The carriage was a simple box girder with two large split trails anchored with spades on their ends. Elevation was

by a rack on the cradle employing a hand wheel. It could achieve 35-degrees elevation, and total traverse was 60 degrees.

Wheels were cast steel with two solid rubber tires. Optional caterpillar wheel shoes of twelve plates could be attached for towing in soft ground. For transport the tube could be withdrawn on the cradle; the trails were closed, and their ends would be held on a towed gun carriage transport limber. There was no provision for a shield.

During the war, 577 complete guns and carriages were ordered in France, with 218 issued and used near the end of the war in Europe. In the US extensive plans were made for production, actively aided by government-funded plants to be operated by arsenals or contractors. Gun tubes were made by the Watervliet Arsenal and Bullard Engineering Works. Carriages

Several 155 mm guns deployed on Waikiki Beach at Fort DeRussy, Oahu, in the 1920s. This gun was issued and heavily used by the coast artillery in addition to the field artillery. Note the caterpillar shoes on the wheels.

were made by Minneapolis Steel & Machinery, and recuperators by Dodge Bros. With delays in finding machine tools, translating plans from metric to English measurements, and acquiring raw materials and skilled labor, only seventy-one were completed by the end of the war—and just sixteen were floated for shipment to Europe. Sources vary, but it seems that the US acquired about 997 155 mm Model 1917/18 guns before 1920. The Marine Corps acquired sixteen immediately after the war.

American- and French-produced guns were virtually the same and interchangeable on carriages. French guns were marked with serial number below the breech; American guns were marked on the muzzle. Both had carriage plates with manufacturing information on the right trail. The gun, along with the howitzer of the same bore, provided the mainstay of heavy artillery between the wars and was used by field and coast artillery in the US and overseas. On November 1, 1939, 979 155 mm guns were reported in inventory, virtually the entire quantity purchased twenty years earlier. The guns participated heavily in the General Headquarters (GHQ) maneuvers of the early 1940s. In May 1941, the first guns were released under lend-lease to the British in the Middle East. Another forty-eight were transferred to the Marine Corps in early 1942. During the Second World War, over sixty were lost in defense of the Philippines, and the guns also saw combat in North Africa and Guadalcanal. In 1943, most were replaced with the new 155 mm M1. One hundred 155 mm GPFs were taken off carriages and mounted on the M12 gun motor carriage in late 1942 and early 1943. A considerable number still exist, including those never given high-speed conversion.

155 mm Gun Model 1917 and 1918

Gun Characteristics

Bore size: 155mm

Construction: Built-up alloy steel

Tube length overall: 232.87 inches

Nominal length: 38.2 calibers

Tube and breech weight: 8,795 pounds

Usual carriage: 155 mm gun carriage Model 1917 and 1918

Weight of gun and carriage: 19,860 pounds

Maximum elevation: 35 degrees

Loading: Separate

Shell weight: 95 pounds

Maximum muzzle velocity: 2,411 fps

Maximum range: 17,700 yards

Builders: Tube: Puteaux, Watervliet Arsenal, Bullard Engineering Works; carriage: Puteaux, Minneapolis Steel

Number built: 997

The 155 mm Model 1917 and 1918 guns survive in considerable numbers. This French-built Model 1917 is in a park in Walla Walla, Washington. The wheels indicate it was never modified to the M3 carriage standard for high-speed towing.

240 mm Howitzer Model 1918

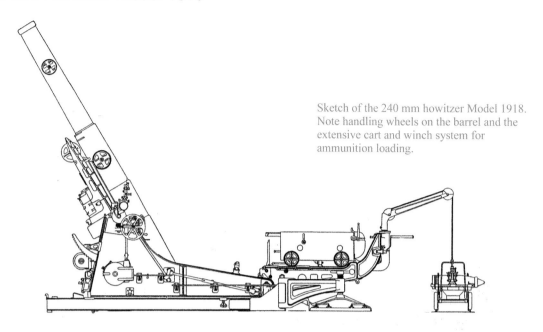

Sketch of the 240 mm howitzer Model 1918.
Note handling wheels on the barrel and the
extensive cart and winch system for
ammunition loading.

Completing the assembly of an early-production 240 mm howitzer
Model 1918 in October 1918.

The 240 mm howitzer was the heaviest regular army siege gun (except for small numbers of railway guns). While the initial American Army was to receive British-designed 8-inch and 9.2-inch howitzers, the second army (of thirty divisions) was to be armed with 240 mm howitzers as its heaviest weapon. This gun was much more powerful, in both shell weight and range, than the British types. There had been a prior effort to design a 9.5-inch howitzer based on a licensed Schneider design. Schneider had basically downsized its successful 280 mm howitzer to American requirements. The intent was for production to be done in the US. In early 1917, orders for forgings were placed at Midvale and Bethlehem, and orders were placed for assembly at Watervliet. On January 3, 1918, the US decided to change the caliber to 240 mm to take advantage of the French offer to help supply ammunition.

The tube and jacket were built-up alloy steel. It was held in a sleigh that also supported the recoil mechanism. The hydropneumatic, constant recoil and tandem counterrecoil cylinders used hydraulic liquid. The howitzer was also equipped with a quick return mechanism. The breechblock used a conventional interrupted screw closure. A distinctive feature on the barrel, two maneuvering rollers aided in mounting the howitzer onto its cradle. The top carriage had two steel flasks and cross transoms. The upper carriage sat on a fixed steel firing platform. An attached winch and arrangements for moving shot carts were included. A quadrant sight and Model 1917 panoramic sight were mounted on the gun.

The howitzer used separate loading. The shells weighed 345 pounds, and were common steel HE or gas types. When emplaced, which was estimated to take 3–12 hours, the carriage could provide 60 degrees elevation and 20 degrees traverse using a pintle bearing at the front. The howitzer was moved by disassembling into four loads for transport.

Orders were issued for the manufacture of 1,200 complete howitzers for the war effort. Gun tubes were ordered from Watervliet Arsenal, using five sources of forgings. Carriage orders started in September 1917 from Watertown Arsenal and Standard Steel Car. Recuperators were ordered from both Watertown and Otis Elevator. It took time to construct and equip plants and to render French plans and specs into manufacturing guides. Only the pilot howitzer was completed by the time of the armistice, but production continued more slowly in the immediate postwar period. Through 1921, 330 240 mm M1 howitzers and carriages were delivered.

Later developments included the M1918M1 with a slightly greater tube diameter, the M1918A1 with changed rifling, and the M1918M1A1, which was the re-lined gun. Howitzers were delivered starting in late 1919. The first twelve were to go to the Philippines to form a heavy counterbattery force for the harbor defenses of Manila Bay. However, the Washington Treaty intervened, and the howitzers were diverted at sea and turned over to the Hawaiian defenses. The guns served there until well into the Second World War. During the interwar years, the inventory of howitzers (in 1926 there were 317 howitzers and 556 carriages) were stored, except for those assigned to the Hawaiian coast defense role. A few were brought

out for the 1940 maneuvers and some were given new transport wagons for high-speed towing. By the time heavy artillery of this size was needed in the Second World War, more modern types were available. None saw combat, and none were transferred in lend-lease.

240 mm Howitzer Model 1918

Gun Characteristics

Bore size: 240mm

Construction: Built-up alloy steel

Tube length overall: 199.6 inches

Nominal caliber: 19.75 calibers

Tube and breech weight: 10,790 pounds

Usual carriage: 240 mm howitzer carriage Model 1918

Weight of gun and carriage: 41,206 pounds

Maximum elevation: 60 degrees

Loading: Separate

Shell weight: 345 pounds

Maximum muzzle velocity: 1,700 fps

Maximum range: 16,390 yards

Builders: Tube: Watervliet Arsenal

Carriage: Watertown Arsenal, Standard Steel Car Co.

Number built: 330

The sole surviving example of a 240 mm M1918 howitzer and its firing platform is on display at the US Army Artillery Museum at Fort Sill, Oklahoma.

Artillery Projects of the 1920s

At the end of the First World War, a special committee supervised the distribution of ordnance surrendered by the Central Powers as part of the war's political settlement. The US received over 3,000 artillery pieces and thousands of other military items. With no need for additional guns following the surge in domestic production, almost 2,000 pieces were distributed to states and territories for war monuments. The military kept 252 for further evaluation or display in its own museum system, and 757 were retained by the ordnance department. Only one piece—the modern German 10 cm LeFH-16 (1916) howitzer was retained for strategic reserve purposes. This howitzer was the only enemy artillery weapon of modern times to be kept in quantity for possible American service.

In 1919, the army formed a committee led by General William I. Westervelt to assess the artillery lessons of the war and formulate future weapon needs. It was known as the Caliber Board or the Westervelt Board. Its conclusion was that all the American artillery weapons used during the war were in need of improvement; lack of range was a particular criticism. The board also recommended a mix of guns and howitzers escalating in size and assigned to corresponding army echelons. The board's selected sizes soon became projects for the ordnance department. While production funding was scarce at the time, the development of many of the Second World War's most important American artillery weapons was rooted in this board's recommendations.

One recommendation was for a new infantry weapon that could replace the 37 mm Model 1916 gun (and thus be useful against machine gun nests and anti-tank service) and the 3-inch Stokes mortar (highly explosive fire to support infantry attacks).

It had to be highly mobile, capable of hand carriage, and have a range of at least 1,500 yards. Work started on this project promptly after the war's end. With the experimental Model 1920 infantry howitzer, it was deemed impractical to combine the two needs—it was asking too much to get a mortar and direct-fire gun in one tube and carriage. Subsequent efforts attempted to develop two separate guns, initially focused on a 1.8-inch gun and a 2.24-inch howitzer. Through prototypes and wooden mock-ups, in 1923 development settled on the 37 mm infantry gun and the 75 mm infantry mortar. These were taken to standardization, and limited numbers were built to allow extended service testing, but never put into full production.

Similar efforts were made to develop the next logical improvement to standard field guns. While the army was pleased with the Model 1897 75 mm gun, 4.7-inch gun M1906, and 155 mm howitzer M1918, it wanted to see improvements, particularly in range. Once again, the program's aim was to fully develop and test an improved design, carry it to standardization, and then put the design on the shelf for immediate use when needed. In the early 1920s, new design programs were initiated for all four of these guns. All were prototyped in the 1920s, and the 75 mm gun and 105 mm howitzer were produced in small batches to create test batteries.

For heavy artillery, a development program was started for a new 155 mm long-range gun and 8-inch howitzer. Also designed was a new "combination" carriage to accommodate either gun. While prototype units were produced, no authority for purchasing additional units was forthcoming. However, the US learned important lessons from these projects.

75 mm Gun Model M1 and M2

The Model 1897 75 mm gun performed favorably during the First World War. The rapidity of fire and stability provided by the recoil mechanism were excellent, but the fixed trail limited its elevation and range. Development of a new 75 mm field gun got underway in the early 1920s. A series of guns and particularly carriages was fabricated and extensively tested from 1920–25. Initial attempts to provide a single carriage with interchangeable 75 mm or 105 mm howitzer gun tubes proved too heavy and clumsy, though they established a concept that was useful in the late 1930s. With a new, longer barrel and split-trail carriage, the Model 1920 75 mm evolved into the single prototype Model 1923E that was standardized as the M1 in 1926. Three more guns and carriages were ordered in 1925 to form a complete battery of four guns intended for rigorous field testing.

These guns were made at Watervliet Arsenal, and the carriages at Rock Island Arsenal. While the Model 1920 gun had been made of lightweight chrome steel, the M1 reverted to "regular" gun steel. The carriage provided a 45-degree elevation and 45 degrees of traverse. The recoil system was hydropneumatic and based on the St. Chamond type used on the M1897. The breech was a drop-block type. Firing was by hammer-type firing mechanism.

While no additional M1 75 mm guns or carriages were ordered and budgets were tighter than ever, developmental efforts did not cease. In 1932 the "new" 75 mm gun M2 was developed, and standardized in 1936. Improvements were mostly in the carriage with a new recoil apparatus and equilibrator springs. Once again, a small quantity of guns and carriages were ordered for trial. Ten were completed (Nos. 1–10) by using the one prototype made in 1929, and nine new guns were produced at Watervliet Arsenal with an order originating on July 5, 1932. This was enough to allow further field testing, and no further production ensued.

Looming over this project were two other considerations. One was the large number of existing 75 mm guns (mostly M1897s along with their considerable inventory of ammunition) that might still prove useful and inhibited the expenditure of

The interwar development of a new 75 mm field gun passed through numerous iterations. This photograph from Aberdeen Proving Ground, dated January 28, 1929, shows a 75 mm M1 No. 1 with spread trails at 0-degree elevation.

scarce dollars for their replacement during the economic depression. Another was the ongoing debate over whether the 105 mm howitzer, with its significantly heavier shell, might better serve the needs of standard divisional artillery. Eventually the latter argument prevailed and the need for a new 75 mm divisional gun disappeared, taking with it all of the interwar developmental projects.

Thus, the few guns produced are rare. They were not issued to units, except when assigned for temporary evaluations. After testing they moved to arsenal storage. Only one example survives—a single 75 mm M2 formerly at the Aberdeen museum, but now presumably in storage pending its assignment to a new facility.

75 mm Gun M1 on Carriage M1

Gun Characteristics

Bore size: 75mm

Construction: Built-up gun steel

Nominal caliber: 37 calibers

Tube and breech weight: 945 pounds

Usual carriage: 75 mm gun carriage M1

Weight of gun and carriage: 3,100 pounds

Maximum elevation: 45 degrees

Loading: Fixed

Shell weight: 15 pounds

Maximum range: 15,100 yards

Builders: Gun: Watervliet Arsenal; carriage: Rock Island Arsenal

Number built: M1: 4, one prototype and three evaluation

A 75 mm M1 field gun on M1E2 carriage during towing trials. Note the lack of any shield on the gun carriage. Photo dated January 16, 1933.

This M2 gun and carriage is the only surviving example of the interwar 75 mm developments. It was displayed for years at the Aberdeen Ordnance Museum, but is presently in storage awaiting the construction of new museum facilities.

105 mm Howitzer Model 1916

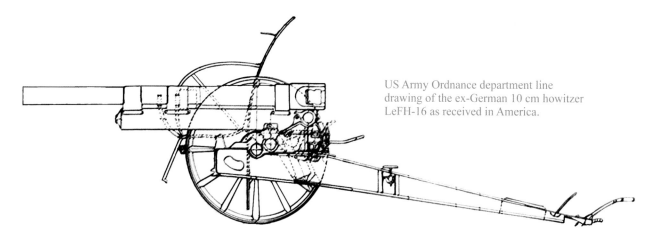

US Army Ordnance department line drawing of the ex-German 10 cm howitzer LeFH-16 as received in America.

More than 1,000 excellent German 10 cm (105 mm) howitzers were among the weapons allocated to the United States at the end of the First World War. This howitzer was the most modern version of a series of German 10 cm field howitzers that started with the Model 1898. It had been progressively lengthened and improved until the LeFH-16 was adopted during the latter part of the war. The carriage was similar to the one used for the most recent 7.7 cm gun. The tube consisted of a built-up tube, jacket, and clip hoop. The 105 mm gun tube was 22 calibers long and had thirty-two lands and grooves with a rifling of ⅔₄₅ progressing to ⅟₁₈. It was equipped with the usual German sliding-wedge breech type. The gun fired a 34-pound HE shell or star shell. Its powder charge was in a brass cartridge case and could use up to nine separate zone loadings.

The simple but durable box carriage held its breech at the axis of elevation—which kept it always at about the same height and eased loading. The gun had equilibrator springs mounted between the trail and carriage. Recoil was checked with a hydraulic brake with spring return to restore the tube's position with the counterrecoil. A hand wheel on the left side of the carriage provided elevation. The box carriage was cut out for the recoil length, and it could provide elevation from -9 to +40 degrees. Only 4 degrees of total traverse was possible on-carriage. The left trunnion held a German-made quadrant sight. German wheels were about 48 inches in diameter and spaced for a 61-inch-wide track.

The US received 3,242 guns and trench mortars. The ordnance department reserved 757 of these guns and mortars. By far the largest quantity was 651 105 mm howitzers. These were kept by the US Army as part of its artillery reserve following the war.

Apparently delivered in 1919, the guns were sequestered in arsenals. In April 1920, Raritan Arsenal reported that it had

Illustration from the *Handbook of Artillery* (1924) of the German 105 mm howitzer Model 1916 on carriage Model 189⁸⁄₀₉. Large numbers of these guns were surrendered to the allies after the First World War ended.

130 in reserve, though they were rusting badly. The green wood used to form muzzle tampions was warping and allowing water into the tubes. It requested and was granted funds to clean them up and repaint the guns and carriages. In September 1920, several batteries' worth of these howitzers were shipped to Camp Knox and Fort Sill for training. The 1924 *Handbook of Artillery* states that the howitzers were retubed and rechambered to take the 105 mm ammunition made for the experimental howitzer model 1920 (the project that would eventually evolve to the famous WWII 105). However there is no confirmation of that action in other ordnance department correspondence, and the lack of surviving department orders to do this work makes it doubtful that the project was ever accomplished.

In 1923 the army discussed using the 650 existing ex-German howitzer carriages for the newly produced 105 mm howitzers. By 1925 that idea was dropped, and the final 130 guns and 650 carriages were authorized for disposal. Soon thereafter, these howitzers seem to disappear from army correspondence.

There are more than a few German Model 1916 105 mm howitzers in existence. In addition to the 600+ kept as ordnance reserve, others went to state distribution for war memorials. At least forty-two survive on display, though without a precise list of serial numbers it is impossible to tell which of these were memorial display items and which may have come from the strategic reserve.

105 mm Howitzer Model 1916 on Carriage Model 1916

Gun Characteristics

Bore size: 105mm
Construction: Built-up alloy steel
Tube length overall: 91 inches
Nominal caliber: 22 calibers
Tube and breech weight: 975 pounds
Usual carriage: 105 mm howitzer carriage Model 1916
Weight of gun and carriage: 3,045 pounds
Maximum elevation: 40 degrees
Loading: Semi-fixed
Shell weight: 34 pounds
Maximum muzzle velocity: 1,460 fps
Maximum range: 11,000 yards

Builders: Rheinmetall, Krupp, others
Number aquired: 620

Numerous examples of the German 105 mm howitzer Model 1916 exist in the US in public memorials and private hands. This piece is in Leominster, Massachusetts.

37 mm Infantry Gun M2

A new infantry support gun was developed as a result of the Westervelt Board's recommendations. What was needed was a highly mobile, light gun to destroy enemy machine gun nests and other forms of resistance (including tanks) deployed with infantry formations. After testing several versions of a 1.8-inch and 37 mm bore size, the army settled on the Model 1923 37 mm infantry gun. According to specifications issued April 1922, one test gun was manufactured at Rock Island Arsenal and shipped to Aberdeen for testing in June 1923. This gun was designated the 37 mm infantry gun M1923E. Following testing in 1924, it emerged much changed, using a new split trail to help with traversing. This was standardized as the M1925E.

The gun tube was of alloy steel. Its most distinguishing characteristic was the encircling counterrecoil spring, which was encased in a large-diameter cylinder surrounding the gun tube. On top of this spring cylinder was the conventional hydraulic recoil tube or cylinder. It had a conventional drop-block breech. The carriage was a straightforward split trail type. The trails were lightly built, perforated to save weight. The carriage allowed elevation from -14 to +21 degrees and a useful maximum traverse of 67 degrees. The accompanying hand-drawn ammunition cart was designated the M2. Total weight with limber and caisson cart was 1,114 pounds. It fired a 1.25-pound HE round, or 1.45-pound AP shot.

As was customary, limited numbers were fabricated to allow extended service testing. Knowing it would probably not get funding for large-scale production, the army intended to perfect new weapon types and standardize them for production, with the provision that the designs were as ready as possible for manufacture should a national emergency warrant. One Model 1925E was built, followed by a rebuilding as the M1925E1 by Rock Island in October 1926. This final model was standardized as the 37 mm infantry gun M1 on carriage M1, effective June

Rock Island Arsenal photograph of the 37 mm infantry gun M2E1 on carriage M1E1 on April 21, 1931, in firing position.

6, 1927. Four more were built and submitted for testing at Fort Benning. Additional minor changes led to a new designation as the Model M2 (both gun and carriage) in 1929.

In 1930–31, twelve M2 37 mm infantry guns were made. Eight new ones were constructed and the four similar M1 guns were modified to the M2 standard. All were completed by June 1931. These twelve were subjected to additional service testing. According to abundant photographs from the period, they also made the rounds to military exhibits and reviews. Apparently by the mid-1930s it was becoming obvious that a high-velocity light gun was needed to deal with the new tanks emerging. The M2 infantry gun was perceived to be ineffective against tanks and was declared obsolete on June 17, 1936.

Surprisingly, several still exist. A pair of 37 mm infantry guns M2 are on outdoor display at a war memorial in Grafton, West Virginia. One still carries its carriage plate stamped M2 No. 5 from Rock Island Arsenal in 1931. A slightly earlier M2E1 is on display at the Rock Island Arsenal Museum.

37 mm Infantry Gun M2

Gun Characteristics

Bore size: 37mm
Construction: Alloy steel
Tube length overall: 29 inches
Nominal caliber: 20 calibers
Tube and breech weight: 93 pounds
Usual carriage: 37 mm gun carriage M2
Weight of gun and carriage: 400 pounds
Maximum elevation: 21 degrees
Loading: Fixed
Shell weight: 1.25 pounds
Maximum muzzle velocity: 2,000 fps
Maximum range: 5,500 yards

Builders: Gun: Watervliet Arsenal; carriage: Rock Island Arsenal
Number built: 12, 4 converted from M1 and 8 new

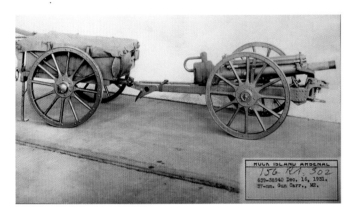

A photo from December 1931 showing the M2 37 mm infantry gun in traveling position with its attendant cart.

One of two surviving 37 mm infantry guns M2 in Grafton, West Virginia.

75 mm Infantry Mortar M2

Concurrent with the 37 mm infantry gun project was the development of a new infantry mortar—a 75 mm weapon capable of increased range. In 1919, development began on a breechloading rifled mortar (also referred to as an infantry howitzer). Initial efforts to create a single weapon combining mortar and direct fire failed, as did the follow-up concept to make a single portable carriage with two exchangeable tubes—a 1.8-inch direct fire gun and a 2.24-inch howitzer. An alternate 75 mm howitzer proved much superior to the 2.24-inch size, and development continued in 1922. The resulting new 75 mm mortar was capable of 45-degree elevation, 10-degee traverse, and weighed approximately 285 pounds. A series of prototypes were designated M1922, M1922E1, and M1923 75 mm infantry mortar.

Model 1922E1 infantry mortar held considerable promise. It had a rifled, breechloading steel alloy tube surrounded by the hydrospring recoil. This spring was contained in a cylinder that wrapped around the gun tube. While not common, a similar application of this design was used with the much earlier naval Fletcher-type field gun from the 1890s. Atop the hydrospring cylinder was the small pneumatic recoil cylinder. Traverse was accomplished by sliding the tube sideways along the axle. The carriage was a simple support of side and transom members, with a long T-shaped pole drag handle to the rear. It could be separated into two pack loads of 179 and 229 pounds.

Continued tinkering with the elevation wheel mechanism resulted in the M1922E3. This version was standardized as the 75 mm infantry mortar M1 on June 10, 1927. Four examples were built in mid-1927 to allow more extensive service testing. Yet additional modification resulted in the 75 mm infantry mortar M2. Sixteen of these mortars were then produced during 1931. The four M1 mortars brought to the new standard joined twelve newly fabricated M2s to provide sixteen required infantry mortars. All were complete by the beginning of 1932.

In 1932 these breechloading rifled mortars were classified as limited standard, indicating that more would probably not be produced. While they had some features of standard service howitzers (and in fact were also similar to German minenwerfers), they still competed with conventional mortars, and the simultaneous appearance of the new 81 mm mortar ultimately condemned their future. Production of this excellent new 81 mm field mortar began sporadically in 1933. The next year, on August 17, 1934, the 75 mm infantry mortar was declared obsolete. It took a couple of years to expend the existing ammunition, but these weapons were no longer in service or even maintained in storage by the start of the war. They saw no combat in their short lives.

Fortunately, several still exist. One mortar was displayed indoors for many years at the old Aberdeen Ordnance Museum. It has recently been moved to storage at Fort Lee pending erection of a new museum. At least one other mortar is in private hands, though occasionally available for viewing at the Knight's Armament Museum in Titusville, Florida.

Developmental prototype 75 mm infantry mortar M1922E at Rock Island Arsenal on February 17, 1925. Note mechanism to slide top carriage along axle to provide traverse.

The surviving 75 mm infantry mortar M1922E1 made in 1927 displayed at the Ordnance Museum at Aberdeen Proving Ground. Note the simple carriage and prominent hydrospring recoil cylinder surrounding the barrel.

75 mm Infantry Mortar M2

Gun Characteristics

Bore size: 75mm

Construction: Alloy steel

Tube and breech weight: 92 pounds

Usual carriage: 75 mm infantry mortar carriage M2

Weight of gun and carriage: 396 pounds

Maximum elevation: 82 degrees

Loading: Fixed

Shell weight: 10.5 pounds

Maximum muzzle velocity: 480 fps

Maximum range: 2,000 yards

Builder: Rock Island Arsenal

Number built: 16 for service tests

A pre-production 75 mm infantry mortar Model M1 on May 20, 1930. Note the simple construction of the carriage and carrying handles attached to the lower ground plate.

High-Speed Modifications

American interest in modernizing the artillery acquired during and immediately after the First World War began in the late 1920s. These early pieces were designed with wooden-spoke wheels for low-speed animal draught—usually no more than 8 mph. While larger pieces such as the 240 mm howitzer M1918 were often towed by tractors, wheels with hard tires indicated relatively low-speed capability. As America was probably the world leader in adopting motor transportation, the interest was not surprising. Frankly, one of the other problems was the daunting prospect of acquiring, maintaining, and transporting large numbers of horses and their feed. Animal transport was simply more expensive and more wasteful of shipping resources. Consequently, projects were begun to design and then convert a substantial part of the army's field artillery to high-speed, motorized, towed transport.

Much of the initial priority was directed toward artillery for the National Guard. As this branch was considered a "standby" force, eliminating the need for large numbers of horses that needed tending and feeding was attractive. Interestingly, most of the funding for the conversion of the M1897 75 mm gun initially came from Depression-era National Recovery Act funds rather than direct army ordnance appropriations.

High-speed conversion projects were designed and implemented to some extent for all three types of 75 mm guns (M1897, M1916, and M1917), and for both 155 mm types (howitzer and gun Models 1917 and 1918). Though mainly used for training rather than for deployment, some of the 240 mm howitzers were also modified. There was even a state-sponsored project for conversion of some 3-inch Model 1905 training guns. Some work was done to prepare specifications for high-speed wheels for the British 6-inch guns and 8-inch howitzers in war reserve status. Projects were started in 1933, and some conversion work was accomplished every year right up until the start of the Second World War.

Army arsenals undertook production of the conversion kits, with one exception. The Model 1897A4 75 mm carriage conversion kits were purchased under contract from the kit designer—the Martin-Parry Corp. It made the kits and sent them out to various stations where the conversion could be accomplished with regular tools and knowledgeable ordnance personnel. Incidentally, Martin-Parry also sold kits to the British for their 18-pounder guns, 4.5-inch howitzers, and to the Dutch East Indies for the US Marine Corps MkVII landing guns. All other conversion equipment was supplied by the army; in most cases the Rock Island Arsenal was entrusted with this task. Generally the modification parts were distributed to posts or storage facilities and installed on-site.

These modifications addressed only the towing situation. They did not otherwise modernize or improve the gun or howitzer's capabilities. A good example is the new carriage for the French 75 (the M2A2), developed simultaneously with the M1897A4 high-speed carriage. Under the budget restraints of the 1930s, it was realized that a wholesale conversion to the new, split-trail carriage would not be forthcoming, and the high-speed variant was a practical and affordable step for lower-priority formations.

75 mm Field Gun Model 1897 on Carriage Model 1897A4

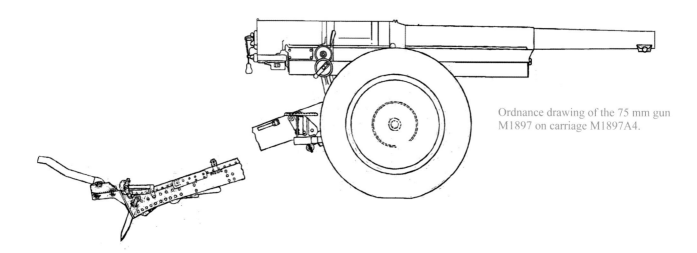

Ordnance drawing of the 75 mm gun M1897 on carriage M1897A4.

While studies had been conducted in the late 1920s, serious attempts to modify the large stock of 75 mm Model 1897 guns began in 1932. A memo in 1933 outlined the army's desire to modify existing guns for high-speed towing by trucks. National Guard units and ROTC training units were to be equipped first, followed by the regular army (except cavalry units, which of course would continue to need horse-capable artillery). Appropriations for these modifications followed and continued for several years.

The kit conversions involved removing the carriage's seats, wooden wheels, and crank brakes. The existing axle was too high for compact pneumatic tires; a rig to drop a new lower axle on each side was required to carry the steel disk wheels and pneumatic tires. Appropriate brakes were added. Changes increased the carriage weight by 350 pounds and raised the gun axis height by 4 inches; otherwise there were

no changes in elevation, traverse, or gun performance. On January 18, 1934, it was standardized as the gun M1897A4 on carriage M1897A4. In mid-1934 the first fourteen National Guard field artillery regiments received their adaptor kits. By late 1936, 650 sets had been authorized for installation in regular army units, but no funding was ever received to convert the almost 2,000 additional guns in storage. By October 1941, 871 conversions had been authorized, but only 605 were reported accomplished.

The simple modifications worked as expected. Guns of this type were used extensively in the 1940–41 GHQ maneuvers involving many National Guard divisions. None were supplied to overseas garrisons, which were less dependent on the M1897 type 75mm. In any event, the 105 mm howitzers replaced this conversion before any units were shipped overseas. They saw no combat in American hands, and surviving examples are rare.

US Army photograph from November 26, 1936, of the "kit" or adaptor manufactured by the Martin-Parry Corporation to modify the M1897 75 mm carriage to the high-speed M1897A4.

ORD
7377

July 1933 view of one of the prototype evaluation battery M1897A4
gun carriages at Fort Bragg, North Carolina.

Early version of the M1897A4 modifications. The gun is doing precisely
what the alteration was intended for—allowing motorized towing.

Very few of the almost 1,000 transitional M1897A4 carriages still
exist. Three are at Fort Sill, like this one inside the artillery museum.
One other, although restored with an incorrect wheel type, is at a war
monument in Cranston, Rhode Island.

75 mm Field Gun on Carriage Model 1917A1

In 1933, the ordnance department started efforts to make the Model 1917 75 mm carriage high-speed. Building on experience with the M1897 gun, the department produced adaptor kits internally—though Martin-Parry had developed a similar rig for Canada and bid on the chance to supply the US Army. Kits used many of the same 1897A4 parts, including disc wheels, tires, and brakes. New lunettes were attached to the guns. First orders occurred in January 1934, and all adaptor kits were collected at Rock Island Arsenal, though modifications were simple enough to do at the posts. First kits were sent to Hawaii (48) and the Philippines (24). Additional sets were made later, but only about half of the 900 remaining M1917s were converted to the high-speed M1917A1.

The remaining Model 1917 75 mm guns, whether converted to high speed or not, were slated for deletion as the 105 mm howitzer began production. Two hundred guns were supplied to Finland after its winter war with the Soviet Union. Great Britain received 395 guns following its catastrophic loss of artillery at Dunkirk. Except for a handful at arsenals or depots, all remaining American guns were assigned to the Philippines or Hawaii at the start of the war. There were 174 Model 1917s in the Philippines, in about a two-to-one ratio of high-speed to unconverted, in the hands of both the American and Philippine armies. All were lost in the subsequent campaign of 1941–42. Another forty-eight were at sea; they were soon landed in Java and lost there as well. Hawaii had the remaining quantity. Its guns were replaced with 105 mm howitzers by mid-1942, and after a period of service as beach defense and reserve guns, were scrapped at war's end. Only three M1917s exist today in the US. The only high-speed M1917A1 left is an exported gun at the Royal Canadian Artillery Museum in Shilo, Canada.

ROCK ISLAND ARSENAL

710-39391 April 28, 1933
Carriage, Gun, 75-mm.
M1917E2 (British).

Rock Island Arsenal photo from 1933 of the final prototype for the high-speed Model 1917 75 mm gun carriage.

The 75 mm gun Model 1917 was extensively used in the Philippines and Hawaii between the wars in preference to the 75 mm M1897. Here an M1917A1 carriage is on maneuvers on Oahu in 1941.

The only known surviving 75 mm on M1917A1 carriage is at the Royal Canadian Artillery Museum at Shilo, Manitoba. Canada was supplied a number of these guns for training during the Second World War.

75 mm Field Gun on Carriage Model 1916A1

The final high-speed project for 75 mm guns was intended for the Model 1916. In 1936 the army developed the design and parts to modify the existing carriages for high-speed towing, and in 1938 funding was obtained to begin the conversion of the first 180 of 320 units. With a few minor exceptions, this was virtually all the inventory of existing M1916 carriages, though many additional tubes without carriages still existed. After conversion the carriage was designated the M1916A1 (or M1916M1A1 if equipped with the St. Chamond recuperator). The changes were relatively simple—involving new pneumatic tires, brakes, removal of the axle seats, and addition of towing connectors.

There was only a limited number of the 75 mm gun Model 1916A1 in overseas stations at the start of the war. Fourteen guns of this type were part of the artillery reserve in the Philippine department. Apparently some served in a beach defense role, though no specific use in a combat situation has been found. They were lost when the Fil-Am forces surrendered in 1942. Another twelve were in Puerto Rico. When replaced with 105 mm howitzers, the guns were distributed as anti-submarine guns at minor ports in the Caribbean—St. Lucia, Antigua, St. Thomas, St. Croix, and Haiti. Once again, their use in combat cannot be confirmed. Most of the converted high-speed guns were distributed to allies under lend-lease. In early 1941, 150 were supplied to Great Britain (used for training and home defense), and fifty to Greece. Another small allotment was consigned to Yugoslavia but diverted to the Middle East after that country succumbed, and some served with an Australian anti-tank unit in Malaya during the 1941–42 campaign.

One of the few remaining 75 mm guns on Model 1916A1 high-speed carriage still in active US service in April 1942 in Panama.

The initial prototype of the conversion of the 75 mm gun Model 1916A1 on its high-speed carriage at Rock Island Arsenal on July 31, 1936.

Only three high-speed Model 1916 75 mm guns on M1916A1 carriages are known to survive. This one is on display at Colombia's Military Museum in Bogotá, Colombia. The guns were supplied through lend-lease during the Second World War.

3-Inch Gun M1905 High-Speed

One of the oddest high-speed modification projects was for thoroughly obsolete 3-inch guns Model of 1905. A number of private military schools had obtained such guns for training purposes after the First World War. The ammunition was long gone, so they were used only as saluting guns. The New York Military Academy at Cornwall-on-Hudson requested assistance in getting its eight guns modified for towing by truck to events so that its cadets would be familiar with this transport method. The War Department, with the support of Martin-Parry, supplied the modification kits.

The modifications were simple, involving only the drop-down axle attachment, disk wheels, and pneumatic tires. Hand brakes and equilibrators were deemed unnecessary because the guns wouldn't actually fire service charges. Negotiations occurred in early 1939, and the work was accomplished in early 1940. Martin-Parry handled it as a no-cost accommodation. There is some indication of a similar transaction with a western military school. Several survive on the academy's campus, doing their best to confuse artillery historians.

One of the surviving 3-inch Model 1905 guns given high-speed modifications including disk wheels and pneumatic tires in 1940. It is at the New York Military Academy.

155 mm Howitzer M1917A1 and M1918M1 on Carriages M1917A3 and M1918A3

The 155 mm howitzer high-speed project started in 1933, though at a slow pace. A four-wheeled design by Martin-Parry was rejected in 1935, but in 1936 an urgent request from the National Guard for units to be towed by trucks accelerated plans. A modification of the existing carriage emerged in 1937 as Model 1918E3. Two years later, conversion kits were being distributed. Initial conversions included 154 in the army and 156 in the National Guard.

As finally adopted, the M1918A3 and M1917A3 carriages were equipped with high-speed wheel bearings and pneumatic tires. They had a drawbar for towing (previously adopted on the M1918A2 carriage). The modification of Model 1917 and 1918 carriages for high-speed towing was accomplished at government arsenals. Most were done at Rock Island Arsenal, but Raritan Arsenal also appears on some surviving carriages. The carriages received a new information plate (still on the right side of the trunnion support) with location of modernization, model, and date. There was no effect on performance. Handbooks report a heavier howitzer and carriage weight of 8,184 pounds.

On November 1, 1939, 2,103 155 mm howitzers were reported in American inventory, of which 423 had been modified for high-speed towing. Efforts to convert the remaining inventory accelerated in 1940–1941. By June 1940, almost 600 were reported converted. It appears that virtually all remaining 155 mm howitzers were provided with modernized carriages by the start of the war. (In the US inventory, several hundred older, non-converted type were disposed of through lend-lease). While quite a few "A3" howitzers served in combat theaters, many more stayed in the continental US as training pieces. After the war all were declared obsolete and disposed of. Over 100 are known to still exist.

A 155 mm M1918 howitzer on M1917A3 high-speed carriage, conversion made at Rock Island Arsenal in 1940. The gun is on display in Marysville, Ohio.

155 mm Gun M1917A1 and M1918A1 (GPF) on High-Speed Carriage M3

In December 1930, a project was begun to allow the 155 mm gun to be towed at a speed of at least 20 mph. By 1936 the first units using Timken air brakes and pneumatic tires had been designed. The original axles could still be used—resulting in a relatively simple conversion process. By December 1936, the M3 carriage type was standardized and production of the first fifty-two units (once again for the National Guard) begun. Eventually all 155 mm GPF were slated for conversion. On June 30, 1941, 654 were converted or under an authorized schedule. Based on the relatively large number of existing unconverted carriages on display, it appears that the final 300 or so were not converted to high-speed M3 carriages.

Converted carriages were given steel disk wheels, pneumatic tires, and air brakes. The M2 carriage limber (the two-wheeled limber the trails were carried on during towing) was also upgraded to an M3 designation and given pneumatic tires and disk wheels. Preferred towing vehicles were the 7.5-ton truck or M4 tractor. When carriages were modified they were supplied with a new carriage plate identifying the site or arsenal, model type, and date. Most modifications were done at the Rock Island Arsenal; however, the Benicia Arsenal also produced some new carriages.

The 155 mm on high-speed M3 carriage was the preferred gun supplied to units deployed overseas. Except for a mix of types in the Philippines, all the guns sent to North Africa, Italy, and with the Marine Corps were the M3 type. These guns continued to be an important coast artillery weapons as well. Both the unmodified and high-speed modified carriages survive today as display and museum items. The major point of identification is the difference in wheels.

Several good examples of the 155 mm M1917 and M1918 guns on high-speed carriage M3 remain on display in the US. This representative is at Fort Stevens, Oregon.

240 mm Howitzer M1918M1 on High-Speed Carriage M1918A2

As the 240 mm howitzer was only operated from a prepared position on a flat firing platform, the changes made to facilitate high-speed towing were limited to the transport vehicles. The original M1918 howitzer was assigned four transport wagons for gun tube, top carriage, cradle, and platform. Additional wagons carried accessories and tools. The wagons averaged about 15,000 pounds fully loaded. The provision of motorized towing enabled these loads to be consolidated in two new vehicles weighing 30,000 and 25,000 pounds. One carried the tube and cradle, the other the lower carriage and platform. The transport wagons M4 and M5 were equipped with large-diameter pneumatic tires. A vehicle with A-frame and tools along with a truck-mounted crane accompanied these new wagons.

New pneumatic tires of a standard commercial size were fitted. The modifications to the wagons allowed them to be towed at speeds up to about 35 mph. They were also equipped with air brakes. The modified carriages were designated M1918A2.

Only forty-eight 240 mm M1918 howitzers received the new transport wagons. Even then it appears that the major rationale was not for modernizing them for combat deployment, but to use them for training on something similar to the wagons and tractors projected for the new 8-inch and 240 mm heavy artillery types being developed. None of these modernized howitzers were deployed to combat theaters; they stayed in the US for training or as reserve defense material in Hawaii. The 240 mm Model 1918 was declared obsolete in 1944, though apparently it wasn't scrapped until after the war.

None of the modified (for that matter, even the unmodified) transport wagons still exist for the 240 mm M1918 howitzer.

Army Technical Manual TM9-340 illustration of the new, high-speed transport wagons for the M1918 240 mm howitzer. Note how the barrel and carriage are transported on separate wagons.

Pack Howitzers

The US Army had been looking for a replacement for the old Vickers 2.95-inch mountain gun since the early 1900s. The Model 1908 and 1911 mountain howitzers were developmental steps, but there were no First World War requirements for this type of gun. However, postwar the Caliber Board (also known as the Westervelt Board) recommended a new pack weapon. It suggested requirements for a gun of 3-inch bore, firing the same projectiles as the standard divisional gun, having a 45-degree elevation, range of 5,000 yards, and capable of breaking into pack loads of about 225 pounds each. At this time a shield was not seen as necessary. Subsequently two units were made of an initial M1920 design with differing breech mechanisms. Modifications led to a series of improved M1923 types. Finally in 1925, the M1923E2 passed evaluation and preliminary service tests. It was standardized as the M1.

The success of the M1 75 mm howitzer led to its use on three separate mobile field carriages and several self-propelled mounts. The original development, standardized in 1927, was for a pack gun useful in mountain and jungle terrain. The M1 pack carriage could disassemble into six loads and was issued to mountain troops. During the war substantial numbers were supplied to China. The most-used carriage was the M8 developed for airborne use. Essentially an M1 pack howitzer modified with pneumatic wheels for towing, the M8 eventually served the US Army and Marine Corps as a light artillery piece in a great number of situations. It was also favored by British forces when supplied as a lend-lease item.

Finally, responding to the needs of the cavalry branch for a new divisional gun, the same 75 mm M1 howitzer was placed on a new carriage. Developed in the late 1930s, the M3 field howitzer carriage entered production right before the Second World War and featured a modern design with split trail and protective shield. Unfortunately, it appeared as mounted troops were being phased out and was never extensively produced. Small numbers were used by miscellaneous specialized units and others supplied to allied nations, particularly China. The 75 mm pack howitzer also proved popular on self-propelled mounts. A limited number of mountings on halftracks (T30) were produced early in the war. Far more successful and numerous were mountings of specially produced M2 and M3 75 mm howitzers on the M8 HMC (an M5 Stuart tank with turret-mounted howitzer) and the LVT-4 (amphibious tractor with a similar turret mount).

A new infantry gun was developed late in the war. The concept of a light gun accompanying infantry units for direct fire had fallen out of favor after the abortive efforts of the early 1920s. At that time, the design of a 2.24-inch gun was completed and a few were made, but it suffered from underfunding like so many projects of the time. By the early 1940s, attention turned to creating lightweight anti-tank weapons (such as the bazooka). However, a request for a suitable hand-transport weapon for jungle warfare in the Pacific was urgently pressed. In this case the ordnance department displayed the urgency required. A quickly designed 37 mm gun, based on the 37 mm anti-tank gun married to a modified 0.50-caliber machine gun tripod, seemed able to meet the need. In a short time a useful number were assembled for army use in the waning days of the war.

The extended life of the pack howitzer and relatively compact size has meant that many examples survive as saluting guns, memorial guns, and in military museums around the world. They are complemented with fewer numbers of the 75 mm field howitzer and 37 mm T32 infantry gun.

Sketch of the M1A1 75 mm howitzer on the M1 pack carriage.

The new 75 mm pack howitzer had several ingenious features. The tube was centrifugally cast and cold-worked. The gun attached to a breech ring with an interrupted, threaded screw. This assembly was cradled between a bottom and top sleigh. The top portion was held in place by a distinctive curve-shaped, lead-filled weight. Recoil and counterrecoil were achieved with hydropneumatic springs mounted under the bottom sleigh. The tube had uniform rifling of $\frac{1}{20}$, with twenty-eight grooves and lands. Rate of fire was expected at six rounds per minute in short bursts, three for prolonged firing. The gun fired semi-fixed ammunition and had four variable powder charges available. It was supplied with HE, HEAT, chemical, or smoke projectiles. Gun model, serial, weight, and inspection data were stamped on the breech housing on the angled face above the breech opening; a plate on the carriage contained the carriage manufacture information. The gun was initially made at Watervliet Arsenal, but later three other contract firms also produced it. Several facilities made the carriages.

The first carriage developed was intended for disassembling as pack equipment. It was a box-trail steel carriage pierced with circular cut-outs to help conserve weight. The carriage was hinged partway down its length for folding to ease handling, or as a disassembly point. Six fairly equal weight pack loads for animal transport could be made. The carriage was equipped with an axle and small wooden spoke wheels with steel rims. On the carriage was a panoramic sight M1 and direct-fire 3-power telescopic sight M5. During the war it served mostly in Burma and the South Pacific. A small number persisted with the 4th Artillery in the United States until the late 1950s.

The second major carriage (M8) was developed for airborne use, either as a complete assembly for gliders or broken into segments for parachute dropping. While it used the same M1 gun and most of the lower chassis and trail of the pack carriage, it was equipped with steel disk wheels and pneumatic tires and had a different lunette for towing. The carriage weighed about 70 pounds more due to these changes. Gun performance and equipment was the same for these two types. Paracrates were produced for the airborne M8 howitzers and first employed in Southern France in August 1944.

Production of the 75 mm howitzer and its carriages started slowly. M1 pack carriages equipped the 2nd and 4th Field Artillery Regiments with guns for serious field evaluations. Between September 1940 and December 1944, 4,939 75 mm howitzers were produced, most of them on M8 carriages. They were widely used in most theaters, but were particularly useful in the Pacific, Southeast Asia, and Italy. The Marine Corps used a substantial number in the Pacific theater. In fact, the Marines had begun replacing their 75 mm field guns with 75 mm pack howitzers in the summer of 1939. Although eventually upgraded to 105 mm M3 howitzers, the 75 mm type was quite useful throughout the Pacific campaigns due to its high mobility.

Additionally, over 1,600 guns and carriages were supplied to allies in Great Britain (826), China (637), France (68), and Latin American countries (60). Postwar the gun and carriage (M8) was redesignated the M116. They lasted a long time in US inventory and other countries. Even in 1986, they were reported in service in at least nineteen foreign nations.

An evaluation battery of M1A1 pack howitzers was dispatched to the American-Mexican border to garner field handling experience. This photo dates from that experience in April 1927.

75 mm Pack Howitzer M1A1

Gun Characteristics

Bore size: 75mm

Construction: Steel

Tube length overall: 52 inches

Nominal caliber: 15.9 calibers

Tube and breech weight: 341 pounds

Usual carriage: Carriage M1 or M8

Weight of gun and carriage: Gun: 1,269 pounds; carriage 1,339 pounds

Maximum elevation: 45 degrees

Loading: Semi-fixed

Shell weight: 14.7 pounds (HE)

Maximum muzzle velocity: 1,250 fps

Maximum range: 9,489 yards

Builders: Gun: Watervliet Arsenal, Draper Corp., General Electric, Crowder Division of American Type Founders; carriage: J. G. Brill, Rock Island Arsenal

Number built: 4,939 on M1 or M8 carriages

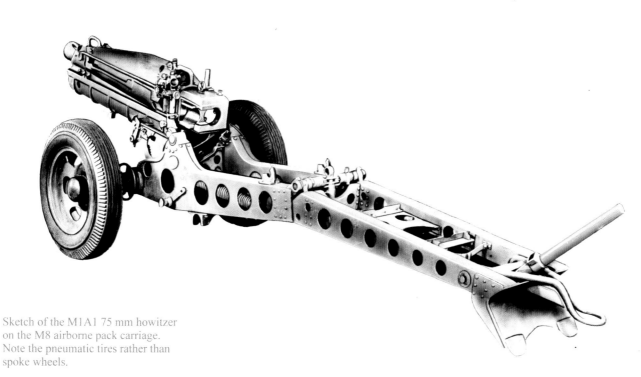

Sketch of the M1A1 75 mm howitzer on the M8 airborne pack carriage. Note the pneumatic tires rather than spoke wheels.

75 mm pack howitzer M1A1 on pack carriage M8 being used by the
Marine Corps on Peleliu in September 1944.

75 mm pack howitzer on wheeled carriage M1 of
the Mars Task Force in Burma during 1945.

Only a few pack howitzers on M1 pack carriages exist in the United States, like this example (actually the precursor M1923E1) at the National Museum of the Marine Corps near Quantico, Virginia.

On the other hand, pack howitzers on M8 airborne carriages are plentiful. Over seventy are on display in the US and many others are at foreign museums. This howitzer and carriage are on display in Vernon, Texas.

75 mm Pack Howitzer M1A1 on Field Howitzer Carriage M3

The army's cavalry branch required a field gun for its divisions. After the First World War it attempted to use the standard Model 1897 75 mm gun, but found its characteristics and high-speed towing capabilities lacking. In the 1920s, a project was begun to see if the newly developed 75 mm pack howitzer could be equipped with a specially designed carriage to serve the branch's purposes. In 1931, characteristics for a new carriage were worked out, and in fiscal year 1934 funds were supplied to manufacture a pilot model. Fifteen were ordered for service tests in the late 1930s. A project to develop a new limber and caisson persisted for a considerable length of time; the new light limber M4 and light caisson M2 were not standardized until as late as February 1943. Even the army's ordnance department was frustrated that it took over ten years to yield a gun that required only forty-eight units.

The last developed field howitzer carriage T2E3 was standardized as M3A1 in December 1935. The cavalry's field howitzer carriage had a full split trail with tubular legs. The carriage could give elevation from -9 to +50 degrees and 22.5 degrees of traverse left and right. A firing pedestal in front of the axle could be lowered and the wheels raised to provide a stable firing platform. Unlike the two pack carriages, there was no provision for disassembly to allow separate transport. The finished carriage could be towed by horse or motor vehicle. A separate development effort in 1940 led to a hard steel shield on a carriage designated M3A2. The last variant was the M3A3 standardized on March 5, 1942. This carriage followed a new policy of adopting combat-type wheels (7.50 × 16 inches). Older carriages were progressively modified to this standard when re-equipped with the new wheels. The howitzer and upper carriage were exactly the same as the M1 pack howitzer.

In July 1936, the first standard order for the M3A1 was placed at Rock Island Arsenal for twenty-four carriages. Subsequently, 748 M3A1 and M3A3 carriages were ordered, most of them fabricated in 1941. One hundred fifty-seven were produced at Rock Island. A contract on September 29, 1940, ordered 591 from Gar Wood Industries. Not all of these were completed as finished field howitzers. Perhaps as many as 312

Ordnance illustration of the 75 mm field howitzer with shield on M3A3 carriage.

howitzers were not delivered due to their tubes being taken for motorized mounts T30, but some of the excess parts (trails and lower carriage components) were used in manufacturing M3 carriage mounts for the 105 mm light howitzer, whose carriage was roughly based on the 75 mm field howitzer.

A number of these 75 mm field howitzers were delivered to the 1st and 2nd Cavalry Divisions—though the latter was soon dismantled and never saw combat. Photos show field howitzers deployed to the Iceland garrison. The gun also proved useful to China, which obtained about 125 during the war. In American service it did not survive into the postwar era.

75 mm Pack Howitzer M1A1 on Field Howitzer Carriage M3

Gun Characteristics

Bore size: 75mm

Construction: Steel

Tube length overall: 52 inches

Nominal caliber: 15.9 calibers

Tube and breech weight: 341 pounds

Usual carriage: 75 mm howitzer carriage M3A1, M3A2, M3A3

Weight of gun and carriage: 2,224 pounds (M3A3 with shield)

Maximum elevation: 50 degrees

Loading: Semi-fixed

Shell weight: 14.7 pounds (HE)

Maximum muzzle velocity: 1,250 fps

Maximum range: 9,489 yards

Builders: Gun: Watervliet Arsenal, General Electric; carriage: Rock Island Arsenal, Gar Wood Industries

Number built: 748 (312 diverted to T30 mounts)

Only a single surviving 75 mm field howitzer is known to exist in the US; this unit was formerly at the Aberdeen Ordnance Museum.

Almost 60 M3 75 mm field howitzers in storage at the 173rd Ordnance Depot at Makum, India, on July 16, 1945—probably awaiting delivery to Chinese forces.

37 mm Infantry Gun T32

While cannon companies were used for part of the war with infantry regiments, battalions and companies had only organic mortars and heavy machine guns as heavy armament. Experience with jungle warfare in the Pacific and in Europe's mountainous terrain dictated the need for a light, preferably man-handled gun. In November 1943, a special "jungle warfare" committee from the chief of ordnance office toured the region and collected input from the South and Southwest Pacific theaters. Their report stated that certain weapons designed for jungle warfare

be developed and issued as soon as possible. What was needed was greater firepower in hand-carried guns for standard infantry formations. One promising artillery project already under development was selected for urgent procurement.

The 37 mm weapon selected for development pulled parts from several proven guns. It used the same vertical-sliding breech mechanism and powder chamber as the 37 mm anti-tank gun model M3. The breech ring was attached by an interrupted screw to a shortened, separate tube 50 inches long. The

Crew from the 34th Division load a 37 mm T32 infantry gun on T9 tripod mount in Italy, March 6, 1945.

hydrospring recoil mechanism was a shortened version from the 37 mm M4 carriage. The simple tripod T9 was a modified M3 0.50-caliber machine gun mount with traversing and elevating mechanisms on the traversing rod between the two long, rear tripod legs. On the carriage it could be maneuvered to a 12-degree elevation and -5-degree depression. The gun was usually equipped with a 3-power T126 telescope on mount T103. It fired fixed HE shells M63, AP shot M80, or canister M2 rounds, all previously developed for the M3 anti-tank gun. Five men could carry the gun with backpack loads weighing between 39 and 70 pounds. The resulting flat trajectory weapon, with its compact, 23-inch height, was well-suited to the task.

Production was initiated relatively quickly. On December 30, 1943, the US Army's Research and Development Service ordered 200 complete units. Incremental additional orders through January 1945 brought the total number of guns and carriages produced to 650. The primary manufacturer was the York Safe and Lock Company. Distribution was made to units training in the United States. The guns were deployed to combat units in 1945 for campaigns in Italy, Luzon, and Okinawa. While not particularly innovative, it was satisfactory. The gun was marked with the usual serial, production, and inspection marks on the left side of the breech ring. The carriage had an identification plate attached to the tripod head.

It is doubtful that this expedient, never standardized weapon survived into the postwar period. There is no evidence of its further service or supply to allies. While there may be some examples in private hands, only two specimens are known to survive on display.

37 mm Infantry Gun T32

Gun Characteristics

Bore size: 37mm

Construction: Steel

Tube length overall: 54.5 inches

Nominal caliber: 30 calibers

Tube and breech weight: 110 pounds

Usual carriage: 37 mm Gun T9 tripod mount

Weight of gun and carriage: 264 pounds

Maximum elevation: 12 degrees

Loading: Fixed

Shell weight: 2.42 pounds (M63 HE shell)

Maximum muzzle velocity: 1,500 fps

Maximum range: 7,750 yards

Builders: York Safe & Lock

Number built: 650

There are only two known examples of the 37 mm T32 on display. This specimen is at the Rock Island Arsenal Museum.

Second World War Field Guns

The basic divisional field gun was arguably the most important class of artillery of the Second World War. A new American generation of guns was developed between the wars, though production didn't really get started until right before the conflict. The "French 75" that equipped the army in the First World War made one final appearance. Though modified with a modern split carriage and capable of high-speed motorized towing, nothing could be done about the relatively small size of the explosive charge. Pursuing the same expansion of power and range flexibility of the larger howitzer that led the British to the 25-pounder and the Germans to their 10 cm feld haubitze, the American 105 mm howitzer eventually emerged as the best compromise to mobility, range, and throw weight.

At the time, the divisional artillery concept embraced multiple battalions of "standard" field guns equal to support its number of infantry regiments, and a heavier battalion to provide counterbattery and special heavy interdiction coverage. Two guns were developed for this latter purpose—the 155 mm M1 howitzer and the 4.7-inch gun. The howitzer followed the mission doctrine of the previous Model 1917/18 howitzers, but the modern replacement was a much more capable weapon. The 4.7-inch gun, modified late in its development to 4.5 inches to simplify ammunition supply with the British gun of this size, struggled to find an appropriate role in combat. While the gun worked as designed and the carriage was the same as for the 155 mm howitzer, the shell's payload weight was just too small.

It was never produced in quantity and was the only significant pre-war artillery development to fall by the wayside.

In April 1942, American infantry divisions were provided with cannon companies for the first time—one company to each of the three infantry regiments. These were companies with six howitzers designed to give dedicated artillery support to the regiment and its battalions. At first this was supplied by halftrack or self-propelled gun carriages carrying 105 mm guns, but the preference was for towed 105s. This need turned out to be nicely filled by the development of the light 105 mm howitzer M3. Production was rapidly ramped up (aided, fortunately, by a corresponding decrease in demand for 75 mm pack howitzers), and most infantry regiments were equipped with a cannon company of six M3 105 mm howitzers. This proved to be a good fit of weapon to organization.

While the fully modernized 75 mm gun had a brief role as a substitute for an anti-tank gun, it was quickly relegated to stateside training. Just one battalion armed with this gun saw combat during the war. All of the more modern field guns were used—in fact three of them (the two types of 105s and the 155 mm howitzer) were the most heavily used American artillery pieces of the war. They were made in large quantities, and because they were extensively supplied to allies through lend-lease during the war and after the conflict through various military assistance programs, they have been involved in military combat ever since. Some even continue to serve with the armies of smaller nations. Numerous guns still exist on memorials and in military museums worldwide.

75 mm Field Gun on Carriage M2

In the late 1930s, two projects were started to modernize the considerable inventory of Model 1897 75 mm guns in the army's inventory. The first was a simple (and inexpensive) modification that added new high-speed towing wheels to existing guns. While this allowed motorized towing, it did nothing to improve range (elevation) or traverse (leverage against tanks). Initially this modification was limited to National Guard guns. For the regular army, a more radical improvement involved a new split-trail carriage, wheels, and shield. This was accomplished with a new carriage for the existing M1897 gun in 1934—standardized as the M2 carriage.

The familiar M1897 or "French 75" gun was used on these new carriages. Several thousand still existed in the late 1930s. Described on page 86, it was a 34.5-caliber nickel-steel tube and the original French-designed, eccentric Nordenfelt-type screw breech.

Existing guns were modified as gun model 1897A4, and any newly produced guns would become model 1897A2. On both of these the notable barrel guide piece and barrel jacket were removed when mounted in the new carriages.

The M2, M2A1, and M2A2 carriages were split-trail type. The wide split (60 degrees) permitted a high elevation (46 degrees). The compact carriage could deliver a 45-degree right and 40-degree left traverse important for any anti-tank role. Disk wheels with pneumatic tires and brakes allowed high-speed towing. Equilibrator springs were standard, along with a straight steel shield for crew protection. The M2 carriages had a deployable jack under the carriage that could be used to support the carriage weight in firing position. In 1941, an improved M2A3 carriage was introduced. It had shorter (by 19 inches) trail legs and improved drawbar, and the supporting jack was replaced with extended curved segments mounted inboard of each wheel. Both carriage types used a combined recoil and counterrecoil cylinder mounted underneath the tube and cradle. Sighting equipment included an M12A1 panoramic sight, an M14 elbow telescope, and an M5 range quadrant. A range of shells including HE with various fuses, chemical shell, shrapnel, AP shot, and semi-AP shot were available. Guns continued to carry their old markings on the muzzle face or above the breech; the new carriages had manufacturing information on a plate on the right trunnion support.

Production of the new carriage started slowly with the M2A2 in 1936. Less than 200 had been made by the end of 1939. Meaningful quantities were not delivered until 1940 and 1941. A November 25, 1941, report stated that 554 M2A2 and 188 M2A3s were in service with field and anti-tank units. The source of the tubes was

Ordnance publication retouched photograph of the 75 mm gun M1897A5 on carriage M2A3. The final modification of carriage for the French 75. Note the split trail and high elevation achievable.

existing spare stocks and older (unmodified) M1897 guns on original spoke-wheel carriages. Complete production numbers are not available, but 918 were reportedly built between July 1940 and November 1941. Some were assigned to divisional battalions pending replacement by 105 mm M2 howitzers. This gun briefly became the primary anti-tank gun, once again an acceptable substitute until production of new types could meet demand.

An important type in the late 1930s and early 1940s, the 75 mm M1897 on M2 carriages were mostly assigned training responsibilities once war started. The only combat deployment of the type was the twelve guns of the 2nd Battalion, 131st Field Artillery. This unit was on the way to the Philippines when Pearl Harbor was attacked. It was diverted to Java, where it fought and was captured in March 1942. At home, many of the guns were removed from their carriages and used to arm the halftrack GMC M3 in 1941–1942. The 75 mm M1897 types were declared obsolete on March 8, 1945. A considerable number of 75 mm guns on M2A2 and M2A3 carriages exist in museums and at war memorials throughout the US.

75 mm Field Gun Model 1897A4 on Carriages M2A2 and M2A3

Gun Characteristics

Bore size: 75mm

Construction: Built-up, nickel steel

Tube length overall: 107.125 inches

Nominal caliber: 34.5 calibers

Tube and breech weight: 1,026 pounds

Usual carriage: 75 mm gun carriage M2A2 or M2A3

Weight of gun and carriage: 3,400 pounds (with M2A3 carriage)

Maximum elevation: 45.5 degrees

Loading: Fixed

Shell weight: 14.6 pounds (M48 HE)

Maximum muzzle velocity: 2,000 fps (M2A3)

Maximum range: 13,950 yards (M2A3)

Builders: Gun: various as per M1897; carriage: Rock Island Arsenal, Parish Pressed Steel

Number built: Approximately 1,250

The 75 mm gun, on either the M2A2 (pictured here in Murfreesboro, Tennessee) or M2A3, is a common site at war memorials, museums, and veteran service clubs. Over 100 still exist.

US Army photograph from Rock Island Arsenal showing the first 75 mm M1897 on M2 carriage on June 26, 1936. Note the support jack folded directly under the carriage and lack of a shield.

ROCK ISLAND ARSENAL
156 RA-87
752-41062   June 26, 1936
75-MM., Gun Carriage, M2.

105 mm Field Howitzer M2A1

This highly successful weapon was the result of a methodical and lengthy development program. After the First World War, artillery boards advocated the adoption of a mobile howitzer of medium weight to replace the 155 mm in divisions. German war prize 10 cm howitzers were put into reserve, and a program was begun to develop a domestic howitzer of this size. After much trial and successive modification, the 105 mm howitzer M1 was standardized in 1927. During the Depression, production was slow. Ten M2 guns were ordered as test units in 1930, and the design was standardized in May 1934. The final M2A1 howitzer was standardized in March 1940 and typically placed on the M2A1 carriage (developed after removing the electric brakes) or M2A2 (with an enlarged shield and new screw traverse). The howitzer was commonly towed by the 6×6 truck.

The standardized howitzer had a 24-caliber nickel steel tube. It had thirty-four grooves and 1/20 uniform rifling. The improved M2A1 howitzer had a minor modification of added bearing strips on the bottom of the breech. The breech was a horizontal sliding wedge, fed by a prominent shell-loading cradle. Above the tube was the hydropneumatic recoil cylinder. The M2A1 and M2A2 carriages were single-axle, split trail type equipped with spring equilibrators for stability. They also had pneumatic tires capable of high-speed road towing. On its left side, the carriage usually carried an elbow telescope M16 and panoramic sight M12A2. The carriage allowed for elevation from -5 to 64 degrees and on-carriage traverse of 45 degrees. A new shield design was introduced on the more numerous M2A2 carriages. It consisted of several sections and hinged-down upper panels. Eventually thirteen different ammunition types were supplied for this howitzer (HE, HEAT, and smoke among them). Ammo was semi-fixed with seven possible charges, but loaded as complete rounds. The manufacturing information was marked on the breech housing; the carriage plate with similar data was attached to the left trunnion support.

Limited production started in 1940 but accelerated later that year when it was decided to equip all three of the infantry division's light battalions with 105s instead of 75s. By January 1942, plans called for production of 600 complete howitzers per month. The howitzer was also emplaced on self-propelled mounts, the M7 "Priest" in particular. Primary production contractors included three firms for the tube (Vilter, Chain Belt, and United Engineering & Foundry), and four for the carriage (Rock Island Arsenal, Pullman-Standard, American Locomotive, Parish Pressed Steel). A total of 8,536 units were completed during the war. The Marine Corps adopted the howitzer in 1942, eventually replacing most of its pack howitzers. They were also supplied to allies; primary benefactors were Great Britain, China, France, and several Latin American countries.

Rock Island Arsenal illustration of the 105 mm howitzer M2A1 on M1A1 carriage in January 1941.

The piece saw large-scale war service, used by 264 battalions in virtually every theater the Americans fought.

Production continued postwar, ending in 1953 with 10,202 guns. Re-designated the M101A1 105 mm howitzer, it served in US regular and National Guard units through the Korean and Vietnam Wars. In 1977, it was reportedly supplied to sixty-eight countries, making it the most widespread artillery piece ever produced. After replacement in American forces, some of these howitzers became available for public memorials. Over 100 were supplied to communities and most are still on display.

105 mm Howitzer M2A1 on Carriage M2A1

Gun Characteristics

Bore size: 105mm

Construction: Nickel steel

Tube length overall: 101.35 inches

Nominal caliber: 22.5 calibers

Tube and breech weight: 1,080 pounds

Usual carriage: 105 mm howitzer carriage M2

Weight of gun and carriage: 4,980 pounds

Maximum elevation: 64.25 degrees

Loading: Semi-fixed

Shell weight: 41.75 pounds

Maximum muzzle velocity: 1,550 fps

Maximum range: 12,500 yards

Builders: Howitzer: Vilter, Chain Belt, United Engr Foundry, Watervliet Arsenal; carriage: Rock Island Arsenal, Pullman-Standard American Locomotive, Parish Pressed Steel, San Jose Manufacturing

Number built: 10,202 (1934–1953)

The 105 mm howitzer served all over the world during three major wars. This one is with the 1st Cavalry Division in Korea in 1951.

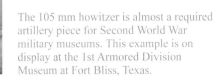

The 105 mm howitzer is almost a required artillery piece for Second World War military museums. This example is on display at the 1st Armored Division Museum at Fort Bliss, Texas.

4.5-Inch Gun M1

The Westervelt Board recommended a light corps gun 4.7 to 5 inches in caliber. It was to fire a round of about 60 pounds at least 18,000 yards. The board envisioned it sharing a common carriage with a new 155 mm howitzer. A new carriage Model 1920 was developed, with the recognition that requiring it to share the howitzer carriage would limit elevation and traverse. Eventually the Model 1922E gun on Model 1921E carriage was perfected. During these years the US Army knew it wouldn't be given money for large-scale production and wisely chose to develop weapons that could be produced once a need emerged. The project matured slowly, but by 1939 the 4.7-inch gun T3 on the 155 mm howitzer carriage T1 was completed. The last change came in April 1941 when the gun was re-sized to a 4.5-inch bore to share common ammunition with the British. That decision seems peculiar, as that concession was not required on any other American artillery piece, with the possible exception of the 57 mm anti-tank gun. Ultimately, the relatively small shell size was the gun's major flaw.

The tube was the usual built-up alloy steel construction. It had a stepped-thread interrupted screw breech. Below the tube

was the hydropneumatic recoil cylinder. The split trails could be opened to 60 degrees. The carriage was equipped with spring equilibrators to compensate for unbalanced weight distribution. The M1 carriage could allow 65-degree elevation and a left-right traverse of 26.5 degrees each direction. Firing was stabilized using a deployable firing jack. M65 HE round ammunition was usually issued. The M12 panoramic sight was included, and the carriage also had telescope mount. A small but adequate steel shield provided crew protection. Like its partner gun, the plan was to use the M5 high-speed artillery tractor for towing. Guns were marked in the usual fashion on the muzzle face and on a plate attached to the carriage's right trunnion support.

Production did not start until September 1942. In fact, despite the design readiness, the 4.5-inch and companion 155 mm howitzer were among the last major artillery programs to begin American production—to some extent justified by the relative abundance of serviceable, older Model 1917–18 155 mm howitzers. One tube manufacturer (Watervliet) made the gun, though original production schedules had allocated some of the work to Yuba Manufacturing. The Rock Island Arsenal and three

The last developmental model before the change to a 4.5-inch bore caliber, this is the 4.7-inch gun T3 on carriage T1 at Aberdeen on April 10, 1941.

commercial firms made the carriages. Between 1942 and 1944, only 426 4.5-inch M1 guns and carriages were produced. Just sixteen battalions were armed with the gun, all serving in the European theater. None were supplied to allies under lend-lease.

While the gun basically fulfilled its mission, it threw a shell that was too light. In addition, the power, accuracy, and range of the new 155 mm howitzers and guns left little room for this size of gun. When the war ended in September 1945, it was quickly removed from service and later scrapped or donated. Few 4.5-inch guns exist today; less than a dozen are in memorial and museum displays. Their similarity to the companion 155 mm howitzer has led to misidentification in some museum displays.

4.5-Inch Gun M1 on Carriage M1

Gun Characteristics

Bore size: 4.5 inches

Construction: Nickel steel

Tube length overall: 187.6 inches

Nominal caliber: 42 calibers

Tube and breech weight: 4,200 pounds

Usual carriage: 4.5-inch gun carriage M1

Weight of gun and carriage: 12,466 pounds

Maximum elevation: 65 degrees

Loading: Separate

Shell weight: 54.9 pounds

Maximum muzzle velocity: 1,920–2,275 fps

Maximum range: 21,125 yards (super-charge)

Builders: Gun: Watervliet Arsenal; carriage: Lufkin Foundry, Caterpillar Tractor, Western-Austin, Rock Island Arsenal

Number built: 426

Surviving 4.5-inch guns exist, like this representative outside a National Guard armory in New Braunfels, Texas. The casual observer needs to look twice to distinguish it from the 155 mm howitzer.

Though few in number, the 4.5-inch gun M1 saw combat in Europe during the war. Here, a unit in the 90th Division prepares a gun in Luxembourg in January 1945.

105 mm Howitzer M3

Ordnance pamphlet sketch of the 105 mm howitzer M3.

Unlike other common American field guns, the M3 howitzer was not developed methodically. Rather, it began relatively late as an effort in 1941 to create a 105 mm weapon for new formations requiring a lightweight alternative. The primary intended users were regimental cannon companies and airborne divisions (which already had the 75 mm pack howitzer). An attempt was made to marry a standard M2 105 mm howitzer to the M3A1 75 mm field howitzer carriage. The 105 mm barrel was shortened and the carriage strengthened with a stronger trail and recoil mechanism. Few adjustments were needed to accept the larger tube. The result was a highly serviceable weapon.

The shortened barrel was just 66 inches long, 27 inches shorter than the M2 105mm. The weapon's overall length was 13.1 feet. It was relatively light at 2,495 pounds. The barrel had thirty-four grooves and a uniform $\frac{1}{20}$ rifling. The breech was the 105 mm horizontal sliding-wedge type. The carriage held the two spring equilibrators. The configuration could provide a nominal 30-degree elevation, though removal of the stops could increase that to as much as 65 degrees if necessary. On-carriage traverse was 22.5 degrees left and right. The gun fired the same semi-fixed ammunition as the divisional 105 mm gun, usually the 33-pound HE round, though the propelling charge was made smaller. There were five zone charges and maximum range was published as 8,295 yards (7,250 yards with the 30-degree elevation). Gun information was stamped on the top surface of the breech housing and gave model, manufacturer, serial number, year, weight, and inspector's initials. Carriage information appeared on an attached plate on the carriage side.

This wartime photograph of a 105 mm M3 howitzer clearly shows how the wheels could be lifted and the gun supported by its firing pedestal.

The design was standardized in February 1943 and soon entered production. One thousand nine hundred and sixty-five were made in 1943, 410 in 1944, and 205 in 1945. Total production was 2,580 howitzers and carriages. Two commercial facilities made the gun, and one commercial and one government arsenal made the carriage. Part of the carriage production was met by diverting unused components of 75 mm field howitzer M3A1 made at Gar Wood Industries (310 sets of trails and lower carriages).

In April 1942, infantry cannon companies were authorized to accompany each US infantry regiment. The new, light but still relatively powerful M3 howitzer was perfect for this use. While there was some reorganization, and even temporary suspension of the cannon company concept, for much of the war each regular infantry regiment was assigned a company with three platoons of two 105 mm M3 howitzers each. The gun also went to two glider battalions of the 82nd Airborne Division. Normally it was towed by a Dodge 6×6 truck, though it could be handled by other 1.5-ton trucks or a jeep. It saw action across a wide range of theaters and combat conditions. In fact, this howitzer is credited with firing the second largest number of rounds by American field artillery in the war (second only to the divisional 105 mm M2 howitzer). It was generally not made available for export, though two went to England, ninety-four to American-supplied French infantry divisions, and eighteen to Latin American countries.

The 105 mm M3 left American service soon after the Second World War. Many were donated as memorial and museum guns and given to allies after the war under military assistance programs.

105 mm Howitzer M3 on Carriage M3

Gun Characteristics

Bore size: 105mm

Construction: Alloy steel

Tube length overall: 66 inches

Nominal caliber: 16 calibers

Tube and breech weight: 995 pounds

Usual carriage: 105 mm howitzer carriage M3

Weight of gun and carriage: 2,495 pounds

Maximum elevation: 65 degrees

Loading: Semi-fixed

Shell weight: 33 pounds (HE)

Maximum muzzle velocity: 1,550 fps

Maximum range: 8,295 yards

Builders: Gun: United Engineering & Foundry, Chain Belt; carriage: Rock Island Arsenal, Gar Wood Industries

Number built: 2,580

Almost thirty 105 mm M3 howitzers exist on display, several at military posts like this example at Fort Bragg, North Carolina. At least another dozen are in overseas museums, reflecting the widespread postwar distribution as part of military assistance.

155 mm Howitzer M1

An ordnance department illustration of the new 155 mm howitzer M1 being towed.

In the early 1920s, developmental work was initiated for a new 155 mm howitzer of increased range to replace the Model 1917/18 howitzers. However, funding soon evaporated and no new weapons were standardized or produced. The effort proved valuable when the project was restarted in 1939. A model was standardized on May 15, 1941. While eventually it was made in substantial numbers, the adequate inventory of recently modernized Model 1918 howitzers made the project low priority early in the war.

The barrel was monobloc construction and had an interrupted-screw breech, and the variable recoil system was hydropneumatic. The split-trail carriage was intended, with minor modifications, to carry the 4.5-inch gun M1 or the 155 mm howitzer M1. The carriage could achieve an elevation of -2 to +65 degrees and a left-right traverse of 26.5 degrees. It was equipped with spring-type equilibrators. Intended for high-speed road transport, it had pneumatic tires and air brakes. An M12 panoramic sight and telescope mount M25 provided on-carriage sighting. Howitzers were marked on the muzzle face and below the breech opening; a plate on the right side of the trunnion contained carriage data.

The howitzer fired a 95-pound round using separate-loading ammunition. The primary shell was high-explosive, but chemical and smoke were also available. Two sizes of powder charge could be assembled for the seven zones of fire. Ammunition was not interchangeable with the previous Model 1918 type howitzers. By all accounts, this weapon was known for its uncanny accuracy. It was both well-liked and well-performing. The M5 high-speed tractor was the preferred towing vehicle, but it was certainly towable by any large truck on roadways.

Some 4,135 155 mm M1 howitzers were produced during the war, starting in October 1942. It was one of the types that continued in production long after the war with little modification. Through the 1950s, 10,300 howitzers were manufactured. Watervliet Arsenal and Yuba Manufacturing were primary producers for the barrel; there were six contractors for the carriages, including Oliver Corp., Lufkin Foundry, and Rock Island Arsenal.

There was early debate about deployment—was this a corps artillery piece or best suited to infantry divisions? The answer turned out to be the infantry divisions, as the 155 mm howitzer was standard equipment for the heavy battalion of each division's artillery regiment. But large numbers were also used in non-divisional battalions serving corps and armies. Over 160 army artillery battalions were organized using this howitzer. The Marine Corps also adopted the howitzer for its heavy corps artillery functions. By 1944, the 155 mm M1 howitzer was being used successfully in every US military theater of any significance.

During the war, substantial numbers were supplied to Great Britain (236), China (36), France, and several Latin American countries. The howitzer continued its long service record after the war and was designated M114 in 1962. It was extensively used in Vietnam and beyond. Minor carriage modifications to the firing jack were made postwar. A large re-tubing program in the 1980s featured different rifling to allow the gun to use new ammunition types. The weapon was one of the primary types supplied to American allies—over forty other nations used it in their artillery, some well into the early twenty-first century. In the 1950s, it became a popular item for donation to veteran associations and memorials. Army documents list 285 155 mm howitzers distributed in the US, and over 100 have been verified as on location. Numerous examples also survive in military museums and displays in foreign locations.

Probably between 250–300 155 mm M1 and M114 howitzers still exist in the United States, many at memorials, armories, and museums. This nice example with firing jack deployed is at the state park at Fort Miles, Delaware.

155 mm Howitzer M1 on Carriage M1

Gun Characteristics

Bore size: 155mm

Construction: Nickel steel, monobloc construction

Tube length overall: 149.2 inches

Nominal caliber: 23 calibers

Tube and breech weight: 3,825 pounds

Usual carriage: 155 mm gun carriage M1

Weight of gun and carriage: 12,800 pounds

Maximum elevation: 65 degrees

Loading: Separate

Shell weight: 95 pounds

Maximum muzzle velocity: 1,850 fps

Maximum range: 16,000 yards

Builders: Howitzer: Watervliet Arsenal, Yuba Manufacturing; carriage: Oliver Corp., Lufkin Foundry, Caterpillar Tractor, Western-Austin, Link-Belt, Rock Island Arsenal

Number built: 10,300

The 155 mm howitzer was extensively produced and used postwar. Here, an M1 is on the firing range with American soldiers in Grafenwehr, Germany, in 1947.

Second World War Heavy Artillery

First World War experience and the immediate postwar recommendations of the Westervelt "Caliber" Board reinforced the army's awareness that heavy artillery would be needed in future conflicts. Efforts were made in the early 1920s to develop new heavy pieces, including an 8-inch howitzer, 8-inch gun, and 240 mm howitzer. These projects were soon shut down for lack of funding. The ordnance branch was the major proponent of heavy artillery. Field artillery was focused on mobility, and even up until the early part of the Second World War few saw the need for anything larger than a 155 mm gun.

The eventual development of four new weapons depended on a key assumption about using common carriages. Planners realized that the weight and firing stress of a gun and a larger howitzer were similar and they could be expected to share carriage design. Thus a new 155 mm gun and 8-inch howitzer could share a carriage, as could a much larger 8-inch gun and 240 mm howitzer. This was also true of the smaller 4.5-inch gun and 155 mm howitzer field pieces. This approach eased design efforts, simplified spare parts supply, and facilitated machine tooling for manufacturing plants.

The 155 mm gun and 8-inch howitzer received the initial attention. The tubes eventually selected were fairly conventional in design. They also benefited by being cold-worked. That was a new way of strengthening the tubes using hydraulic pressure during fabrication, a technique being refined by the army's arsenals. However, the carriage was the really innovative part. Four dual-wheel bogie sets provided excellent towing capacity. Also, the wheels could be raised and the carriage set on flat ground, creating a stable firing platform. The large, heavy guns could be moved quickly and fired accurately.

The larger pair of guns was the last started. A new 240 mm howitzer and an 8-inch gun developed during the late 1930s were intended to provide heavy reserve artillery for army-level units. However, the artillery branch and the service force did not see a role for anything larger than a truly mobile 155 mm gun. Heavy guns could only fire from positions that took hours to prepare, and movement of the weapons involved multiple specialized vehicles. Nonetheless, the ordnance department pushed to develop larger artillery. Guns of this size were found necessary in almost all armies. The resulting designs were successful but did not become available until the later campaigns and few were produced

The new heavy field artillery was not given the same production priority as anti-aircraft and anti-tank guns. None of these weapons became available in quantity until the campaigns of the last two years of the war. However, the quantity and quality of American heavy artillery was felt in the European and Pacific theaters. Each type was made available for lend-lease, with Great Britain the primary recipient.

After the war, these models were retained. Except for the 8-inch gun, many were distributed to allies under military assistance programs. They fought again in the Korean War, and some models made it to later conflicts, too. Many examples of the 155 mm gun and 8-inch howitzer exist around the world on public display, though the two larger guns are today quite rare. In 1949, the US Army began to scale up a 240 mm gun to 280 mm size and developed an elaborate transport system to create the M65 atomic cannon. While only twenty were manufactured and the weapon actively served for just a handful of years during the Cold War, it was the ultimate in size and power for American mobile field artillery.

The 155 mm M1 "Long Tom" gun in an ordnance department illustration. The innovative wheel set is clearly visible.

This was a 1920s project to replace one of the expedient guns acquired during the First World War. Seen as a replacement for the 155 mm GPF, work was done to find an improved-range 155 mm gun that could share a mobile carriage with a new 8-inch howitzer. The project was revived in the early 1930s, resulting in the innovative eight-wheeled carriage. The gun was standardized as M1 in July 1938, and production began in October 1940. Four preliminary test guns and an initial order for twenty more went to equip the 36th Field Artillery Regiment.

The gun tube was a cold-worked, built-up alloy tube of 45 calibers. It had forty-nine grooves and uniform rifling twist. It was fitted with an interrupted stepped-thread breech mechanism.

After the first twenty M1 guns, the model was changed to M1A1 where the threads were cut directly into the breech ring as opposed to a breech bushing. Under the barrel was the hydropneumatic variable recoil mechanism. Prominent pneumatic equilibrators were positioned on either side of the barrel. The gun had a lengthy split trail. It could achieve an elevation from -2 to 63 degrees. Utilizing a pintle mechanism, on-carriage traverse was 30 degrees left and right. The gun fired a 95-pound projectile using separate loading up to a useful 25,715-yard range. The usual HE, chemical, and AP shells were supplied. The ammunition was not interchangeable with the previous Model 1918 155 mm gun. The gun's relatively long range led to its nickname Long Tom.

One of the early-production 155 mm M1A1 guns at the GHQ maneuvers in the United States in August 1941. Note that the gooseneck is not part of the gun and has replaced the organic limber in this exercise.

For transport, the trails were closed and the gun tube retracted back on the carriage and locked to a support. The ends of the trails were placed on a two-wheeled heavy carriage limber, which in turn was connected to a towing vehicle. Heavy 6×6 trucks and M4 18-ton tractors were the preferred prime movers. On carriage sights were a telescope and the M12 panoramic sight. Production was spread between army and commercial facilities. The tubes were made at Watervliet Arsenal and Mesta Machine. Carriages were fabricated at Rock Island Arsenal and Pettibone Mulliken Corp. Altogether, 1,882 completed guns were delivered through June 1945. Guns were marked above the breech and on the muzzle face; the carriage plate was attached to the right trunnion support.

Organized into complete battalions, they were mainly used at the corps artillery level. Forty-nine battalions were equipped with the 155 mm M1 gun during the war—forty in Europe and seven in the Pacific saw deployment. It first saw combat in Tunisia in 1943 and was involved in most campaigns thereafter. The British received 184 guns as lend-lease, and another twenty-five went to the rearmament of French forces. The M40 gun motor carriage used the 155 mm M1 gun, and 418 of this vehicle were made during the last year of the war. The 155 mm gun M1 was redesignated the M59 after the war. The gun was extensively used in Korea and some served in Vietnam. In 1977, 120 were still in US Army reserve. Over a dozen nations were supplied quantities under the military assistance program. Major recipients were Denmark, South Korea, and Israel. Many kept these well into the 1980s. Few examples remain today—perhaps as many as half are in foreign museums.

155 mm Gun M1A1 on Carriage M1

Gun Characteristics

Bore size: 155mm

Construction: Built-up alloy steel

Tube length overall: 253 inches

Nominal caliber: 45 calibers

Tube and breech weight: 9,595 pounds

Usual carriage: 155 mm gun carriage M1

Weight of gun and carriage: 30,600 pounds

Maximum elevation: 63 degrees, 20 minutes

Loading: Separate

Shell weight: 94.71 pounds

Maximum muzzle velocity: 2,800 fps

Maximum range: 25,715 yards

Builders: Tube: Watervliet Arsenal, Mesta Machine; carriage: Rock Island Arsenal, Pettibone Mulliken

Number built: 1882

There are several 155 mm M1 (later designated M59) guns spread around military museums and memorials in the world, due to their wide postwar distribution. This is one of a pair of M59 guns at the Martyr's Memorial in Amman, Jordan.

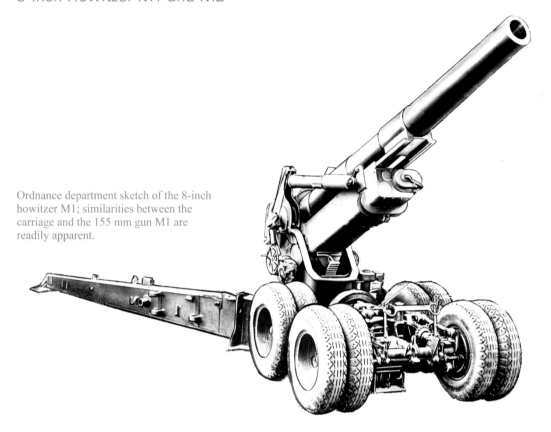

Ordnance department sketch of the 8-inch howitzer M1; similarities between the carriage and the 155 mm gun M1 are readily apparent.

Replacement of the First World War's British-American 8-inch howitzer was begun immediately after that war. It was considered the largest that could be accommodated on a conventional carriage. The project was curtailed in the 1920s, though progress on a tube had progressed well. Combining it with the new 4-bogie wheeled carriage designed for the 155 mm M1 gun perfected in the late 1930s was a major step forward. The howitzer was intended to be a General Headquarters reserve weapon for issue to independent heavy battalions. Final design work and tube production was entrusted to the Hughes Tool Co. The design was standardized as the M1 8-inch howitzer in April 1938. A relatively minor change in method of breech attachment resulted in the M2 howitzer.

The 8-inch howitzer was a cold-worked, 25-caliber, built-up tube. The tube had sixty-four grooves and uniform rifling of $\frac{1}{25}$. It had the usual interrupted-thread, step-cut breech mechanism. A percussion hammer was used for the firing mechanism. The carriage was mostly identical to the 155 mm gun M1 carriage. It had the same hydropneumatic, variable recoil mechanism and pneumatic equilibrators on either side of the barrel and cradle. With a shorter barrel, the gun could achieve an elevation of 64 degrees and the same total traverse of 60 degrees. It fired with separate loading ammunition. Powder charges could be loaded for seven different zones. A 200-pound HE shell could be fired to a range of 18,510 yards. In service, the 8-inch M1 and M2 howitzers were praised for their inherent accuracy.

The carriage transport was basically the same as for the 155m M1, except the shorter barrel could stay in battery and did not have to be withdrawn on the carriage. The familiar telescope and M12 panoramic sight were on-carriage fire control devices. Either 7.5-ton 6×6 trucks or the 18-ton M4 high-speed tractor were used to pull the howitzer. The howitzers were marked on the breech and muzzle ends, and the carriage data appeared on the right trunnion support.

Production did not start immediately; the first orders for twenty-five units came with the June 30, 1940, munitions program. Howitzer tubes were made by Hughes Tool Co. and Watervliet Arsenal, carriages by Pullman-Standard Car and Pettibone Mulliken. By June 1954, 1,006 were delivered.

During the war, the howitzer was used in equipping fifty-nine heavy artillery battalions; thirty-eight of these were sent to Europe, and only three served in the Pacific theater. First combat was in Italy in November 1943. They served with distinction at Salerno, Anzio, and the battles around Monte Cassino. They played an important role in all the Northern European campaigns. A significant portion of the guns made went to the British under lend-lease; they acquired 610 units during the war. An additional forty-eight were put on self-propelled carriages as the M43 gun motor carriage in late 1945. The Marine Corps also showed interest in the howitzer and began the process of acquiring these 8-inch howitzers, but this was not accomplished during the war. After the war, the gun was re-designated the M115 8-inch howitzer. It was used in Korea and Vietnam; in fact, some 200 were still in army inventory as late as 1978. It proved popular as a weapon supplied to allied armies under military assistance programs. In addition to serving many NATO partners, as late as 1986 it was serving with India, Iran, Japan, Jordan, Korea, and Taiwan.

Army records show over fifty distributed for museums and memorials since the 1970s. A popular and impressive display piece, many are still serving this purpose.

8-Inch Howitzer M1

Gun Characteristics

Bore size: 8 inches

Construction: Built-up, alloy steel

Tube length overall: 209.6 inches

Nominal caliber: 25 calibers

Tube and breech weight: 10,240 pounds

Usual carriage: M1 8-inch howitzer carriage

Weight of gun and carriage: 31,700 pounds

Maximum elevation: 64 degrees

Loading: Separate

Shell weight: 200 pounds

Maximum muzzle velocity: 1,950 fps

Maximum range: 18,510 yards

Builders: Howitzer: Hughes Tool, Watervliet Arsenal; carriage: Pettibone Mulliken and Pullman-Standard Car

Number built: 1,006

Many examples of the 8-inch howitzer M1 still exist; in fact, they substantially outnumber their companion 155 mm pieces even though fewer were built. This piece is at an American Legion in West Manchester, Ohio.

During the Second World War, the Pacific required fewer pieces of heavy artillery than most other theaters. Nonetheless, units armed with 8-inch howitzers (like those in action on Leyte in late 1944) were deployed in the western Pacific as the war progressed.

240 mm Howitzer M1

The heavy 240 mm howitzer M1918 proved disappointing in firing tests of the early 1920s. Recommendations for a replacement soon emerged. Some new design work took place starting in 1925 but was curtailed when funding stopped. Then in 1934, work on a new, heavy split-trail carriage for a 240 mm howitzer or 8-inch gun began, with some useful results but no new production. Work on a new heavy howitzer finally began seriously in April 1940. Hard-pressed with design work, the ordnance department contracted with construction equipment firm Bucyrus-Erie to complete the design elements and to manufacture a pilot. The result was the new 240 mm howitzer M1 and its carriage with transport wagons and prime movers and an 8-inch gun M1 as a companion piece. Work started and the pilot was delivered in January 1942. The howitzer was standardized in May 1943, though production had already started.

The 34-caliber tube was of built-up alloy steel. The tube had sixty-nine grooves and rifling of $\frac{1}{25}$ uniform twist. It was connected to an interrupted-screw breech mechanism. The constant-recoil mechanism was mounted below the tube and consisted of two hydropneumatic cylinders. The counterrecoil mechanism was also two cylinders, mounted atop the tube. The unit also had hydropneumatic equilibrators. Transported in two main sections, once erected, large split trails were spread on either side of an excavated pit to allow recoil at high angles. Elevation was by spur gears; the howitzer could move from +15 to +65-degrees and traverse 22.5-degrees left and right.

The 360-pound HE shell with separate-loaded powder had four primary zones of range. This ammunition was not interchangeable with the 240 mm rounds for the M1918 howitzer. Two transport wagons (M2A1 and M3A1) were developed to carry the tube and carriage. Later tracked versions (T16E1 and T17E1) were also adopted and used to a limited extent. The wagons could be moved by a heavy truck or the M6 38-ton high-speed tracked mover.

Finding the right manufacturing facilities for the 24⅜-inch project was a problem. These were extremely heavy pieces requiring precision manufacturing relatively late in the war when machine tools, materials, and skilled labor was short. Watervliet Arsenal was the only facility capable of providing the finished tubes. Carriages were made by Bucyrus-Erie, Watertown Arsenal, and the S. Morgan Smith Co. Hannifin Manufacturing provided the recoil mechanisms, and Bucyrus and Pullman-Standard made the transport wagons. Orders were always limited in number. Although a large number of howitzers were projected, orders were reduced as the war turned to the allied favor, and then increased when it was realized that heavy artillery would be needed for German and Japanese fortifications. By the end of production in May 1945, 315 240 mm howitzers were made.

The howitzer was first issued to the 5th Army in Italy, where it was well regarded. During the war, twenty-one battalions were organized, fifteen served in Europe, and five in the Pacific. Also, twenty-eight 240 mm howitzers M1 were lend-leased to Great

One of the early 240 mm howitzers M1 in firing position at Aberdeen Proving Ground on February 2, 1942. This was howitzer serial No. 2.

Britain. At war's end a development project for a GMC version (T-92) was underway, but it was only in the test phase. The howitzers were kept in US inventory for a number of years after the war and discarded in the late 1950s. A dozen were used in Korean combat service in 1953. About thirty were supplied to Taiwan, where they were emplaced in hardened bunkers and some still exist. Only one American survivor is known, appropriately at the US Army Artillery Museum at Ft. Sill, Oklahoma.

240 mm Howitzer M1

Gun Characteristics

Bore size: 240mm

Construction: Built-up nickel steel

Tube length overall: 336 inches

Nominal caliber: 34 calibers

Tube and breech weight: 25,100 pounds

Usual carriage: 240 mm Howitzer Carriage M1

Weight of gun and carriage: 64,700 pounds

Maximum elevation: 65 degrees

Loading: Separate

Shell weight: 360 pounds

Maximum muzzle velocity: 2,300 fps

Maximum range: 25,255 yards

Builders: Tube: Watervliet Arsenal; carriage: Bucyrus-Erie, Watertown Arsenal, S. Morgan Smith

Number built: 315

One of the twelve 240 mm howitzers M1 deployed with the American forces in Korea in December 1953.

The only surviving 240 mm M1 howitzer in the United States is displayed on its transport wagon at the US Army Artillery Museum at Fort Sill, Oklahoma.

8-Inch Gun M1

This was the last major new artillery piece to be developed and go into production during the Second World War. Though it was planned as a companion to the new 240 mm M1 howitzer, it was placed in second priority to that gun (and the carriage and transport wagons and tractors they would share). Like its companion, it was designed as a GHQ reserve weapon, deployed in dedicated battalions as needed to interdict enemy communications and provide long-range counter-battery fire. An early design project was started in 1919 but suspended in 1924. It resumed in 1939 and accelerated quickly in 1940, and under wartime conditions advanced rapidly. Prototypes were evaluated, and the completed gun was standardized in 1942 as the 8-inch Gun M1.

The 8-inch tube was cold-worked alloy steel with a shrunk-on jacket. The breech mechanism was the same type of interrupted stepped-screw as that used on the 240 mm howitzer. It fired a 240-pound HE shell with separate loading. At elevation and maximum muzzle velocity, a range of 35,000 yards was possible, the longest of any American mobile gun. In fact, there was considerable worry over the possibility of a short barrel life because of erosion due to its high velocity. Several solutions were proposed, but nothing was implemented. The gun also used a hydropneumatic constant recoil mechanism. This M7

mechanism, while similar to that on the 240mm, had a pair of unequal-length cylinders mounted above the gun tube.

The carriage was similar to that developed for the M1 240mm, except the much longer gun could not be elevated as high. On-carriage elevation, even with excavated pit, was a minimum of 10 degrees and a maximum of 50 degrees. It was standardized as the Carriage 8-inch Gun M2. Like its companion, it used two pneumatic-tire transport wagons to carry it to location, towed by heavy trucks or the M6 high-speed tractor. A mobile crane was also needed. Still, it took only an estimated one to two hours to erect the gun in its position. The gun was equipped with the usual M12 panoramic sight and an M1 elevation quadrant.

Watervliet Arsenal made the gun tube. Bucyrus-Erie, S. Morgan Smith, and Watertown Arsenal provided the carriages, and Hannifin Manufacturing made the recoil cylinders. The first manufacturing order for fifty-three was authorized on April 2, 1942. First deliveries were in September 1942, and orders fluctuated considerably from 1942–44 as the war progressed in fits and starts. In all, 139 8-inch M1 guns and carriages were produced through 1945.

Eight artillery battalions were organized using the gun, five serving in Europe, three in the Pacific. The first combat

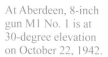

At Aberdeen, 8-inch gun M1 No. 1 is at 30-degree elevation on October 22, 1942.

use was in Italy in April 1944. Seventeen guns were supplied to Great Britain, where they were used in super heavy batteries as the 8-inch Gun Mark I. At war's end a self-propelled mount was under development as the T-93 using major parts of the M-26 tank, but no production decision had been made and only trial units were fabricated. The guns lasted another decade in storage before being disposed of. Fortunately, three examples still survive at military museums.

8-Inch Gun M1

Gun Characteristics

Bore size: 8 inches
Construction: Built-up nickel steel
Tube length overall: 409.5 inches
Nominal caliber: 50 calibers
Tube and breech weight: 30,000 pounds
Usual carriage: 8-inch gun, M2 carriage
Weight of gun and carriage: 69,300 pounds
Maximum elevation: 50 degrees
Loading: Separate
Shell weight: 240 pounds
Maximum muzzle velocity: 2,950 fps
Maximum range: 35,000 yards

Builders: Tube: Watervliet Arsenal; carriage: Bucyrus-Erie, Watertown Arsenal, S. Morgan Smith
Number built: 139

One of three surviving 8-inch guns M1. This one is at the 45th Infantry Division Museum in Oklahoma City.

An 8-inch gun M1 tube on its cannon transport wagon M1. Another wagon carried the carriage M2. Both wagons are assisted by a mobile, truck-mounted crane M2.

280 mm Heavy Motorized Gun M65

The year 1949 saw development of a large cannon capable of firing a nuclear warhead. Miniaturization of warheads had only progressed so far at this time; the smallest practical shell dictated a gun of at least 280 mm bore. Chiefly designed by engineer Robert M. Schwartz at Picatinny Arsenal, the new design borrowed heavily from an abortive 240 mm gun project of the Second World War and from studies of captured German K5 railway carriages from the same conflict. In remarkably short time, using some design research that had continued from late in the war, the new design was completed, allowing fabrication of two 240 mm test guns. They were evaluated with the new T72 carriage in 1950. These guns weighed 18,000 pounds and had a range of eighteen miles.

The tube for the 280 mm was a conventional design with an interrupted, stepped-thread breechblock and an electrical contact percussion hammer firing mechanism. The tube was 46.4 calibers long. Separate loading ammunition of HE, dummy, and nuclear types were made available. Weight of a round varied from 550 to 600 pounds. The adopted T72 carriage showed considerable innovation. The gun was supported in a cradle suspended between two stout side members resembling a railroad mount. Each end of this carriage was elevated onto one of two specialized wheeled maneuvering tractors. These were powered by a 375-horsepower engine and were in contact with each other by telephone, and could travel up to 35 miles per hour. Upon reaching a firing position, the gun was lowered with its firing platform, which could traverse 360 degrees. It took just fifteen minutes for both erection and dismantling into firing position. A double-recoil system was used; both the barrel and the carriage had pneumatic recoil mechanisms. The carriage allowed for a 55-degree maximum elevation and left to right traverse of 15 degrees (without using the 360-degree central pivot). The carriage was equipped with panoramic telescope M12A7C.

Army Technical Manual TM 9-338-1 illustration of the 280 mm gun T131 on carriage T72 with its two dedicated transport vehicles.

Army Signal Corps photograph of three complete units of the 280 mm M65 gun. Pictured with the 59th Field Artillery in Germany during the late 1950s.

Twenty units were built, with Watervliet Arsenal fabricating the gun, Watertown Arsenal fabricating the carriage, and Baldwin Locomotive making the chassis. Initially the gun was designated T131, but eventually was standardized as the Model 65. It also acquired the nickname atomic cannon. The first complete gun was ready for display at President Eisenhower's 1953 inauguration parade. The gun was only fired once with an atomic warhead. As part of a series of test detonations, a single round was fired on May 25, 1953 at Frenchman's Flat, Nevada, in what was known as the Grable test. The 15-kiloton device successfully detonated at a seven-mile range.

Separate field artillery battalions were organized to operate the weapon. It appears that battalions in Europe were equipped with six guns each (three firing batteries each of two guns), while continental US battalions had a single gun per firing battery. Some of the technical and deployment details for this gun are still classified. Active units were deployed for several years to Germany. In 1955 the 663rd Field Artillery Battalion took its 280 mm guns to Okinawa. Activated units served from about 1953 until 1962.

Despite the innovations with the carriage and its transports, the gun was still difficult to maneuver and rapidly deploy, particularly in narrow European streets. The 30,000-yard range also proved disappointing. Further reductions in the size of nuclear munitions meant that 8-inch and 155 mm shells with nuclear capability would soon become available. That spelled the end of these guns. In 1962 they were removed from deployment and within two years declared obsolete. Their size and unique capabilities made them popular as museum display pieces. One 240 mm prototype and seven 280 mm M65s survive.

280 mm Heavy Motorized Gun M65 on Carriage T72

Gun Characteristics

Bore size: 280mm
Construction: Built-up alloy steel
Tube length overall: 512.5 inches
Nominal caliber: 46.4 calibers
Tube and breech weight: 42,970 pounds
Usual carriage: 280 mm gun carriage T72
Weight of gun and carriage: 94,000 pounds
Maximum elevation: 55 degrees
Loading: Separate
Shell weight: 600 pounds (HE T122)
Maximum muzzle velocity: 2,500 fps
Maximum range: 31,200 yards

Builders: Tube: Watervliet Arsenal; carriage: Watertown Arsenal
Number built: 2 240 mm prototypes, 20 280 mm production guns

Several 280 mm M65 guns are on display. This nicely restored unit is at the US Army Artillery Museum at Fort Sill, Oklahoma.

Anti-Tank Guns

The US Army lagged behind most other nations in developing dedicated anti-tank weapons during the interwar period. In May 1919, a Caliber Board (Westervelt Board) report suggested that the anti-tank situation could best be handled by developing appropriate AP rounds for existing guns, while allowing for the future development of dedicated weapons. Finally in the late 1930s, efforts were made to develop an infantry-accompanying gun, resulting in the 37 mm M3. Adequate for opposing light tanks, the dramatic increase in European (German) tank size and armor during the war soon made it obsolete. In fact, the development story of American anti-tank artillery (and truthfully most other countries) is one of being forced to rapidly upgrade gun size and power repeatedly as the war went on. Consequently, virtually all guns developed after the 37 mm were assembled from gun tubes and carriages either adopted from other nations (the 57 mm story) or from existing parts originally intended for other purposes (the 3-inch and 90 mm guns).

Thankfully, American production capacity was such that, once approved, designs could be manufactured relatively quickly. Furthermore, the hurried nature of the programs meant that the vast majority of the guns, carriages, and recoil mechanisms were produced under contract with private industrial firms new to armament production.

Throughout the Second World War there was a significant difference of opinion within the US Army about the true utility of towed anti-tank weapons. Most field commanders and representatives of the Tank Destroyer and Armored Forces command were strongly in favor of self-propelled tank destroyers.

With American production capacity and abundant finances, there appeared to be little reason not to use the most mobile weapon possible. On the other side of the argument, the infantry and airborne branches argued for guns as lightweight as possible to facilitate tactical utility. Army command, represented by General Leslie McNair, was impressed with German AT tactics using carefully concealed, towed guns. Starting in early 1943, top-down orders for production of 57mm, 3-inch, and 90 mm anti-tank guns were issued. However, with the development of each new type, opposition emerged from the advocates of mobile motor mounts and projects were often delayed and production reduced.

Many of these guns still exist. The end of the war saw a sudden cancellation of existing orders, and the controversy over the form of future anti-tank capabilities was settled in favor of tank destroyers or simply more tanks. Also, the new generation of bazookas and recoilless rifles appeared to satisfy the needs of the infantry. On June 1, 1945, the table of equipment for infantry divisions dropped all organic, towed anti-tank guns. The guns in inventory were no longer needed, even by a much-reduced army. For a few years towed guns stayed with the specialized light divisions (like airborne), at least through the mid-1950s. Many were available for distribution as memorial guns. Based on survivor counts, a much higher percentage of anti-tank guns (of all five types discussed here) survive today than any other gun type of the First or Second World War cannon. In fact, the 3-inch anti-tank gun has more surviving examples on public display than any other American rifled gun.

37 mm Anti-Tank Gun M3

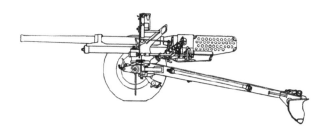

Sketch of the US Army 37 mm M3 anti-tank gun.

The first dedicated American anti-tank gun was eventually standardized and produced as the M3 37 mm gun. After years of experimenting with commercial and ordnance department designs, requirements for an infantry-accompanying weapon were formulated. In the late 1930s, the ideal design was thought to be a light, highly mobile gun capable of firing armor-piercing and high-explosive ammunition and of operated by a single soldier. A Rheinmetall 37 mm Pak-36 gun purchased and imported to Boston in July 1936 offered solutions to many of the design requirements. The ordnance department combined the features of their own prototypes with those of the German gun, and in late 1938 standardized the T10 gun as the M3 and the T5 carriage as the M4. It is important to note that the American gun was not a licensed-built German weapon, though it reflected some of the German gun's characteristics.

The single-forging tube had twelve grooves of a uniform $\frac{1}{15}$ twist. The gun was capable of firing fifteen to twenty rounds per minute. Firing was by trigger. The trigger, sighting, and elevating gear were on the same side to be operated by one man. The breechblock was a vertical sliding wedge. A version threaded on the end of the barrel for a gas deflector to suppress dust generation was introduced as the M3A1 gun. However, this suppressor was damaged when the canister shot was fired, so while guns were issued threaded, they were not supplied with the device itself. Recoil was absorbed by a hydrospring, and normal recoil was 20 inches. Tests credited the gun with armor penetration of the APC shot of 2.1 inches at 1,000 yards. Other versions of this gun were widely used in American light and medium tanks, amphibious tractors, and armored cars.

The carriage was a split-trail, two-wheeled type with pneumatic tires. It was named M4A1 when production started in January 1942. It had an added release mechanism for free traverse on the shoulder bar. The carriage provided 30-degree traverse left and right, 15-degree elevation, and 10-degree depression. An M6 sighting telescope was mounted. The intended towing vehicle was a light truck, but often the quarter-ton jeep was used.

Production orders began in late 1938, but useful quantities were not delivered until early 1940. Production of the gun began at the Watervliet Arsenal, though soon contractors were used (York Safe & Lock, United Shoe Machinery Corp., and National Pneumatic Company). Carriages were initially made at the Rock Island Arsenal, then at Duplex Printing Press,

Ordnance department illustration of an M3A1 37 mm anti-tank gun on carriage M4A1 with attached muzzle gas deflector.

Muncie Gear Works, and York Safe & Lock. Production ended in 1943 with a total output of 22,920 (including spare tubes). Most of the guns served with US forces. Small quantities were shared with South American countries, Canada, Great Britain, Russia, and France. Only China received a large allocation under lend-lease, acquiring 1,669 guns. The 37 mm guns were marked with manufacturer, date, and serial number on the side of the breech housing; carriage information appeared on a plate on the trail.

The gun was issued to the anti-tank platoons and companies of infantry battalions, regiments, and divisions starting in 1940. The Marine Corps also extensively employed the gun. First combat was in the Philippine campaign of 1941–42. The gun was present in North Africa and Italy. As tanks became more heavily armored, it rapidly became obsolete in the European theater and was little used after 1943. However, in the Pacific it was useful against the lightly armored Japanese vehicles, bunkers, and personnel, and served well to the end of the war. Dropped from the army's inventory postwar, many survive as memorial guns.

37 mm Anti-Tank Gun M3 on Carriage M4

Gun Characteristics

Bore size: 37mm

Construction: One-piece steel auto-frettage tube

Tube length overall: 82.5 inches

Nominal caliber: 53.5 calibers

Tube and breech weight: 191 pounds

Usual carriage: 37 mm gun carriage M4 & M4A1

Weight of gun and carriage: 912 pounds

Maximum elevation: 15 degrees

Loading: Fixed

Shell weight: 1.91 pounds (AP), 1.61 pounds (HE)

Maximum muzzle velocity: 2,600–2,900 fps (AP–HE)

Maximum range: 12,850 yards

Builders: Tube: Watervliet Arsenal, York Safe & Lock, United Shoe Machinery Corp., National Pneumatic Company

Carriage: Rock Island Arsenal, Duplex Printing Press, Muncie Gear Works, York Safe & Lock

Number built: 22,920 guns, 18,937 carriages

The 37 mm anti-tank gun is a popular display item for both service and private artillery museums. This item was formerly part of the Littlefield collection in Portola Valley, California.

57 mm Anti-tank Gun M1

The American 57 mm anti-tank gun came close to never being developed. As soon as it became obvious that tank armor was growing beyond the penetration capabilities of the 37mm, the army began looking for a more powerful gun. As early as September 1940, the chief of field artillery requested a larger gun than the 37mm. Debate swirled between the ordnance department and the branch chiefs about whether to go straight to the 3-inch/75 mm size or develop a new gun in the 47–57 mm range. This was influenced by the British experience with their own 57mm. In fact, that gun (known as the 6-pounder) was soon scheduled to be manufactured by contractors in the US as a lend-lease item, and there could be economies in cost and time if the US adopted it, too. On June 21, 1941, the manufacture of a pilot gun was authorized.

Eventually the decision was reached to produce a virtual copy of the 6-pounder as the 57 mm gun M1. There were only two significant differences between the British and American versions. The M1 had a longer barrel, reflecting the capability of American machine tools versus what was available in England. The American-produced gun was 16 inches longer (thus a full 50 calibers) than the first British production. The carriage M1A1 had US-type wheels and tires. The design was handicapped by relatively low striking energy and, for much of its service life, the availability of only solid AP shot. Near the end of the war,

an HE round became available, along with new discarding-sabot shot obtained from the British.

The forged steel barrel was equipped with a vertical sliding wedge breech. The gun had a hydrospring recoil mechanism. Still, it was known for its violent kick during recoil. It was capable of only direct fire with an M18 telescopic sight and standard M1 aiming circle. The carriage had a single axle and conventional split trail. Starting with production in September 1942, the carriage M1A2 discarded the traversing mechanism

Ordnance illustration of the 57 mm M1 anti-tank gun from a technical manual.

A US-supplied 57 mm gun in service with South Korean forces during the Korean War in 1950.

in favor of a free traverse via the operator's shoulder bar; the M1A3 incorporated a new drawbar and lunette. The gun on carriage had a 45-degree left-to right-traverse and provided a 15-degree elevation and 5-degree depression. The original British-type sights were replaced with a new M69C telescopic sight manufactured by Eastman Kodak. A protective shield with a distinctive scalloped upper edge was included, and supplemental side shields could be carried separately.

The first production order was issued in August 1941. Altogether, 18,406 guns and 15,845 carriages were made (complete, assembled units totaled 15,367). It saw only limited use in a self-propelled or armored vehicle role. Some 5,352 guns and carriages were supplied under lend-lease, and the British took 4,242 of these. Other countries accepting them were France, Brazil, Bolivia, and Chile. Gun information appeared on the side of the breech housing; carriage data was on an attached plate.

The prime mover was the 1.5-ton 6×6 truck (WC-62 or 63). The gun was urgently needed in Europe following experience with the 37 mm in North Africa. In January 1943, it was ordered to replace the 37 mm gun in most infantry divisions. It served until the end of the war in European and Pacific theaters—even though its capabilities were sorely tested by the latest German armor types. The gun was soon phased out of US Army service, though it served with Korean forces during the Korean War.

57 mm Anti-Tank Gun M1

Gun Characteristics

Bore size: 57mm

Construction: steel monobloc auto-frettage tube

Tube length overall: 117 inches

Nominal caliber: 50 calibers

Tube and breech weight: 755 pounds

Usual carriage: 57 mm gun carriage M1A3

Weight of gun and carriage: 2,700 pounds

Maximum elevation: 15 degrees

Loading: Fixed

Shell weight: 12.56 pounds (AP)

Maximum muzzle velocity: 2,700–2,900-fps (APC–AP)

Maximum range: 10,860 yards

Builders: Gun: War Supplies, American Type Foundries, Yoder Co.; carriage: War Supplies, International Harvester, Parish Pressed Steel, Rock Island Arsenal

Number built: 18,406 guns, 15,845 carriages

A favorite for displaying at veteran service clubs, this example of a 57 mm anti-tank gun is at an American Legion in Elmer, New Jersey.

Ordnance manual illustration of the M5 3-inch anti-tank gun.

This was the primary towed American anti-tank gun deployed in large numbers during the war. Like its predecessor, it was developed hurriedly from existing weapons. The project started in late 1940 following reports of heavier tanks from the campaign in France. Once again, the obvious limits of lighter guns were evident, and the ordnance department looked for a solution that could be put into production rapidly. It combined the 3-inch anti-aircraft gun tube T9 and the 105 mm howitzer M2 gun carriage. Pilots were ready late in 1941. After trials, debate continued about the need for towed anti-tank artillery, and in the fall of 1942 an acceptable design was standardized for initial production.

The gun tube was basically that used in the successful (and already in production) M2/M3 series of 3-inch AA guns. It was made of forged nickel steel. The breech was a conventional horizontal sliding wedge with a continuous-pull firing mechanism. The gun was capable of fifteen to twenty rounds per minute in short bursts, though five rounds per minute was more generally obtainable for sustained firing. The gun was supplied with HE, AP, APC, and smoke rounds. Armor penetration was published as 4 inches at 1,000-yard range. While primarily intended for direct fire, the carriage allowed a 30-degree elevation and the mount was equipped with a panoramic sight to allow use of HE rounds in a conventional artillery role.

The initial carriage was similar to that of the M2 105 mm howitzer, including shield. The hydropneumatic recoil allowed a recoil of 42 inches. Spring-type equilibrators were used. The two-wheeled split carriage allowed a traverse of 22.5 degrees left and right and had electric service brakes. However, a new

Signal Corps photograph of a 3-inch anti-tank gun in the Second World War.

M6 carriage was soon developed. It had a sloped armored shield recognizably different from the older carriage. All guns except some deployed for proving ground and training work in the US were reconfigured to the M6 carriage type. The M3 halftrack was the gun's designated prime mover.

Production began in December 1942 on an initial requirement of 1,000 units. All the tubes were made at Vilter Manufacturing of Milwaukee. The carriages were provided by Pullman-Standard Car of Chicago, and M9 recoil mechanisms were made at Rock Island Arsenal. The M6 (sloped-shield) carriage supplanted the M1 starting in October 1943. Altogether, 2,500 guns and 2,850 carriages were constructed when production ended mid-1944. Virtually all production was for US forces, and none were provided to lend-lease partners. Manufacturer information, serial number, inspector, and weight were stamped on the top of the breech housing. Carriage information appeared on an attached oval plate on the left trunnion support.

The gun was used mostly to equip the towed anti-tank battalions assigned at the army level, rather than divisional artillery. While projects were begun for dedicated prime movers based on full-tracked vehicles, none of these proved successful and the usual prime mover remained the M3 halftrack. While not an outstanding gun in performance or handiness, the weapon provided adequate service in the campaigns of 1944–45. Several towed battalions figured heavily in the Ardennes fighting that winter. Not unexpectedly, they were more useful when integrated with infantry in defensive positions rather than as stand-alone tank killers. This gun was not favorably viewed or needed for Pacific operations. The towed battalions were quickly dismantled at the end of the European conflict and the guns declared obsolete and disposed of by the end of 1945.

3-Inch Anti-Tank Gun M5 on Carriage M1 and M6

Gun Characteristics

Bore size: 3 inches

Construction: Built-up nickel steel

Tube length overall: 157.4 inches

Nominal caliber: 50 calibers

Tube and breech weight: 1,600 pounds

Usual carriage: 3-inch gun carriage M1

Weight of gun and carriage: 5,109 pounds

Maximum elevation: 30 degrees

Loading: Fixed

Shell weight: 12.87 pounds (AP), 15.44 pounds (HE)

Maximum muzzle velocity: 2,600–2,800 fps (AP–PC)

Maximum range: 16,100 yards

Builders: Gun: Vilter Manufacturing; carriage: Pullman-
     Standard Car

Number built: 2,500 guns, 2,850 carriages

The 3-inch anti-tank gun is no doubt the single most common memorial gun on display, as several hundred survive. This piece is in a public park in Galion, Ohio.

Ordnance illustration of the 90 mm anti-tank gun.

The 90 mm was yet another development program for a more powerful anti-tank gun. Begun in early 1943, it was to some extent driven by the combat appearance of the German Mk VI (Tiger) tank. This gun took advantage of a powerful anti-aircraft gun already in production—the 90 mm M1 gun. It was described as a high-velocity, flat-trajectory anti-tank weapon. The gun had a 50-caliber tube rifled with thirty-two grooves. It was built of a one-piece tube threaded to accept the breech ring. The breech mechanism was a semi-automatic vertical sliding type that had a manual firing mechanism built into the traversing hand wheel. The gun was provided with HE, AP, and APC ammunition. It had a penetration of 122 mm of armor at 1,000 yards—more importantly, it could penetrate the frontal armament of a Mark VI at twice the distance a 3-inch anti-tank gun could.

The first production carriage (T5E2) was a two-wheeled, split trail conventional design. Recoil was handled by a T25 hydropneumatic mechanism. The legs could be splayed at 60 degrees, and it could be maneuvered with a castor wheel on the end of the left trail. A conventional ring and shank type of lunette was included for towing. The carriage had a left-to-right traverse of 30 degrees and an elevation of 18.5 degrees. Elevation and traverse hand wheels were on the left side of the cradle.

Army photograph of the 90 mm anti-tank gun on T5E1 carriage during May 1944 evaluations.

The carriage featured a direct fire M79E1 sight telescope, a M12A6 panoramic telescope, and a quarter-inch-thick angled shield. Electric brakes were incorporated for the carriage wheels. Plans for a dedicated M39 prime mover built by Cadillac never matured; other vehicles were eventually assigned this role. It took only thirty seconds to emplace the gun for action.

A second, quite interesting type T9 carriage was designed and a pilot produced. Drastic design efforts were implemented to reduce the considerable weight of the production model. The gun shield acted as a prime structural support, with the wheels attached directly to it. The trails attached to the top of the shield, and they could be swung around in the same direction as the barrel to reduce overall towing and shipping space. The weapons weighed about 3,000 pounds less than the T5E2. Two further alternative carriage designs were also produced in pilot form.

On September 7, 1944, the ordnance committee classified the 90 mm T8 on carriage T5E2 for limited procurement. While production was started, it was never of the scale of the previous anti-tank guns. Initial requirements were pegged at 600 units, but in January 1945 that was reduced to 200, the number finally delivered. The gun was produced at Watervliet Arsenal, the carriages at Link-Belt, and the recoil mechanism at Rock Island Arsenal. Gun information (arsenal, inspector, weight, serial number) was carried on the breech ring top surface. Carriage information was on a brass plate mounted under the barrel cradle.

As the most powerful US anti-tank gun to reach production, it was one of the last to be eliminated. Despite its size and weight, it was used by airborne formations in the towed capacity (self-propelled mounts being too heavy to air transport). It saw action in the Korean War, and units were provided to the Korean Army. By the late 1950s, it too was deleted from inventory and many were contributed as memorial guns.

90 mm Anti-Tank Gun T8 on Carriage T5E2

Gun Characteristics

Bore size: 90 mm

Construction: Alloy steel

Tube length overall: 186.15 inches

Nominal caliber: 50 calibers

Tube and breech weight: 2,290 pounds

Usual carriage: 90 mm gun carriage T5E2

Weight of gun and carriage: 7,700 pounds

Maximum elevation: 18.5 degrees

Loading: Fixed

Shell weight: 24.1 pounds

Maximum muzzle velocity: 2,700 fps

Maximum range: 21,400 yards

Builders: Gun: Watervliet Arsenal; carriage: Link-Belt

Number built: 200

Surprisingly, many of the T8 90 mm guns survive, particularly at American Legion posts in the Midwest and South. This sample is on outdoor display (serial No. 189 from 1945) in Sharonville, Ohio.

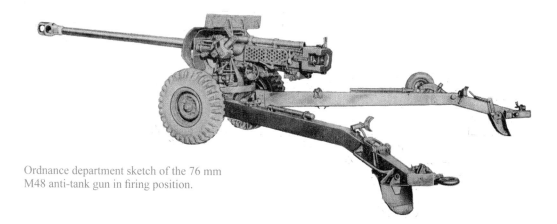

Ordnance department sketch of the 76 mm M48 anti-tank gun in firing position.

During the Second World War, a project had been started for an anti-tank gun based on the 76 mm model that was being installed in tanks and tank destroyers. In May 1943, two pilot guns were produced. While performance looked good, the projected time to fully develop such a gun was not available, and it never progressed to standardization or procurement status.

This project was revisited in the early 1950s, given the need for a lightweight, low-silhouette but powerful towed anti-tank gun for the army airborne divisions. A new 76 mm gun had been developed for the M41 Walker Bulldog tank and was adopted for this project. The 76 mm one-piece tube was

fitted with a horizontal sliding breechblock. The long, 60-caliber tube had the performance and weight profile desired.

The barrel was the usual one-piece alloy steel construction and was typically equipped with a double-baffle muzzle brake. A new lightweight, split-trail carriage with a small, curved shield was developed. A lever-operated firing mechanism was mounted on the left side. The carriage provided a maximum elevation of almost 21 degrees and a depression of 14 degrees. On-carriage traverse was an impressive 30 degrees left and right. The unit became the T124E2 gun, with the T78 recoil mechanism and new carriage designated T66. Intended for direct fire only, it was equipped with the T149 sighting

The 76 mm anti-tank gun on field maneuvers (designated "Flashburn") with the 82nd Airborne Division at Fort Bragg, North Carolina, on May 3, 1954.

instrument and 5-power telescope. Firing was by a lever on the left side of the cradle.

The gun was supplied with a comprehensive modern range of ammunition types. Those included the T64 high-explosive round with both point-detonation and mechanical time fuse, the T128 armor-piercing with tracer round, hyper-velocity AP rounds, discarding-sabot rounds, smoke, and training rounds.

Limited numbers were produced for this specific use—just seventy-six were ordered. The tube was made at Watervliet Arsenal and the gun carriage was made at Standard Engineering. First inroduced in 1951, most of the production occurred in 1952. The gun information was stamped on the top of the breech housing, tube serial on the breech face in front of the breech recess, and the carriage information was carried on an oval brass plate attached to the right trunnion support. In 1954, the weapon was reclassified as the M48 anti-tank gun. The gun was issued only to the support companies of airborne infantry regiments and the anti-tank platoons of the airborne division headquarters. Crew was normally composed of squad leader, gunner, assistant gunner, and four ammo bearers. The quarter-ton command truck (jeep) was the recommended mover.

The gun did not have a long service life, and by 1956 it was reclassified as limited standard. As far as we know, it was never supplied to other countries as military assistance and never saw combat. It was probably declared obsolete and removed from service in the early 1960s. Existing guns were distributed as memorial pieces, and a surprising number survive. At least twenty are on display in the United States.

76 mm Anti-Tank Gun M48 (T124)

Gun Characteristics

Bore size: 76mm

Construction: One-piece alloy steel

Tube length overall: 198.75 inches (with brake)

Nominal caliber: 60 calibers

Tube and breech weight: 1,280 pounds

Usual carriage: 76 mm Gun Carriage T66

Weight of gun and carriage: 3,493 pounds

Maximum elevation: 21 degrees

Loading: Fixed

Shell weight: 15 pounds (HE), 14.6 pounds (AP)

Maximum muzzle velocity: 1,400 fps (HE), 3,200 fps (AP)

Builders: Gun: Watervliet Arsenal; carriage: Standard Engineering

Number built: 76

Many of the 76 mm anti-tank guns were distributed as monument guns—at least twenty are known to exist. This gun at an American Legion in Ragland, Alabama, bears serial number No. 73, made by Watervliet Arsenal in 1953.

Navy Field and Landing Guns

Naval vessels had carried light field guns for use in special landing detachments for many years. An entire line of howitzers had been developed for this purpose by naval ordnance designer John A. Dahlgren. Typically called a boat howitzer, these light guns could be carried in special boat carriages, and once transferred ashore, fitted to light, wheeled carriages. A special feature was the ability to be moved by hand, as it was difficult to find horses during an emergency. These guns were employed with success during and after the Civil War.

A continuous series of rifled breechloading guns, generally of 3-inch bore caliber, was developed or purchased by the US Navy from 1875 until just after the First World War. Advanced for its time, the first domestically produced modern gun was the navy's steel 3-inch breechloading howitzer of the late 1870s. This was followed by a short-lived 6-pounder. In 1895 the Mark I 3-inch was developed by the navy's bureau of ordnance. This tube, modified and fitted to a new carriage with a hydrospring recoil cylinder, became the Mark I Mod 1 on Mark II carriage produced in the early 1900s. This was the last field gun the navy developed in-house. The navy also designed and produced boat and land carriages for its common 1-pounder Hotchkiss revolving and 1-pounder semi-automatic guns. Besides the US Navy, the Revenue Marine Service and even several state naval militia organizations purchased field guns for use independent of navy orders.

In the years before the First World War, each battleship, large cruiser, and smaller gunboats carried one or two field guns. As the navy grew, so did the need for additional guns. Between 1904 and 1910, the navy purchased guns developed by Bethlehem Steel (designated Mark IV). A couple of years later, the navy bought fifty Rheinmetall designed guns (Mark VII). However, the guns and limbers proved too heavy for landing operations and were turned over to the Marine Corps for use as artillery equipment. Right after the First World War, two additional types were acquired. Designed and supplied by Bethlehem Steel, these were the advanced, split-trail Mark XI landing gun and a few Mark XII mountain guns.

These guns saw action ashore several times. In the Caribbean, navy ships landed detachments with 3-inch landing guns between 1885 and 1923. In a few cases they opened fire on insurgents and local troops. The high point of this type of action was at Veracruz in 1914, where four types of landing guns were provided. Interventions in Haiti, Dominican Republic, and Nicaragua also saw naval landing forces and marine detachments at work with their field guns.

The 1920s and 1930s saw a decline in this tactical concept. Opportunity for instantaneous, unilateral action was dwindling. While large warships continued to be equipped with landing guns, use was uncommon. In April 1939, the navy requested appropriations to purchase 81 mm mortars to replace its existing landing guns in its battleships. In some instances, 37 mm M1916 or 75 mm pack howitzers served as landing gun replacements. By the start of the Second World War, remaining guns were stored at naval districts and no longer routinely issued. Some were left in the Philippines, where they fought out their last action as beach defense artillery with the forces stationed there in 1941–1942. In 1943, the old landing guns were declared obsolete and removed from inventory. Later distributed to museums and memorials, several still survive.

3-Inch US Navy Breechloading Howitzer, 350-Pound

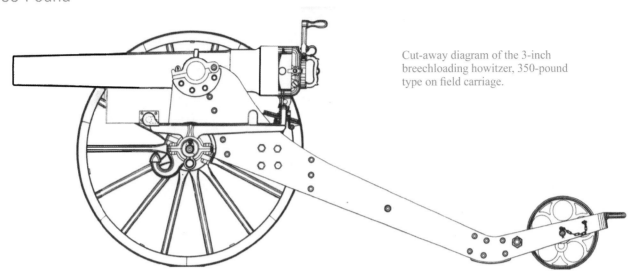

Cut-away diagram of the 3-inch breechloading howitzer, 350-pound type on field carriage.

In the early 1870s, the US Navy, with prodding from the US Revenue Marine Service, began developing a modern boat howitzer. This was unusual in an era when the navy paid little attention to technological developments. Nonetheless, America's first domestically designed and produced rifled breechloading steel cannon came about through these efforts. The gun's intended role was not new—it was to be mounted in ships' boats or taken ashore to support landing parties. Two sizes were developed—a "light" 350-pound model and a "heavy" 500-pound model—that shared projectiles. The two sizes were dictated by the ships' boats—smaller cruisers (frigates) were limited to 350 pounds. Forged steel was coming on the scene, and both gun sizes were produced in hardened bronze and forged steel.

More than a dozen 350-pound experimental guns with differing construction, metal, and breech types were fabricated at the Washington Navy Yard's gun foundry in 1874–75. Most were subsequently melted down, but at least one was accepted as a service gun. Thirteen bronze guns were ordered in 1875, made at the yard with metal from its own foundry. Twelve were assigned to the Naval Academy for training; the thirteenth was issued for ship service. The next forty-two guns were the first American guns to be made of forged steel, a fact that supplier Midvale Steel bragged about for years in its anniversary publications. Except for the construction metal and arrangement of hoops, both types were identical. Forty of these steel howitzers were produced in 1877–1883, and then a final two (Nos. 41–42) were ordered for Colt's Firearms in 1887.

The howitzer consisted of a single-piece tube with two jacketed hoops around the breech end. It had sixteen lands and grooves with uniform right-hand twist. An interrupted-screw breech fit through a right-hand-opening bronze breech collar. The gun fired a 7-pound shell of explosive or shrapnel type. Powder was separately loaded in serge bags. Firing was by friction primer. The original vent had a lengthy path, starting with a nipple on top of the breech ring before making a right turn along the breech axis. Once in service, this design was simplified.

Three carriages were produced. The boat carriage was a simple wooden and bronze raft designed to fit in the bow of larger ship boats. A pivot plate on the carriage had an eye that fit into the boat's bow. It also had two flat rails on which the bronze top carriage slid in recoil. Instructions for use were distributed, and at least thirty-six boat carriages were made, according to the navy's annual reports. However, they were not widely issued, and no action in the late nineteenth century describes their deployment or use.

A new deck carriage was also developed for the gun. This was a short, pivoting gun mount designed for shipboard use, often in constricted broadside situations. Six were reportedly made. The most common carriage was the wheeled field carriage composed of two thin, quarter-inch steel check plates with riveted transom pieces. The tail of the trail was angled up and held a 12-inch-diameter maneuvering bronze wheel. Under the breech was a double-screw elevating mechanism capable of achieving about 20 degrees of elevation. Wheels were 3-foot-diameter with oak spokes and had a bronze brake that could be tightened on the axle to lessen recoil; otherwise there was no built-in recoil mechanism.

Howitzers were marked on top of the tube with an acceptance anchor; on the base ring with foundry, registry number, and weight, and on the right trunnion face with caliber and year. The left trunnion face had the inspector's initials. Carriages were marked on the right side near the trunnion seat. Crew was normally calculated at twelve men, though more might be needed on draglines. Two ammunition boxes, ten rounds each, were fitted above the axle on either side of the barrel. The howitzers and carriages pre-date the navy's system of ordnance marks, and they were never referred to in terms of model designation. Also, while these were not howitzers in today's terms (high-angle fire with variable powder charges), they were consistent with their immediate Dahlgren predecessors.

The steel, 350-pound howitzer seemed to be the navy's preferred landing weapon. Most were assigned to warships. These guns were used in the 1885 intervention in Colombia. However, by 1892–93, improved guns were on the horizon, and they began to be moved to state naval militias and other training stations. Despite this, some were issued to auxiliary ships in the Spanish-American War. In 1909–12 many were authorized for distribution as memorial guns to GAR posts and municipalities. While some of these were melted down in the scrap drives of the Second World War, at least fifteen bronze and steel guns survive in public or private hands.

3-Inch Breechloading Howitzer

Gun Characteristics
350-pound
Bore size: 3 inches
Construction: Bronze or steel
Tube length overall: 46 inches
Nominal caliber: 13 calibers
Tube and breech weight: 318–360 pounds
Usual carriage: BLH 350-pounder field carriage
Weight of gun and carriage: 760 pounds
Maximum elevation: 20 degrees
Loading: Separate
Shell weight: 7 pounds
Maximum muzzle velocity: 1,087 fps
Maximum range: 4,794 yards

Builders: Washington Navy Yard
Number built: Bronze (13) Steel (42)

A 3-inch, 350-pound breechloading howitzer with crew aboard USS *Pensacola* in the mid-1880s.

While the 350-pound breechloading howitzer is hard to see in this photograph, the image is historically significant. This photo from 1888 was taken aboard USS *Alliance*; in 1885 this ship put this gun ashore in Aspinwall, Colombia, in an intervention to protect American interests.

The 350-pound breechloading howitzer seems to have survived in considerable numbers. Here is bronze No. 1 on display in Prophetstown, Illinois.

3-Inch US Navy Breechloading Howitzer, 500-Pound

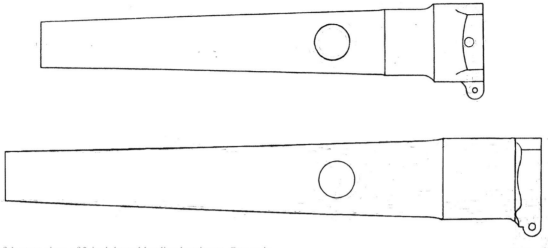

Outlines of the two sizes of 3-inch breechloading howitzers. On top is the size and shape of the 350-pound type, below is the 500-pound design. Note the two breech hoops for the smaller gun versus the larger one. Both have a lug on the bottom of the breech to attach the carriage's elevating screw.

This larger, heavier version of the 3-inch breechloading howitzer was intended to be produced simultaneously with its lighter companion. In reality, it was produced slightly later and for a longer period of time than the 350-pound type. It was also made in bronze and steel. Only three initial bronze pieces were made in 1876–77. One was used in experiments firing fixed metallic ammunition. The other two were issued to USS *Talapoosa*. One was lost when the ship wrecked in 1884, but the other was salvaged and survives in private hands in California. Thirty-three 500-pound steel guns were produced between 1879 and 1888. Forgings were provided by Midvale Steel, Naylor Steel, and Ames Forge; howitzers and carriages were fabricated at the Washington Navy Yard.

Differences between the two sizes of boat howitzers were minimal. The 500-pound gun was about ten inches longer and had a single reinforcing band around the breech, compared to two in the lighter gun. They used similar carriages, though the larger gun had one degree less elevation and was 100 pounds heavier. While the ammunition was the same, the proscribed powder charge for the 500-pound gun was 1 pound versus three-quarter pound. The greater length gave a higher muzzle velocity and slightly greater range

Four guns with a type of square breech housing were made for and sold to the US Army in 1884. They were quickly passed on to a militia assignment. The Treasury Department's Revenue Cutter Service presented a more significant diversion. It appears that fifteen to twenty-one of these howitzers were ordered for this service. Most then found their way onto the larger cutters. The navy routinely supplied the armament for the Revenue

Cutter Service, including a number of smaller 1-pounder boat guns and landing carriages. Only in a couple of instances did the 500-pound breechloading howitzer serve aboard US Navy vessels in the 1880s. They too were turned over to training facilities and then memorials well before the First World War. No 500-pound howitzers exist on display, but one bronze and at least three steel examples are in private hands.

Rare photograph taken on USS *Trenton* in the 1880s. It shows both a 500-pound breechloading howitzer (closest) next to a 350-pound type (note shorter barrel of the second gun), as well as what looks like a Gatling gun on field carriage in the distance.

3-Inch Breechloading Howitzer

Gun Characteristics
500-pound

Bore size: 3 inches

Construction: Bronze or steel

Tube length overall: 55.7 inches

Nominal caliber: 16.2 calibers

Tube and breech weight: 460–527 pounds

Usual carriage: BLH field carriage

Weight of gun and carriage: 1,035 pounds

Maximum elevation: 19 degrees

Loading: Separate

Shell weight: 7 pounds

Maximum muzzle velocity: 1,140 fps

Maximum range: 4,990 yards

Builders: Washington Navy Yard

Number built: Bronze (3) Steel (33)

Few 500-pound breechloading howitzers still exist; four are known to be in private hands. This steel tube (No. 3) is owned by Donald Lutz of Port Huron, Michigan.

1-Pounder Field Gun (Heavy) Mk V Mod 1 on 1-Pounder Field Gun Carriage Mk I

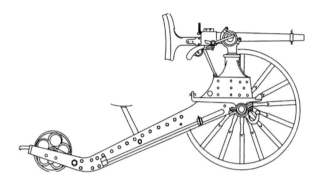

Navy short 1-pounder gun on naval landing carriage. The same carriage was also used to carry Gatling guns.

The 1-pounder (37mm) quick-fire gun was a popular light shipboard gun employed by many navies in the late nineteenth century. It was available in numerous marks with both short and long barrels and light and heavy weight, and was purchased from manufacturers or licensed-built in large numbers in the 1890s and early 1900s. The navy also acquired a boat mount and a landing gun carriage for guns carried as ship armament. The gun's light weight and simple yoke-pivots facilitated dismounting from deck mounts and transfer to carriages.

Both a 20-caliber and 40-caliber gun were used, though the longer type was preferred. The gun was made of a single steel forging and had twelve grooves. A distinctive feature was the light ring around the forward part of the barrel forming a seat for the sight. The trunnion ring was screwed on. Most were held by a yoke that could be relocated to mobile types of carriages. The primary gun intended for the field mount was the 1-pounder, heavy Mk V. This gun and subsequent field carriages were manufactured by the American Ordnance Company (as a licensee of the Hotchkiss patents) and later the Washington Navy Yard. The registry number was engraved on the upper barrel near the breech. Carriage information was marked on a plate.

According to secretary of navy annual reports, the first 1-pounder field carriages were ordered from Hotchkiss in fiscal year 1893, when five carriages and four limbers were acquired. The following year, two more 1-pounder field carriages were obtained for the Connecticut Naval Militia, plus thirty cage stands for 1-pounders for small boats. Confusion about the precise number of field carriages made stems from the fact that several state militias purchased guns from manufacturers, rather than going through the navy's contracting process. One surviving gun in Kentucky was bought for the state militia following the assassination of Governor Goebel in 1901. The 1-pounder field gun was used extensively for state militia training; there may

Postcard illustration of a 1-pounder naval field gun during training with the Treasury Department's Revenue Cutter Service. Card made in 1904.

have been more on active duty in these organizations than on navy ships. The Revenue Cutter Service of the US Treasury Department used many 1-pounders as both a shipboard and landing gun.

Combat deployment appears to have been limited. There are a couple of comments about sending them ashore from gunboats in Caribbean waters. The 1-pounder boat mount was the only replacement for the early 3-inch boat howitzer and extensively allocated to ships in the early twentieth century. Few actual combat deployments occurred—though they fought a spirited duel with similarly-sized Mexican guns in 1914 during the Veracruz action. Their service withdrawal date is unknown, but the allotment to battleships was doubled in 1917 (as boat guns, no additional field gun carriages were supplied) and they probably persisted in inventory until the early postwar period of 1919–1921.

After removal from the navy, many of these guns and carriages were sold to Francis Bannerman. He created a market for "yacht guns"—small cannon used to defend private yachts. Quite a few of these guns remain in private hands; at least eight have been documented in recent years. Few are on display. The Kentucky Military Museum in Frankfurt, Kentucky, owns a gun that was acquired directly for the Kentucky militia.

1-Pounder Gun Mk V on Field Carriage

Gun Characteristics

Bore size: 37mm

Construction: Steel

Tube length overall: 62.37 inches

Nominal caliber: 40 calibers

Tube and breech weight: 100 pounds

Usual carriage: 1-pound field carriage Mk I

Weight of gun and carriage: 436 pounds

Maximum elevation: 15 degrees

Loading: Fixed

Shell weight: 1 pound

Maximum muzzle velocity: 2,000 fps

Builders: Washington Navy Yard, Pratt and Whitney, American Ordnance Company

Number built: Several hundred guns of various types, 20–30 field carriages for US Navy, Revenue Service, militias

The 1-pounder American Ordnance Company naval field gun made in 1900 and now owned by the Kentucky Military Museum in Frankfort, Kentucky.

6-Pounder Field Gun Mk IV and Mk V on 6-Pounder Field Gun Carriage

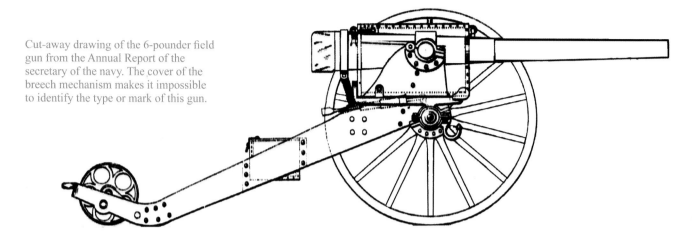

Cut-away drawing of the 6-pounder field gun from the Annual Report of the secretary of the navy. The cover of the breech mechanism makes it impossible to identify the type or mark of this gun.

In 1890, the US Navy designed a replacement for the aging 3-inch boat howitzers. The new gun was a step smaller in bore—just a 6-pounder (57 mm or 2.24 inches). This size had proven itself as a shipboard rapid-fire, semi-automatic gun using fixed ammunition. Appropriations were granted for only a few guns. Midvale Steel provided the necessary forgings, and the first five were fabricated at the Washington Navy Yard. Six followed the first order, but acquisition stopped in 1892 with just eleven guns produced.

The eleven guns followed the size and format of the 6-pounders being used in the fleet as anti-torpedo boat guns. Made of steel, the barrel was rifled with twenty-four lands and grooves. The breeches of nine guns (Nos. 2 and 4–11) featured the Driggs-Schroeder drop-block type and were designated Mk IV field guns. The other two (Nos. 1 and 3) had the Lynch breech mechanism and were designated Mk V. As a field gun needed a round of low ballistic power, the fixed shipboard round was still used, but with a reduced

Illustration from a Driggs-Schroeder brochure of its 6-pounder field gun.

6-POUNDER DRIGGS-SCHROEDER FIELD GUN.

powder charge. The reduced charge also lessened the recoil, so no counterrecoil mechanism was necessary. The carriage followed its predecessor in being a light, steel sheet box trail attached to an axle and side frames. It had a trail maneuvering wheel and typical spoke wheels with brakes to mitigate backward rolling during recoil. As usual, ammunition boxes were carried on either side of the gun. There is no indication that boat carriages were provided.

All eleven guns were finished in 1892. Eight were allocated in two batteries of four each for use in familiarizing cadets at the Naval Academy with landing gun operations, replacing 3-inch breechloading howitzers. Two were assigned to the training ship USS *Constellation*. While there were no technical or performance problems, its relatively small size proved inadequate for field use. The guns did not have a powerful enough shell, and the 2.24-inch projectile was too small to carry a useful shrapnel loading. In fact, the army learned the same lesson with the coast artillery 6-pounder field gun. Within a short time they were slated for replacement with a new 3-inch-sized field gun. In 1898, a number of these guns were removed from the academy and temporarily placed into service to augment coast defenses during the Spanish-American War. For a couple of years after the war, they saw limited service as training pieces at navy yards and with naval militia units.

By 1905 they were no longer in naval inventory. One nicely restored example survives and is the property of the National Museum of the US Navy. It is currently on loan for display in a restricted navy reservation.

6-Pounder Field Gun

Gun Characteristics
Bore size: 2.24 inches
Construction: Steel
Tube length overall: 72 inches
Nominal caliber: 30 calibers
Tube and breech weight: 400 pounds
Usual carriage: 6-pounder field gun carriage
Loading: Fixed
Shell weight: 5.78 pounds
Maximum muzzle velocity: 1,500 fps

Builders: Washington Navy Yard (guns and field carriages)
Number built: 11 (9 Mark IV, 2 Mark V)

The sole remaining survivor of the 6-pounder field gun. It has been recently restored and is on outdoor display at a navy reservation.

3-Inch Field Gun Mk I on Carriage Mk I

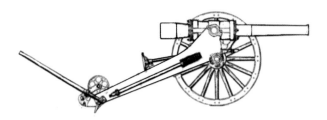

Cut-away illustration of a 3-inch Mk I field gun. This is the early version of what was known as the "Fletcher Gun," without the obvious pressure relief chamber mounted atop the recoil sleeve. Note the raised trail wheel.

Soon after the introduction of the 6-pounder gun, it became apparent that the payload, or shell, was too light for anticipated operations. In the mid-1890s, the navy moved to develop a gun with a larger bore size. While several commercial offerings were examined, the Hotchkiss 10-pounder (2.75-inch) seemed particularly attractive. Efforts were made to manufacture a prototype, but problems were encountered securing an adequate forging. The Bureau of Ordnance moved ahead with its own design for a new 3-inch gun. In late 1893, a type gun using the breech mechanism designed by Lieutenant F. Fletcher was ordered from Pratt & Whitney and tested successfully in mid-1894. Orders for 100 new 3-inch field guns were placed. The first fifty forgings from Bethlehem Steel were ordered for completion at the Navy Gun Factory. The naval facility also made the fifty carriages. These were the first 3-inch guns built under the navy's new Mark designation system. Most were completed in 1896. Another batch of fifty was assigned to the American Ordnance Company, numbered No. 51–100 and delivered in 1897. Thus, 101 guns were built for the US Navy and several others were acquired by state militias (Michigan took at least four).

It was a distinctive design. The conventional tube was made from a single forging, with a Fletcher breechblock. It

A 3-inch Mk I field gun carried aboard USS *New York* about 1900. Guns were typically supplied in pairs to battleships and singly to large cruisers and gunboats.

was fired with a firing lock and spring-loaded firing pin. This was the first naval field gun equipped with a system to moderate the recoil. The gun was surrounded by a sleeve attached to the carriage. Upon firing, the gun moved back, acting as its own recoiling piston rod. Hydraulic fluid was compressed within the cylinder, and counterrecoil springs around the sleeve wall returned the gun to position. Normal recoil was only 7 inches. Underneath the sleeve was a toothed elevating rack. The gun could elevate 10 degrees, and 3-degree traversing train was possible. The rest of the carriage was conventional, with trails on a heavy axle. A maneuvering trail wheel was pinned to where it could be lifted when the gun was stationary. It had open sights. Fixed ammunition was carried in two eight-round boxes atop the axle, on either side of the tube.

There were problems with the design, particularly with fluid expansion when the gun was fired repeatedly. A new bronze recoil sleeve was designed in 1902, but it failed in service trials. Finally an ordnance fix was achieved by attaching a small cylindrical pressure chamber directly atop the recoil sleeve to contain the expanding fluid. One hundred cylinders were ordered

3-Inch Field Gun Mk I on Carriage Mk I

Gun Characteristics

Bore size: 3 inches

Construction: Single steel forging

Tube length overall: 69 inches

Nominal caliber: 21 calibers

Tube and breech weight: 396 pounds

Usual carriage: Field Carriage Mark I and Mark I Mod 2

Weight of gun and carriage: 1,830 pounds with implements

Maximum elevation: 10 degrees

Loading: Fixed

Shell weight: 13 pounds

Maximum muzzle velocity: 1,150 fps

Maximum range: 4,500 yards

Builders: Washington Navy Yard (Nos. 1–50), American
    Ordnance (Nos. 51–100)

Number built: 100, 1 type gun and several units acquired
    by state militias

A modified 3-inch Mk I gun with its Mk I Mod 2 recoil sleeve on display in an exposition in 1915. While it is difficult to see, the added pressure relief cup is directly above the new sleeve.

A 3-inch Mk I gun with unmodified recoil sleeve at the American Legion in Reese, Michigan. This gun was made by American Ordnance in 1901 and carries no registry numbers—indicating that it was purchased directly by Michigan for use by its state naval militia.

in 1902 and 1905, intended to re-equip the existing Mk I guns. The plan was to make the cylinders of steel, but difficulties in passing pressure tests led to the majority being made of manganese bronze. Most guns were retrofitted with the new sleeve in 1905–08, but some surviving examples are without this modification, indicating that at least some missed the corrective effort. After modification the recoil sleeve and mechanism were designated the Mk I Mod 2. While there is some suggestion that even this fix did not correct all the difficulties with this gun, it remained in service for several more years.

The Mk I 3-inch field guns were assigned individually to ships. They saw considerable action in the Spanish-American War—notably the landing at Guantanamo and even with army troops of Astor's Battery in the Philippines. They also served with the marine relief column during the Boxer Rebellion in China. By 1908 they were replaced by new Mk IV guns on battleships but still assigned to cruisers and gunboats. Some went to the US Marine Corps; at least twenty-four were reported at various stations in 1907. In 1914, guns of this type saw combat at Veracruz. After the First World War they were relegated to training establishments; in 1934 they were declared obsolete. Fortunately a few still exist. There are two known unmodified Mk Is; at least six publicly owned models and a few privately owned, modified versions survive.

At least six modified 3-inch field guns with Mk I Mod 2 sleeves still exist, several on display. This representative is outside Dayton in West Carrollton, Ohio.

3-Inch Field Gun Mk I Mod I on Carriage Mk II

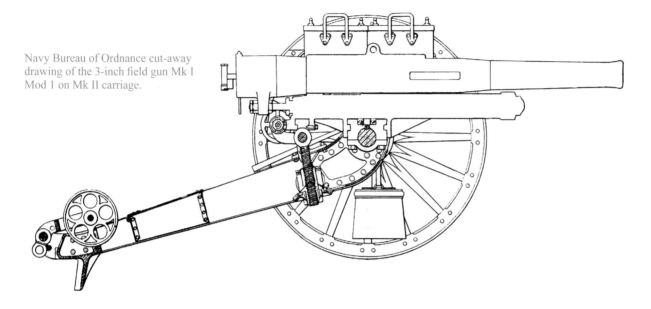

Navy Bureau of Ordnance cut-away drawing of the 3-inch field gun Mk I Mod 1 on Mk II carriage.

The follow-on to the field gun Mk I involved abandoning the troublesome recoil sleeve for a more conventional recoil cylinder. As there was no problem with the gun tube, ammunition, or other features of the Mk I, the navy developed a new model to address the recoil mechanism. Changes to the gun involved simply adding a lug to the underside to connect to a conventional recoil piston. This new tube was known as the Mk I Mod I. The revision to the carriage was more extensive, as it housed the new recoil mechanism, and it emerged as the Mk II 3-inch field gun carriage. Design work took place about 1900. Incidentally, the attempted "fix" to the older Mk I guns was not completed until after orders for the Mk 1 Mod I were placed.

The new gun was built of nickel steel but had the same ballistic performance as its predecessor. The lower carriage was slightly modified. The wheel for the elevating mechanism was moved to the left side, rather than being awkwardly placed directly behind and slightly below the breech. The gear was changed to a shaft bevel gear. Also, the new carriage could manage a small, 3-degree traversing range. The breech mechanism was an improved Fletcher type, including a Tasker firing lock. In this design, the gun was still held by a bronze sleeve. A small hydraulic recoil cylinder was slung beneath the tube, along with the 15-inch counterrecoil springs. The gun still did not have trunnions, as those were part of the sleeve mechanism.

Early photograph of the 3-inch Mk I Mod 1 on its Mk II carriage with limber. Note the identifying recoil cylinder under the gun barrel in this photo and the drawing above.

The usual four ammunition boxes were carried on the carriage, two on top of the axles on either side of the gun. Like its predecessor, no shield was provided. Ammunition was the same as the older Mark I, but subsequent navy landing guns had 3-inch rounds and cartridges with a different configuration.

In 1902, orders for sixty new Mk 1 Mod 1 guns and corresponding Mk II carriages were placed with the Washington Navy Yard. The first thirty-six were quickly completed, but a delay in the forgings for the final twenty-four prolonged their delivery date. The new tubes were given serial numbers 359–418. Guns were marked on the tube above the breech. Carriages were labeled with a carriage plate and numbered 101–160. In 1905, the navy reported that these guns cost $2,461.05 apiece (complete with carriage and implements, but not ammunition). That included royalty payments of $90 each for the patented Fletcher breech mechanism and $35 for the Tasker firing mechanism. Two other guns, destined for transfer to the naval militia (Nos. 906 and 907), were ordered in 1908, bringing the total produced to sixty-two.

Finishing about the time the first Mk IV guns were completed, most of the Mk 1 Mod 1s went directly to smaller navy ships—cruisers and large gunboats. Unlike the earlier Mk Is, it appears that the Marine Corps used this type of gun only occasionally. Two were supplied to the marines for their expedition to Nicaragua in 1909. Representatives were also present at Veracruz in 1914 and Nipe Bay, Cuba, in 1917. Four guns and carriages were sold when Greece purchased USS *Idaho* and *Mississippi* in 1914. Despite the presence of Mk IV and then Mk XI guns, they served on after the First World War. Many armored cruisers had them in the 1910s–1920s. Gunboats USS *Asheville* and *Sacramento* still had Mk I Mod 1 with Mk II carriages in 1934. At that time, however, the navy declared them obsolete except where needed at training establishments. Few of these guns are left; two are on outdoor public display and a third is thought to be in private hands.

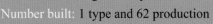

3-Inch Field Gun Mk I Mod 1 on Carriage Mk II

Gun Characteristics

Bore size: 3 inches
Construction: Single nickel-steel forging
Tube length overall: 69.6 inches
Nominal caliber: 21 calibers
Tube and breech weight: 396 pounds
Usual carriage: Field Carriage Mk II
Weight of gun and carriage: 1,383 pounds (without ammunition)
Maximum elevation: 10 degrees
Loading: Fixed
Shell weight: 13 pounds
Maximum muzzle velocity: 1,150 fps
Maximum range: 4,500 yards

Builders: Washington Navy Yard
Number built: 1 type and 62 production

Not many survivors of the 3-inch field gun on Mk II carriage survive, even though sixty-three were fabricated. This nice example is on outdoor display in Montross, Virginia. Note the racks for the ammunition boxes between the gun and wheels.

3-inch High-Powered Field Gun on Carriage Mk III

This gun represented a unique attempt to provide more field guns without purchasing entire gun-and-carriage units. Building on the experience with earlier 1-pounder guns, lighter revolving cannon, and machine guns, the plan was to provide a shipboard carriage that could serve the abundant 3-inch, 50-caliber guns used as anti-torpedo armament on battleships and cruisers. An initial project was authorized in 1904 but was delayed.

In 1907, the navy authorized the construction of a single type carriage, Mark III with limber Mark II. The intended shipboard gun was the Mark III 3-inch, 50-caliber normally mounted on sturdy cage stands. The gun was very powerful compared to a relatively low-velocity, short field gun, and the stresses on a wheeled carriage would be high. The first recoil cylinder proved too short to manage the recoil and had to be lengthened to provide a full 16-inch carriage recoil. Even then, it was often necessary to tie the carriage down during firing. Changes to the first gun carriage involved elevating gear and provision of an army-type Model 1902 sight.

The gun with its slide fit directly onto the carriage. The Mark III navy gun had a 2,700-fps muzzle velocity with a 13-pound common shell. The carriage was sturdily built and provided 15 degrees of elevation and 10 degrees of depression, but no traversing. It had recoil cylinders below the tube. Initial specification did not call for a trail wheel, but all photographs of test guns show one present. Gun and carriage were so heavy that manual drag was almost impossible. It was assumed that draft animals would be obtained once ashore, and harness was provided. Finally in October 1908, an order was placed with the Washington Navy Yard for a series of thirty carriages (Nos. 190–220), slides, and limbers.

No new gun tubes were ordered to go with these carriages; it was assumed that they would be dismounted from the parent vessel if required. The carriages and limbers were delivered from 1908 through 1910. In April 1909, the navy changed its mind. The original plan was to assign the carriages one at a time to ships with 3-inch, 50-caliber semi-automatic guns. Instead, the navy decided to send them to navy yards as reserve.

In July 1909, fifteen carriages and limbers went to Cavite in the Philippines for storage as part of the Advanced Base Force. The other sixteen stayed at Norfolk Navy Yard. Then in June 1914, the Cavite carriages were ordered to the defense of Guam. There they were to meet up with fifteen 3-inch Mark III Mod 7 guns sent out from the mainland. On Guam, ten of the guns were erected on cage stands as fixed armament, the wheeled carriages held in reserve to relocate the guns if the

Navy 3-inch 50-caliber high-powered gun on field carriage Mk III during testing.

tactical situation warranted. The navy defensive plan for Guam was changed after the First World War and eventually dropped altogether. In June 1921, the fifteen guns, carriages, and limbers were returned to the United States. Shortly thereafter, they and their US counterparts were declared obsolete and disposed of. No Mark III landing carriage is known to have served shipboard, and none saw combat. There are no known survivors, though several 3-inch, 50-caliber guns from the early 1900s exist on ship mounts.

3-inch High-Powered Field Gun on Carriage Mk III

Gun Characteristics

Bore size: 3 inches

Construction: Alloy steel

Tube length overall: 154.3 inches

Nominal caliber: 50 calibers

Tube and breech weight: 2,000 pounds

Usual carriage: Field carriage Mk III

Weight of gun and carriage: 8,000 pounds

Maximum elevation: 15 degrees

Loading: Fixed

Shell weight: 13 pounds

Maximum muzzle velocity: 2,700 fps

Builders: Carriages by Washington Navy Yard

Number built: 1 prototype, 30 production carriages

A Mk III field gun carriage with its 3-inch/50 caliber mate, as illustrated in the Secretary of Navy's Annual Report. Note the presence of the trail wheel.

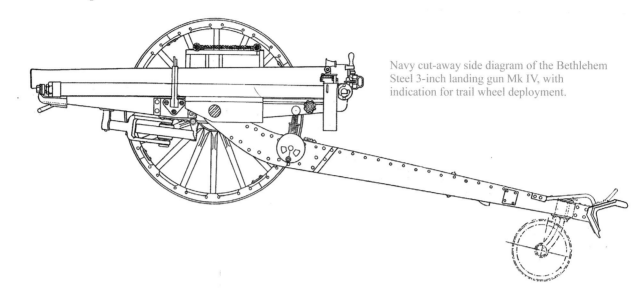

Navy cut-away side diagram of the Bethlehem Steel 3-inch landing gun Mk IV, with indication for trail wheel deployment.

The US Navy's rapid expansion in the early 1900s continued to increase the demand for additional field guns. With only sixty Mk I Mod 1 guns in an acceptable state of service (though the older model continued to be issued), two additional types were ordered. The navy turned to commercial ordnance companies to fill the need. Bethlehem Steel had developed a new landing gun using nickel steel for the barrel and a long recoil for stability. On January 27, 1904, the company solicited an order from the US Navy for twenty-five guns deliverable within a year. The navy accepted the offer three weeks later with few custom changes (modified arrangement of sight brackets, wheel diameter increased from 34 to 42 inches, shield deleted).

The nickel steel tube was a single forging, 23.5 calibers long and had a side-swinging carrier breech. The unique recoil system consisted of two hydraulic cylinders on either side and slightly below the center axis of the tube. Inside the cylinders were springs for the counterrecoil mechanism. A recoil of 30 inches was expected (compared to 7 inches for the Mark I). The twin under-slung cylinders and low profile make the gun easily recognizable in photos. The carriage could achieve a 15-degree elevation and a traverse of 10 degrees left and right.

A navy 3-inch Mk IV landing gun in action at Veracruz, Mexico, in 1914.

With the longer recoil, it was possible to accept a greater muzzle velocity of 1,540 feet per second. This increase caused the navy to designate this gun and subsequent models a "landing gun" versus a "field gun." The mount was equipped with peep sights for direct fire, though instructions were also issued for use with indirect fire.

The carriage was otherwise conventional, with capacity for two ammunition boxes, each with twelve stored rounds. The ammunition was different from that of previous Mk I types, though both used fixed 3-inch rounds. The tube was marked with registry number on its upper surface above the breech. The carriage had a plate with identification information on the top of the trail just below the breech.

Only twenty-five guns were produced. They were given naval 3-inch registry numbers 624–648. A carriage (numbered 162–186) and one limber were supplied with each gun. Delayed by a fire at Bethlehem Steel, they were delivered in 1906–07. The intention was to deploy them exclusively to new battleships—older and smaller ships would continue service with the Mk I Mod 1 guns on Mk II carriages. Their lifetime experience was almost exclusively with the landing forces on battleships (the Marine Corps received only two).

The guns served well until Mk XI landing guns replaced them fifteen years later. The navy's prompt response to the Veracruz conflict in 1914 provided the Mk IV with its only combat action. The gun was still listed as standard equipment in the 1920 *Landing Force Manual*, though apparently it was replaced by fifty-six new Mk XI 3-inch guns in the early 1920s. In 1934, the navy declared them obsolete and authorized their donation as decorative or memorial pieces. Only five are known to survive today; one is displayed on the museum ship USS *Texas*.

3-Inch Landing Gun Mk IV on Carriage Mk IV

Gun Characteristics

Bore size: 3 inches

Construction: Single forging, nickel steel

Tube length overall: 74.35 inches

Nominal caliber: 23.5 calibers

Tube and breech weight: 576 pounds

Usual carriage: Field Carriage Mk IV

Weight of gun and carriage: 1,717 pounds

Maximum elevation: 15 degrees

Loading: Fixed

Shell weight: 13 pounds

Maximum muzzle velocity: 1,650 fps

Maximum range: 5,000 yards at 15 degrees
8,800 yards at 50 degrees

Builders: Bethlehem Steel

Number built: 25 (Serial Nos. 624–648)

With only twenty-five units built, the Mk IV 3-inch landing gun has relatively few survivors. An example is on display at the battleship *Texas* State Historic Site in La Porte, Texas.

3-Inch Landing Gun Mk VII

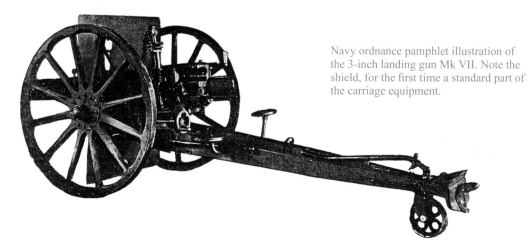

Navy ordnance pamphlet illustration of the 3-inch landing gun Mk VII. Note the shield, for the first time a standard part of the carriage equipment.

The development of yet another landing gun quickly followed the acquisition of the Mk IV. Again, a design developed by private industry was selected, this time outside the United States. German artillery manufacturer Rheinische Metalwaaren und Machinenfabrik (often referred to as "Ehrhardt" after its founder and chief designer) had previously supplied the US Army with 3-inch field guns. For the navy, a type landing gun was acquired and evaluated. Particularly appealing was the long-recoil design, which provided great improvements in steadiness during firing. Two subsequent orders, each for twenty-five guns, carriages, and limbers, were produced for the navy by the American and British Manufacturing Company, on behalf of Rheinische. The guns were given serial numbers 1055–1079 (contract of September 27, 1909) and 1153–1177 (contract of September 25, 1911). These fifty were delivered between January 1911 and September 1912.

Made of nickel steel, it consisted of a one-piece tube with three bands shrunk onto the tube. The gun was 77.95 inches long and 23 calibers. It had twenty-eight grooves, with a twist varying from 3 degrees to 7 degrees at the muzzle. The breech mechanism was a European-style horizontal sliding wedge, withdrawing to the right side. Ammunition boxes—seventy-two fixed rounds—were carried on an Mk IV limber. Long-recoil was controlled by a hydraulic brake cylinder and four counterrecoil springs. The gun had an 18-degree elevation and 24-degree train. It was equipped with a modern panoramic sight, and a steel shield protected the crew. In 1917, ten guns were modified with brakes, a strengthened carriage, and a new type of shield. The gun was a substantial advance over the previous Mk IV type—and was initially slated to replace it on battleships starting with the new USS *Michigan* class.

However, the design soon proved too heavy as a ship landing gun—though one would think that the navy would

The Mk VII 3-inch landing gun essentially became the standard field piece for the Marine Corps between 1911 and 1918. Here a gun and its limber are exercised at the New York Navy Yard.

have been well aware of weight limitations when writing the specifications. While the addition of a shield added several hundred pounds to the carriage and when fully loaded, the limber was far heavier than preceding models. As the guns were produced and accepted, they were sent to navy yards and depots. Within six months, all—except a few retained at proving grounds, one lent to the army for evaluation, and several that went to shipboard—were reassigned to the Marine Corps, which had been requesting its own organic artillery for some time.

In Marine Corps hands, the guns saw considerable action. They were usually assigned to specialized artillery companies or battalions with marine provisional regiments and brigades. Prior to the First World War, guns were deployed to stations in the Philippines, China, Guam, Oahu, and Guantanamo. They supported expeditions to Nicaragua (1912–14), La Paz (1914), Veracruz (1914), Haiti (1915–16), and Dominican Republic (1916–17). While not sent to Europe in the First World War, the guns served with several other expeditions shortly postwar— Virgin Islands (1919) and Nicaragua (1923). Two guns were turned over to Czech forces in Siberia during the 1919 expedition to Vladivostok. The final unit assignment appears to have been the battery with the marines' 39th Company in Peking in 1925–27. When the marines were re-armed with army weapons between the wars, these guns moved into storage. Six were lost in the Philippines when Cavite was captured in 1941 (though they were just in storage there). Most of the remaining guns were sold to the Dutch East Indies in 1941. The guns were converted to high-speed wheels with the help of parts supplied by the Martin-Parry Corporation, but only made it as far as Australia, where they were apparently used for training. One remains in a private collection in Australia, and another is on display near Cairns.

3-Inch Landing Gun Mk VII

Gun Characteristics

Bore size: 3 inches

Construction: Nickel steel, single barrel forging

Tube length overall: 77.95 inches

Nominal caliber: 23 calibers

Tube and breech weight: 539 pounds

Usual carriage: Field gun carriage Mk V

Weight of gun and carriage: 1,710 pounds

Maximum elevation: 18 degrees

Loading: Fixed

Shell weight: 13 pounds

Maximum muzzle velocity: 1,650 fps

Maximum range: 6,000 yards at 15 degrees

Builders: Rheinische (type gun only), American and British Manufacturing

Number built: 51

Marines man a Mk VII 3-inch landing gun in 1916 during operations near Santo Domingo, Dominican Republic.

3-Inch Landing Gun Mk XI

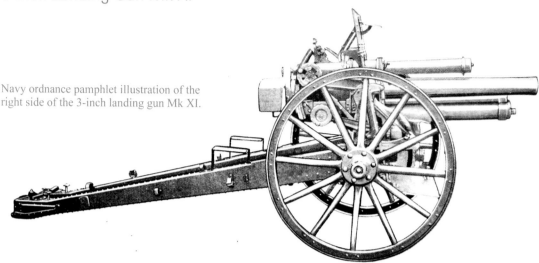

Navy ordnance pamphlet illustration of the right side of the 3-inch landing gun Mk XI.

The final and most modern naval landing gun was the Mark XI. Bethlehem Steel developed it to navy specs in early 1917. Production was initiated during the war but was delayed because of higher priorities. It was originally intended to be issued to the new capital ships of the 1916 Naval Act. After the Washington Treaty, Mk XIs were sent to remaining battleships, heavy cruisers, and larger gunboats.

The gun had some fairly modern characteristics. Still relatively short at 77.5 inches (another 23.5-caliber gun), it was built of alloy steel as a jacket shrunk onto the tube and equipped with the Mark XI drop-block breech. Hydropneumatic recoil and counterrecoil cylinders were attached above and below the gun tube, respectively. It was chambered for fixed ammunition and fired by either a lanyard or handle. The carriage had a modern split trail, allowing for an impressive 50-degree elevation and 45-degree traverse. A standard panoramic sight for indirect fire was provided. Crew protection was supplied with a 0.25-inch-thick shield. The carriage had no provision for ammunition boxes; those were carried on the corresponding limber Mk VII. The wheels were 48 inches in diameter with twelve spokes, still intended for manual drag. Muzzle velocity was 1,650 fps. Attempts were made to evaluate the use of the St. Chamond hydropneumatic recoil cylinder on these guns (as was being done with the similar army 75 mm Model 1916 field gun), but they were all issued with their designed hydraulic recoil system.

For some reason, photographs of the 3-inch Mk XI landing gun are quite rare. This one is on deck with its limber on an early American "Dreadnaught" battleship.

Bethlehem Steel received a contract dated March 12, 1917, for fifty complete units (gun, carriage, and limber) at $15,250 each. Production was delayed until early postwar; deliveries were made in 1919–21. The guns were assigned serial numbers 2104–2153. An additional six guns (Nos. 4975–4980) and carriages were soon added to the order for naval militia units. The guns were marked on the side of the breech housing; carriages had an attached plate on the trail.

The guns moved quickly to service on capital ships. The first battleship to receive the new landing gun was USS *Tennessee* on May 24, 1921. This type was also intended to equip the twelve cancelled battleships and battle cruisers scrapped by the Washington Treaty. With only fifteen battleships in American inventory after 1923, guns were made available on cruisers and large gunboats; ships such as USS *Cleveland, Birmingham, Galveston, Denver, Rochester,* and *Tulsa* carried the Mk XI. Opportunities for use declined in the interwar period, and it is doubtful that the type saw action in China or the Caribbean. However, in late 1940, fourteen of these guns had been concentrated in storage at the 16th Naval District at Cavite, Philippines. With war approaching, they were transferred to the US Army, along with 8,000 rounds of ammunition for use as interim training and beach defense weapons. While several schemes proposed issuing them to Philippine Army units in the southern islands, they remained in greater Manila Bay in defensive roles until surrendered with American forces in April 1942.

When replaced by lighter weapons in 1940–41 (such as the 81 mm mortar), the remaining guns were kept in storage at navy yards and depots. They were declared obsolete (mid-1943) and scrapped, though a few were distributed as museum and memorial pieces. Five survive today, only three of which are on display.

3-Inch Landing Gun Mk XI on Carriage Mk VI

Gun Characteristics

Bore Size: 3 inches

Construction: Alloy steel

Tube length overall: 77.5 inches

Nominal caliber: 23.5 calibers

Tube and breech weight: 624 pounds

Usual carriage: Field Carriage Mk VI

Weight of gun and carriage: 2,300 pounds with implements

Maximum elevation: 50 degrees

Loading: Fixed

Shell weight: 13 pounds

Maximum muzzle velocity: 1,650 fps

Maximum range: 7,800 yards

Builders: Bethlehem Steel Corp.

Number built: 56

Five surviving examples of the Mk XI landing gun are known. This gun, with limber but with wheels needing attention, is in the Trophy Park at the Norfolk Navy Yard.

3-Inch Mountain Gun Mk XII

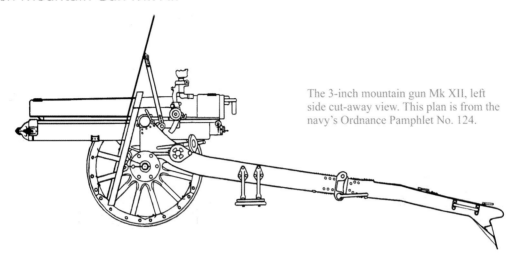

The 3-inch mountain gun Mk XII, left side cut-away view. This plan is from the navy's Ordnance Pamphlet No. 124.

The campaigns of 1914–1916 in mountainous terrain such as Haiti and the Dominican Republic convinced the Marine Corps of a need for its own mountain artillery. It was impressed with the army's M1911 mountain howitzer, which had been given a service trial at Vera Cruz in 1914. In August 1915, the marine commandant called for two batteries of mountain guns or howitzers to be obtained for use in rough terrain like that encountered in recent small wars. The utility of pack material (guns disassembled into 200-pound pack loads) with high-angle firing capability was stressed. In early 1917, the navy's Bureau of Ordnance asked three firms about purchasing a small quantity of such guns. Once again, Bethlehem Steel had a commercial

design that fit the needs. The company described it as the "3-Inch Mountain Gun, Mark L and Carriage Mark B." This was a light pack gun and carriage weighing just over 800 pounds. To be clear, this was a mountain gun firing just a single-sized round, not a howitzer with variable charges.

The tube was a short 15-caliber nickel-steel forging with a breech hoop shrunk onto it. Two lugs projected from the top of the tube to facilitate handling as pack equipment. The breech mechanism Mk XIII had a conventional interrupted screw block that opened with a single-motion handle. The chamber was fitted for fixed ammunition, and the tube had twenty-four grooves and lands rifled in a uniform twist of 1 to 25. Firing was by a percussion

The only known deployment of the 3-inch mountain gun Mk XII was with the marines in Nicaragua. Several guns were used there, perhaps the complete inventory. This photograph from 1928 shows one of these guns with hinged trail raised and placed on a towing limber.

mechanism with a lanyard or handle. Recoil was absorbed with a hydraulic cylinder. It was designed to be divided into four mule loads: tube, carriage, trail, and wheels with shield. The weapon was capable of a respectable 25-degree elevation, 5-degree depression, and 4.5-degree traverse. It had small, 29-inch-diameter spoke wheels and a 0.15-inch-thick steel shield cut-out around the wheels. It was provided with open sights and a panoramic sight on the left, with range quadrant carried on the right.

Bethlehem Steel received a contract to fabricate just four of these mountain guns. There was no prototype or type gun made. It is not known if Bethlehem had any additional foreign commercial customers for the type. Completed and accepted in 1921, the four guns were numbered 5482–5485. They were marked with registry number, inspector, and date on the upper surface of the barrel just forward of the breech hoop. Carriages were marked with a plate on a trail leg. The guns were initially dispatched to storage at the Washington Navy Yard.

Their only known use was with the Marine Corps in Nicaragua. While American military presence in this county extended for many years between the wars, a large peacekeeping force was dispatched in 1926 to help mediate a civil war. Photographs from 1928 show a battery of these mountain guns being transported in pack mode. They probably never saw combat.

In 1937, the navy moved to eliminate the type. The army was offered four of the guns (described as "excess" to requirements) in storage at the Marine Corps base, San Diego. The army accepted two as museum pieces, one each for the Aberdeen Ordnance Museum and the Fort Sill Artillery Museum. The Fort Sill piece managed to avoid the scrap drives of the Second World War and still exists on display.

3-Inch Mountain Gun Mk XII on Carriage Mk VII

Gun Characteristics

Bore Size: 3 inches

Construction: Single forging, nickel steel

Tube length overall: 48 inches

Nominal caliber: 15 calibers

Tube and breech weight: 205 pounds

Usual carriage: Field Carriage Mk VII Mod 1

Weight of gun and carriage: 821 pounds

Maximum elevation: 25 degrees

Loading: Fixed

Shell weight: 13 pounds

Maximum muzzle velocity: 1,100 fps

Maximum range: 4,000 yards at 15 degrees

Builders: Bethlehem Steel

Number built: 4

Somewhat surprising, one Mk XII 3-inch mountain gun still exists. Transferred from the navy to the army's museum system in 1937, gun No. 5484 is on indoor display at the US Army Artillery Museum at Fort Sill, Oklahoma.

Producers of American Mobile Artillery 1875–1953

The following list of firms or government facilities produced finished US mobile artillery cannons or carriages from 1875–1953. Space did not permit inclusion of firms that might have supplied forgings, recuperators, wheels, limbers and caissons, optical equipment, or parts. It was also impossible to include full corporate histories, including acquisitions, mergers, corporate reorganizations, name changes, and final liquidations. The intent is to provide a brief overview of the major contributors and their major products in the supply of modern mobile artillery.

Government Facilities

Benicia Arsenal, Benicia, California. Established in 1851 as the first western ordnance supply depot. Generally served as a regional storage and repair facility with no major manufacturing capabilities. However, this arsenal converted some 155 mm Model 1917 and 1918 gun carriages (the GPF) to high-speed M3 standard just before the Second World War. The arsenal was inactivated in the 1960s.

National Armory, Springfield, Massachusetts. Utilized during the Revolutionary War from 1777, this was one of the oldest government ordnance facilities. While primarily participating in small arms and ammunition production, it produced a few early army 3.2-inch gun carriages and the type carriage for the first 5-inch siege gun. The facility closed in 1968.

Raritan Arsenal. Raritan, New Jersey. Established in early 1918 as a major ordnance storage and shipping center to supply the AEF in Europe. Continued postwar as a regional storage and repair facility, this arsenal converted some 155 mm Model 1917 and 1918 gun carriages (the GPF) to high-speed M3 standard just before the Second World War. The arsenal closed in 1964.

Rock Island Arsenal. Rock Island, Illinois. Created in 1862 by Congress as a major regional arsenal. With the construction of the Field Gun Carriage shop, it became the primary army facility for production of field artillery carriages from the 1890s through the Second World War. Most carriage types were made here for the army. During the two world wars a large number of outside firms were engaged in carriage production, but often Rock Island was responsible for early prototype construction and ongoing service production. Between the wars Rock Island made or oversaw many

conversions to high-speed capabilities, and after the Second World War overhauled existing weapons and produced additional guns and howitzers.

Washington Navy Yard, Washington, DC. This was one of the original ship construction yards funded at the start of the US Navy, on the north shore of the Anacostia River. In the 1840s it began to specialize in light foundry work, steam engine castings, anchor fabrication, and gun production. The 1883 congressionally sanctioned Gun Foundry Board selected this yard to become the navy's primary gun factory. The navy's Bureau of Ordnance called it the Naval Gun Factory until 1945, when it officially adopted that name. The original Dahlgren boat howitzers were made here beginning in 1849, and heavy ship ordnance was produced starting in 1854. Navy 3-inch breechloading howitzers, 3-inch Mk I, and Mk I Mod 1 were made at the factory in the 1870s–1900s. Also, many of the 6-inch and 7-inch navy gun tubes used by the Marine Corps and US Army on mobile carriages during the First World War were originally products of the Navy Gun Factory. The establishment still exists, mostly for administrative functions.

Watertown Arsenal, Watertown, Massachusetts. A Boston-area ordnance facility acquired in 1816 and completed in 1819 beside the Charles River. During the Civil War it built field and seacoast carriages. While it supplied early army gun ordnance, in 1892 it was converted to the manufacture of seacoast carriages. It had limited but useful forging and metal shops, and participated in field artillery carriage production on a number of occasions. It produced five of the first 3.2-inch guns in the 1880s and both the 5-inch siege gun carriages and 7-inch siege mortar carriages. The arsenal's forging capabilities were used to make forgings for the 3-inch Model 1911 mountain howitzer and to produce some of the 240 mm Model 1918 howitzer tube forgings in 1918–1919. During the First and Second World Wars it made carriages for the heavy 240 mm howitzers, and in the Second World War made completed 155 mm M1 guns. The facility closed in 1967.

Watervliet Arsenal, Watervliet, New York. Created as a government ordnance facility in 1813 in Gibbonville on the west bank of the Hudson River near Troy, New York. In 1883 the Gun Foundry Board recommended that this arsenal become the army's dedicated gun factory. Subsequent funding fulfilled this commitment. From 1889 on, virtually all the army's field and seacoast guns were developed at this arsenal. It had limited forging capability and depended on commercially produced forgings. The shop's capacity was adequate for most of the next thirty years, although commercial producers supplemented large orders. By far, it is the most mentioned source of US Army guns in the modern period. During the First World War it produced 75mm, 4.7-inch, 155 mm guns, and 240 mm howitzers. During the First and Second World Wars the arsenal was expanded and increased production, but demand was so high that new commercial sources were enlisted to meet the requirements. Carpenter shops were added in the First World War to build caissons and wagons. This arsenal almost never made gun carriages. The facility served through the Second World War when it produced over twenty types of field, AA, seacoast, and tank guns from 37 mm to 240 mm in size. Watervliet Arsenal is still an army ordnance facility, though cannon production is much reduced.

Private Facilities

American and British Manufacturing Company. See American Ordnance Corp.

American Brake Shoe & Foundry Company, Erie, Pennsylvania. An industrial company incorporated in 1902 specializing in brake shoe production and parts. It operated several plants in Pennsylvania and Ohio. It received government assistance for construction of a new plant at its Erie manufacturing site to produce barrel assemblies and finished 155 mm Model 1918 howitzers. An order was granted in August 1917 for 3,000 howitzers. In one of the more successful such contracts, 1,172 barrel assemblies were completed by the armistice and some were supplied to France. The company still exists.

American Locomotive Company, Schenectady, New York. Created by the merger of several companies, American Locomotive was founded in 1901. Its major product was steam locomotives. During the Second World War, it managed the construction and operation of a government plant to produce carriages for the 155 mm gun and 105 mm howitzer M2. The firm survived until the 1960s, when it was acquired and eventually dissolved.

American Ordnance Corporation, Bridgeport, Connecticut. Founded in 1895 by acquiring financial interest in the Driggs Ordnance Company, the ordnance works of William Cramp & Sons, and the American plant of French Hotchkiss Ordnance—which it represented as both exclusive agent and domestic manufacturer. The plant made guns, ammunition, lathes, and other machine tools. It produced light guns (up to 3 inches), carriages, and ammunition for the army and navy. The company made some of the army's 3.2-inch guns, 2.24-inch Mk III coast artillery field guns, Hotchkiss 1.65-inch and 3-inch mountain guns and carriages, Hotchkiss 37 mm and 47 mm revolving cannons and field carriages, army M1902 and M1905 3-inch guns and carriages, and parts for the 3-inch saluting gun. It made a portion of the navy's Mk I 3-inch field guns and many of the navy's 1-pounder semi-automatic guns and field carriages. In 1902 it reorganized to become the American and British Manufacturing Corp. It also manufactured all fifty navy Mk VII landing guns as a subcontractor for Rheinische (Ehrhardt). The firm secured a considerable amount of foreign business, particularly in Latin America. It existed through the First World War, but went into receivership in 1921. The plant building was razed in 1940.

American Rolling Mill Company, Middletown, Ohio. Firm incorporated in 1899 by inventor George Verity, producing rolled steel and sheeting mostly for construction. In 1917, it took over a contract originally granted to the Mosler Safe Co. of nearby Hamilton, Ohio, to produce 155 mm Model 1918 carriages. It received contracts to produce 1,270 carriages at a rate of three per day. Difficulties delayed most deliveries until early postwar. The firm shortened its name to ARMCO and still exists.

American Type Founders, Elizabeth, New Jersey. Founded in 1892 as an industry consortium trust by twenty-three type foundries to produce standardized linotype. Later it manufactured and marketed printing presses. During the Second World War, it contracted to outfit a plant and manufacture 57 mm anti-tank guns. It produced 12,092 57 mm M1 anti-tank guns, delivering the first unit in May 1942. The foundry additionally produced 75 mm M1 pack howitzers at its Crowder Division during the war. Business declined in the postwar period, and the firm closed in 1993.

Baldwin Locomotive Works, Eddystone, Pennsylvania. Established in 1831, this was a long-standing producer of railroad locomotives. The firm incorporated in 1909. During the First World War, it began production of ordnance and formed the Eddystone Ammunition Corp. subsidiary. The locomotive division contracted to build the MkV tracked 7-inch gun mounts for the US Navy and Army in addition to 14-inch railway artillery equipment. In the Second World War, it produced military railroad equipment and army tanks and made 3-inch/50 AA guns for the navy.

Bethlehem Steel, South Bethlehem, Pennsylvania. A large American iron and steel company started in the 1830s to make rails and wheels for the railway industry. It became the Bethlehem Iron Company and incorporated as Bethlehem Steel Corporation in 1904. The company purchased technical expertise from the British Whitworth Company in 1886 to make ordnance-grade forged steel for armor plate and guns. Beginning in the early 1890s, it provided gun forgings to both services. Later (1910s–1920s) it added facilities for assembling guns and building carriages and artillery vehicles. Bethlehim Steel provided about half of all army gun forgings and a large number to the navy. It supplied a large number of finished 8, 10, and 12-inch seacoast guns as part of a "Hundred-Gun Contract" to the US Army. It also supplied almost seventy large seacoast gun carriages and all sixty of the 3-inch Model 1902 RF gun and pedestal for coast defense. In field artillery, the company produced some of the 3-inch Model 1905 field guns and 6-inch Model 1908 howitzer carriages. It produced all the finished 37 mm Model 1917 infantry guns, many 75 mm guns Model 1916, all the 75 mm guns Model 1917, all the navy's Mk IV and Mk XI landing guns and Mk XII mountain guns. During the First World War it produced 9.2-inch howitzers on behalf of Vickers for British and subsequently American orders. Many naval gun forgings and finished guns were supplied to that service through the Second World War. Bethlehem Steel also produced large numbers of field artillery vehicles in WW1 and had success selling ordnance to foreign governments. It purchased many of the assets of Midvale Steel and Ordnance Company in 1923 and continued to supply ordnance through the Second World War and modern age. The company shut down in 1998.

Bucyrus-Erie Company, South Milwaukee, Wisconsin. A mining equipment company founded in 1880 in Bucyrus, Ohio. As Bucyrus Foundry and Manufacturing Company, it moved to South Milwaukee in 1893 and merged with Erie Steam Shovel Company in 1927. Production specialized in heavy earth-moving and excavation equipment, particularly for the mining industry. As Bucyrus-Erie Company it accepted funding for construction and operation of a plant to produce heavy 240 mm howitzer and 8-inch gun carriages during the Second World War. The firm survived until 2011 when it was purchased by Caterpillar.

Bullard Machine Tool Company, Bridgeport, Connecticut. Created in 1880 as the Bullard Machine Tool Works, and incorporated in 1894 as the Bullard Machine Tool Company. It specialized in machine tools, particularly metal boring machines. During the First World War, it was contracted to build and operate a new facility in Bridgeport for production of four 155 mm Model 1918 guns per day. In November 1917, it was given an order to produce 1,400 155 mm gun tubes. By April 1919, 250 were completed, and the others were finished the following year. The firm produced ordnance material in the Second World War and disappeared through various mergers in the early 1960s.

Caterpillar Tractor Company, East Peoria, Illinois. A heavy farm and construction equipment manufacturer founded by Benjamin Holt. It relocated to a new plant in East Peoria, Illinois, in 1910 and incorporated as the Holt Caterpillar Company. During the First World War it produced a wide range of tractors and prime movers for the war effort. In 1925 it merged with the Best Tractor Company and emerged as the Caterpillar Tractor Company. During the Second World War, the company received funding to equip and operate a plant to produce 155 mm M1 howitzer and similar 4.5-inch M1 gun carriages. It still exists.

Chain Belt Company, Milwaukee, Wisconsin. Founded in 1891 by inventor D. W. LeValley, this company specialized in manufacturing conveyors, elevators, hoists, and concrete mixers. During the Second World War, it was appointed to oversee the construction of facilities and operate a plant making guns and howitzers for the army. The company fulfilled a contract for 105 mm M2A1 and M3 howitzers and the 155 mm gun M1. The firm lasted until it was acquired in the early 1970s and operates today as Rexnord.

Colt Patent Fire Arms Manufacturing Company, Hartford, Connecticut. Organized since 1855, Colt is best known for its pistols and other small arms. However, occasionally it delved into the business of supplying services for light artillery production. Colt was the subcontractor making almost all of Gatling's machine guns with field and shipboard mounts. During the Second World War, it installed breech mechanisms on 37 mm guns.

Detrick & Harvey Machine Company, Baltimore. A specialized manufacturer of metalworking machinery and precision-made parts, founded in the 1880s. It made thirty-seven disappearing and balanced pillar seacoast carriages for 5-inch and 6-inch guns for the army's coast artillery and 4.7-inch howitzer Model 1908M1 carriages for the field artillery.

Dickson Gun Plant, Houston, Texas. A new facility funded with government money and operated under contract with Hughes Tool Company. On the north side of Houston, the new plant, constructed in 1942 for $29 million, was capable of producing centrifugally cast gun tubes. During the Second World War it produced 155 mm M1 guns and 8-in howitzer gun tubes. The tubes bear the name Hughes Tool Co. rather than Dickson. After the war, the plant ceased operation, though eventually other firms used parts of the structure.

Draper Corporation, Hopedale, Massachusetts. A firm with a long history dating to the early nineteenth century when Ira Draper invented fabric milling equipment. Eventually coalesced as the Draper Corporation in 1917, it made looms, threshing machines, spinners, and other weaving/textile machinery. At one point, it was the world's largest producer of power looms. During the Second World War, the firm was contracted to produce large numbers of the 75 mm pack howitzer M1. In 1967, Rockwell International purchased the firm, and in the 1970s the plant closed.

Driggs-Seabury Gun & Ammunition Company, Derby, Connecticut. Incorporated in May 1897 by Louis Driggs, who had just departed from the nearby American Ordnance Company. The new firm included the Seabury Gun Company (around since the mid-1890s to commercialize Lieutenant Seabury's breech patents). The plant was in Derby, formerly used by Brady Manufacturing. It made light 1, 3, and 6-pounder and 3-inch RF guns, carriages, and ammunition for the army and navy. It also made the army's 2.24-inch M1898 and M1900 guns and field carriages for coast defense. In 1904, the company moved to a new plant in Sharon, Pennsylvania. The old plant was taken over by the US Rapid Fire Gun and Power Company. Driggs-Seabury purchased Savage Arms in 1915. After the First World War, the company was reorganized as Savage Arms Corp. and relocated to Utica, New York.

Duplex Printing Press Company, Battle Creek, Michigan. A firm founded in the 1890s to commercialize the patents of Joseph L. Cox for his two-sided (duplex) printing presses. It quickly grew to become the largest producer of these complex machines. During the Second World War, it managed construction and operation of facilities to produce 37 mm anti-tank gun carriages. It produced 9,973 37 mm anti-tank gun carriages during the war. In 1947, the Chicago Printing Press Company acquired the company.

Gar Wood Industries, Detroit. Founded in 1922 as the Wood Hydraulic Hoist & Body Company by Garfield A. Wood, inventor and speedboat racer. It commercialized hydraulic hoists for dump trucks. It also produced truck bodies and equipment, road machinery, commercial hoists and winches, and eventually a line of speedboats. In 1933, it assumed the name Gar Wood Industries. During the Second World War, it converted a manufacturing plant for production of carriages for 75 mm M3 field howitzers and 105 mm M3 field howitzers.

General Electric, Schenectady, New York. Formed by merging several firms, including those created by Thomas Edison in 1892 as the Edison General Electric Company. GE operated many diverse businesses and plants. In the Second World War, it accepted government contracts to establish and operate a plant to manufacture 75 mm M1 pack howitzers and M3 field howitzers at the firm's Erie works. General Electric still exists as a major industrial conglomerate.

Hughes Tool Company, Houston, Texas. See Dickson Gun Plant.

International Harvester, Chicago. A firm formed by financier J. P. Morgan by merging the McCormick Harvesting Machine Company and Deering Harvester. In 1902, the firm was concentrated around its main plant in Canton, Illinois. It established a strong business manufacturing agricultural motor equipment, both at Canton and another major plant in Rock Island, Illinois. It was a major government contractor during the Second World War, producing 20 mm aircraft cannon and 57 mm anti-tank gun carriages. It delivered 8,909 of the latter during the war. The company continued its basic business postwar and in recent years was named Navistar International Corp.

J. G. Brill Company, Philadelphia. Firm founded by John George Brill in 1868 as a manufacturer of horse-drawn carts and vehicles. It evolved into a producer of streetcars and buses. During the First World War it produced a variety of ordnance, including trench mortars. During the Second World War the firm equipped and operated a plant to produce 75 mm M1 pack howitzer carriages. In 1944, the company merged with American Car & Foundry Company. After the war, it was acquired by Consolidated Vultee Aircraft. The firm continued to operate as a subsidiary, but closed in the 1950s.

Link-Belt Company, Chicago. Founded by William D. Ewart in 1880 to manufacture detachable-link train drives. By 1906 it was known as the Link-Belt Company. During the Second World War, the company operated plants in Chicago, Philadelphia, and Indianapolis. It received a contract to operate and manufacture a plant to produce the 90 mm M8 anti-tank gun carriage. Link-Belt produced all 200 of the carriages made. Later it was sold to FMC Corp.

Lufkin Foundry and Machinery Company, Lufkin, Texas. Firm founded in 1902 to manufacture large iron castings used in railroad and sawmill equipment, and later made valves, pumps, turbines, and other heavy power equipment. During the Second World War it contracted to establish an ordnance manufacturing capability. The company produced carriages for the 4.5-inch M1 gun and 155 mm M1 howitzer. It still exists.

Maryland Pressed Steel Company, Hagerstown, Maryland. Originally established as New York & Hagerstown Metal Stamping Co., it was reorganized as the Maryland Pressed Steel Co. in 1914. It took on British ordnance orders early in the First World War and was later acquired by the Poole Engineering and Machine Co. It assembled all American-made 37 mm infantry guns Model 1916 based on the French Puteaux type. Postwar, it entered aircraft business with Bellanca airplane types.

Mesta Machine Company, Homestead, Pennsylvania. Founded in 1898 by George Mesta with the amalgamation of Leechburg Foundry and Robinson-Rea Manufacturing Companies. It specialized in manufacturing machinery for steel mills. During the Second World War it received funding and a contract to operate a plant for production of 155 mm guns M1A1, which was successfully executed. The firm failed in 1983 with the decline of the American railroad industry.

Midvale Steel Company, Philadelphia, Pennsylvania. Main plant in Nicetown, Pennsylvania, from 1866. In 1872 it became the Midvale Steel Works and in 1880, the Midvale Steel Company. In 1915 it became the Midvale Steel and Ordnance Company, specializing in forged and alloy steels. The first domestic steel company capable of producing steel forgings for cannon, it made some of the first forgings for ordnance of both services. It produced forgings for the navy's 3-inch breechloading howitzer (steel) in the 1870s and the inserts for the army's 3.2-inch conversion of ordnance rifles. Thereafter it became the major supplier of forgings for the navy and army. In the late 1890s, shop facilities were created to produce finished guns and fixed coast artillery carriages, but it was never much of a supplier of finished guns or carriages. It did produce complete 8-inch howitzers of Vickers' Model 1917 and Model 1918 designs during the First World War for British, Russian, and American orders. In 1923, most assets were sold to Bethlehem Steel, although the Nicetown plant continued in the forged gun business through the Second World War. Midvale was sold and the plant closed in the 1970s.

Minneapolis Steel & Machine Company, Minneapolis, Minnesota. Founded in 1902 to make structural steel components for construction. In 1910 it introduced its first tractor, and over the next decades excelled in this work. In November 1917, the War Department contracted with the firm to erect and operate a facility for producing 1,446 155 mm Model 1918 gun carriages and heavy limbers. By April 17, 1919, it had produced some 800 units of this equipment. Like most of these initiatives, the orders were curtailed shortly postwar. The firm merged with others to become the Minneapolis-Moline Power Equipment Company in 1929.

Morgan Engineering Company, Alliance, Ohio. Firm founded in 1868 and moved to Alliance in 1871. In 1877 it became Morgan-Williams & Co. The Morgan Engineering Company was incorporated in 1900. It produced steam hammers and pneumatic equipment but found a special niche making overhead traveling cranes beginning in 1878. It was one of the primary suppliers of disappearing barbette carriages for seacoast material, fabricating over seventy carriages for 5-inch to 12-inch guns. During the First World War, 120 wheeled carriages and limbers for seacoast 5-inch and 6-inch guns Model 1917 were produced. It also built many 8-inch, 12-inch, and 14-inch railway gun carriages. A large contract for numerous 12-inch seacoast mortars on railway carriages necessitated the construction of a new assembly shop in Alliance. Morgan was a major supplier of naval ordnance during the Second World War. The firm still exists.

Muncie Gear Works, Muncie, Indiana. Founded in the early 1900s, it specialized in automotive transmissions, clutches, and air conditioning equipment. Beginning in the 1930s, the company made a long line of outboard motors. In the Second World War, Muncie Gear Works received contracts for production of 37 mm anti-tank gun carriages. It produced 1,869 carriages during 1942–43. After the war, much of the firm relocated to Georgia, where it went out of business in the 1980s.

National Pneumatic Company, Rahway, New Jersey. Organized in 1910 and operated its principal manufacturing plant from 1919. It specialized in equipment for pneumatic door openers and closers and rapid transit vehicles. During the Second World War, it received government funding to expand its plant to manufacture 37 mm anti-tank guns. Seven hundred guns were produced during 1941. Apparently the firm failed or was immediately acquired, as no subsequent contracts are on record.

New York Air Brake Company, Watertown, New York. Created in 1890, it still exists today. It specialized in railroad air brakes and their controls. In the First World War, it received government funding for a new facility and a contract as an operating agent to provide 75 mm gun carriages. It contracted for 400 75 mm Model 1916 carriages for an ultimate capacity of twenty-five per month. It delivered ninety-seven completed carriages through April 17, 1919. The contract ended with a much-reduced quantity for delivery.

Northwestern Ordnance Company, Madison, Wisconsin. A new ordnance facility organized and funded by the US government to produce the 4.7-inch Model 1906 field gun. It was to manufacture the gun tube assembly for this piece. After delays in securing forgings, almost 100 guns were completed by the end of 1918, and several hundred others were made in 1919–20.

Oldsmobile Division, General Motors Corporation, Lansing, Michigan. An automobile manufacturing firm established by Ransom Olds in 1897. The firm was acquired by General Motors in 1907 but continued to operate as a division with its own plant for many years. During the Second World War, the plant became a major supplier of army and navy artillery. Among many products were 20 mm navy AA gun mounts and tank cannon. Oldsmobile also completed orders for 105 mm M2A1 gun barrel assemblies. General Motors discontinued the brand and plant in 2010.

Oliver Corporation, Shelbyville, Ohio. A farm equipment company created in 1929 by the merger of four companies, including the Oliver Chilled Plow Works of South Bend, Indiana. It operated several plants in the Midwest. During the Second World War, it contracted to produce carriages for the 155 mm M1 howitzer at the Shelbyville plant. In 1960, the firm was purchased by White Motor Corporation.

Osgood-Bradley Car Company, Worcester, Massachusetts. A firm dating from 1822 originally making coaches and sleighs, and later railway cars. During the First World War, it received government assistance to expand a plant in Worcester to make the 155 mm Model 1918 carriage. It was granted orders in November 1917 to supply them at a rate of five per day. The company struggled to secure equipment during the war, and most carriages were made after the armistice. Pullman purchased the firm in 1930.

Parish Pressed Steel Company, Reading, Pennsylvania. Company founded in 1905 as the Parish Manufacturing Company. By the 1930s, most of the business was in vehicle and trailer frames and automotive sheet parts. Before the Second World War, it was the prime contractor for the new M2 75 mm gun carriages for the modernized 75 mm gun M1897. During the war it received funding to expand into production of 105 mm howitzer M2A1 carriages, and it also built and delivered 6,536 57 mm anti-tank gun carriages. Postwar, it was absorbed into the Dana Corporation, and the Reading plant closed in 2010.

Pettibone Mulliken Corporation, Chicago. Originally organized in 1880 to make railway track fittings and equipment. During the Second World War, it received funding to build and operate a factory that produced 155 mm M1 gun and 8-in howitzer carriages. In the 1970s, it became simply the Pettibone Corporation and still exists as an equipment manufacturer in Des Plaines, Illinois.

Pratt & Whitney Company, Hartford, Connecticut. Began in 1860 as a specialty provider of machine tools and highly machined steel fabrications. It was contracted by Hotchkiss Ordnance of Paris to manufacture and deliver light naval ordnance. In 1889, it began supplying Hotchkiss 37 mm revolving cannon, and a couple of years later added single-mount 1-pounder (37mm) naval mounts. Pratt & Whitney attempted to market the Sponsel type light guns but had little success. When Hotchkiss bought into the American Ordnance Company, they took their orders with them. Pratt & Whitney continued to supply machine tools to military arsenals. After the First World War (1925) it reorganized as an aeronautical engine company.

Pullman-Standard Car Manufacturing Company, Hammond, Indiana. In 1862, George Pullman established the company to manufacture and operate the famous Pullman sleeper railroad cars. When Pullman purchased the Standard Steel Car Co. in 1934, the name become Pullman-Standard. It operated plants in Butler, Pennsylvania, and Hammond, Indiana. During the Second World War, the Indiana plant was substantially expanded under contract to produce tanks and artillery. It produced carriages for the 3-inch anti-tank gun, 155 mm M1 guns, and 8-inch howitzer. The firm was sold off in parts in the early 1980s.

Robert Poole & Son Company, Baltimore. Created in the 1850s as a foundry and machine shop, it furnished the iron columns for the US Capitol. The company went through several reorganizations and name changes. During the First World War it was known as the Poole Engineering & Machine Co. It supplied the US Army with heavy seacoast mortar carriages in the 1890s, and 12-inch disappearing carriages. During the First World War, it was assigned a contract to supply the American-made 37 mm infantry gun Model 1916 barrels and breeches. Guns were assembled at the firm's Maryland Pressed Steel subsidiary division. It also fulfilled navy contracts for 800 3-inch dual-purpose guns and 4-inch deck guns. The firm no longer exists.

S. Morgan Smith Company, York, Pennsylvania. Firm founded in 1877 by Stephen Morgan Smith, an inventor and industrialist. It specialized in producing hydraulic turbines, particularly for hydro and wind-power applications. During the Second World War it constructed and operated a plant to produce carriages for M1 240 mm howitzer and M1 8-inch guns. Allis Chalmers acquired the company in 1959, and it was eventually bought by Voith-Hydro Corp.

San Jose Manufacturing Company, San Jose, California. During the Second World War, this firm was an interesting example of a civic-based manufacturing pool organized by the local manufacturing association. Using a consortium of small, local manufacturers and bank loans, it rented and equipped a central site as a dedicated munitions plant. It secured a contract for a small number of 105 mm howitzer carriages M2 (at a maximum planned production rate of only thirty-eight per month). However, there were start-up difficulties, and through 1944 none were delivered; it is not known whether any guns were produced at this facility.

Sims-Dudley Defense Company, New York. Created, likely in 1895, to manufacture and sell dynamite guns based on the patents of Winfield S. Sims. A tragic explosion of a demonstration gun in April 1896 did not deter the War Department from purchasing sixteen of the Sims-Dudley 2.5-inch dynamite guns during the early stages of the Spanish-American War. However, other sales did not materialize, and by 1902 the firm's charter was forfeited and it was out of business.

Standard Steel Car Company, Hammond, Indiana. Started in Butler, Pennsylvania, in 1902, it specialized in the rapidly growing market for steel railway cars. A second plant was opened in 1907 in Hammond, Indiana. The government funded and contracted with Standard for expansion of facilities at the Hammond location. They were awarded a contract on November 16, 1917, for 964 240 mm Model 1918 howitzer carriages, to be produced at a rate of two per day. None were produced during the war, but sixty-seven were delivered by April 17, 1919. Orders were subsequently reduced. Standard Steel Car Company was also engaged in a contract for steel forgings for the 155 mm Model 1918 gun at its Burnham, Pennsylvania, plant. The company was purchased and merged with Pullman in 1929.

Studebaker Corporation, South Bend, Indiana. Founded in 1852 and incorporated in 1868 as a wagon and harness manufacturer, and later did large-scale automotive production. In December 1917, it accepted an order for 500 4.7-inch gun Model 1906 carriages, caissons, and limbers for production at its Detroit plant. The order was reduced to 380 in September 1918. Orders were further reduced after the armistice, but several dozen carriages were delivered in 1918–19.

Symington-Anderson Company, Rochester, New York. A new plant and company created to take advantage of government funding for First World War production. Mr. T. H. Symington negotiated with the US to obtain funds to build a plant for field gun fabrication in 1917. The Rochester plant was granted a contract for 640 75 mm guns Model 1916 and 4,300 75 mm gun Model 1897. Through April 17, 1919, the plant delivered 416 Model 1916s and 860 Models 1897s. Soon after that, the contracts were closed, and so was the firm.

United Engineering & Foundry Company, Pittsburgh. A new defense plant built in 1942 for $22 million in New Castle, Pennsylvania, to produce 105 mm howitzers M2A1 and M3. The foundry was contracted to oversee the construction, equipping, and operation of the new facility. It produced numerous examples of both weapons. In 1956, the plant was sold to Mesta Machinery for other manufacturing uses. It closed in 1982, though parts of the structure still house industrial firms.

United Shoe Machinery Corporation, Beverly, Massachusetts. Formed in 1899 with the merger of several firms producing equipment for making shoes, including Goodyear Machinery Corporation. It was incorporated in 1905. The main plant was built in Beverly, Massachusetts, in 1902 as a model "company town." During the Second World War, the company contracted with the government to produce 37 mm M3 anti-tank guns. It survived postwar until it was reorganized as USM Corp., and was taken over in 1976.

Vilter Manufacturing Company, Milwaukee, Wisconsin. Founded in 1887 as a specialty manufacturer of steam engines and custom heavy machinery jobbing. It received government funding for plant facilities and became a major producer of army guns during the Second World War. It produced gun tubes for the 3-inch anti-tank gun and 105 mm howitzer M2A1. The firm still exists, making primarily air conditioning equipment.

Walter Scott & Company, Plainfield, New Jersey. Established in 1884 by immigrant Scottish inventor Walter Scott. It specialized in manufacturing complex printing presses. A new producer of ordnance material for the First World War, the firm received orders for 250 carriages Model 1906 for the 4.7-inch gun Model 1906M1 in mid-1917. Only forty-nine carriages were finished during the war, but others were delivered postwar before the balance of the contract was cancelled. The firm was sold in 1957.

West Point Foundry, Cold Spring, New York. One of four private cannon foundries subsidized by the US government following the War of 1812. The foundry was fully established by 1817. It specialized in large iron castings such as those used in sugar mills and cannon production. Famous ordnance engineer and designer Robert Parrott joined the firm in the 1830s, subsequently inventing the "Parrott Rifle" of Civil War fame. This was the largest American cannon producer of the mid-nineteenth century. However, it could not transition to the steel age of the late 1800s. In the late 1890s it built seven Model 1891 seacoast mortar carriages and finished the assembly of eleven 8-inch steel seacoast guns. It assembled the converted 3.2-inch field guns for the army and secured just one contract for twenty 3.2-inch General Service field guns in the 1880s. The foundry went out of business in 1911.

Western-Austin Company, Aurora, Illinois. Created in 1901 with the merger of F. C. Austin Manufacturing Company and Western Wheeled Scraper Company. Initially based in Chicago, it was later concentrated around its major manufacturing plant in Aurora. It specialized in manufacturing scrapers, graders, and allied road equipment. The company went through several name changes including a reversal of names to Austin-Western Company in 1944. During the Second World War, it secured contracts to build and oversee facilities to produce the similar 4.5-inch gun and 155 mm howitzer M1 carriages. After the Korean War in 1951, the company was acquired and eventually ceased business as a subsidiary.

The William Cramp & Sons Ship & Engine Building Company, Philadelphia. One of the major shipbuilders in Philadelphia, founded in the 1830s and incorporated in 1872. It transitioned from wooden ships to iron and steel by the 1890s, and by the advent of the First World War, it became the leading commercial supplier of US Navy vessels. Cramp had an interest in the gun business, if nothing else to help supply foreign orders. The firm established a gun shop in 1891 and acquired small orders for army seacoast carriages in 1894. It helped launch the Driggs Ordnance Company with a financial investment, plant site property, and management seat. Some of the original Driggs orders were fulfilled in the Cramp shops. It contributed its ordnance assets to the formation of American Ordnance Company in 1895. The shipyard failed in 1927, though it was revived for a short time during the Second World War.

Willys-Overland Motor Company, Toledo, Ohio. An automotive engineering firm created in 1908 when John Willys purchased the Overland Automotive Company. It incorporated in 1912 as Willys-Overland Motor Company and operated several plant locations. The company became an agent for the US government to create a plant in Toledo, Ohio, and in December 1917 contracted for 2,927 75 mm Model 1897 gun carriages, at a rate of seventeen per day. It delivered 1,299 completed carriages through April 17, 1919.

The firm was also active in defense work in the Second World War and is well known as one of the creators of the "jeep." After several reorganizations and mergers, Chrysler purchased it in 1970.

Wisconsin Gun Company, Milwaukee, Wisconsin. A new plant constructed by the Worden-Allen Company for a consortium of metalworking firms in the Milwaukee area to build Model 1916 and Model 1897 75 mm guns during the First World War. By April 17, 1919, the firm delivered 116 of the 160 contracted Model 1916s and 190 of the 2050 Model 1897s. There is no postwar record of the plant's fate.

Yoder Company, Cleveland, Ohio. Founded in 1910 by Carl M. Yoder, a Cleveland draftsman and inventor, to commercialize his patented cold-rolled steel forms, particularly for the automotive industry. It made machinery for cold-rolling steel, brake shoe manufacturing, and electric welding. During the Second World War, the company delivered 3,548 57 mm anti-tank guns. It survived until 2001, when it was purchased and renamed Formtek Inc.

York Safe & Lock Company, York, Pennsylvania. An industrial company founded in 1882 by S. Farry Lauks. The firm specialized in safes, locks, vaults, and other precision steel parts. It became an important ordnance producer for the army and navy during the Second World War and operated four government-funded plants. It produced license-built 40 mm Bofors AA guns for the navy. For the army, it made 37 mm anti-tank guns, over 2,000 37 mm anti-tank gun carriages, and the entire quantity of 37 mm infantry gun T-32. Following the war, the firm failed and by 1947 its plants were disposed of.

Yuba Manufacturing Company, Marysville, California. Founded in 1906 by Wendell P. Hammon to manufacture gold dredging equipment, it branched into other types of mining and material-handling equipment. In the Second World War, it received contracts to produce 155 mm howitzers—at one point operating at a capacity of 155 units per month. After the war, the firm was absorbed into Yuba Consolidated Industries.

Foreign Facilities:

Dominion Engineering Works Limited, Hamilton, Ontario, Canada. A Canadian subsidiary of the Dominion Bridge Company making pulp and paper processing equipment. During the Second World War it converted to production of artillery for Canada and export to allies. The company received American orders for 57 mm M1 anti-tank guns through Canadian War Supplies Ltd. and manufactured 2,766 guns for the United States.

French Arsenals. Two French government arsenals produced 75 mm Model 1897 guns that were supplied to US Army AEF in France. Arsenal Bourges (gun markings "ABS") was the primary maker of these guns during the war, and by far the most common source of these cannons. Some of the earlier guns were produced by Arsenal Tarbes ("ATS") and carry its mark.

F.B.S. French producer of 75 mm M1897 guns, which the US acquired in small numbers during the First World War.

Hamilton Munitions, Ltd., Hamilton, Ontario, Canada. Orders for 105 mm M2 howitzer barrel assemblies were placed through Canadian War Supplies Ltd., which acted as a contracting agent for foreign-ordered munitions. They were ordered rather late, for production in 1945. Most forgings for the tubes came from Quebec foundry Sorel Industries. While over 2,000 assemblies were ordered, it is not known how many were delivered before contracts were closed at the end of the war.

Hotchkiss Ordnance Co. Ltd., Paris, with its plant in St. Denis. Organized in 1876 by American inventor B. B. Hotchkiss, in 1885 it was named La Société Anonyme des Anciens Establissements Hotchkiss et. Cie. The company produced light guns, machine guns, tanks, and other vehicles for many years. It supplied the US Army with 1.65-inch mountain guns and 37 mm revolving cannons, and the US Navy with several sizes of revolving cannon and single-mount 1-pounder, 3-pounder, and 6-pounder semi-automatic guns. Encouraged, particularly by the navy, to acquire or build an American manufacturing site, the company used Colt's Patent Fire Arms plant in the mid-1890s, then bought into and helped create the American Ordnance Company (later renamed American & British Manufacturing) to make and market Hotchkiss proprietary guns. In recent years, it became part of Thomson S.A.

Regina Industries, Ltd., Regina, Saskatchewan, Canada. A Second World War Canadian munitions facility opened in the former General Motors auto assembly plant that had operated in Saskatchewan in 1927–29. It was used for production of gun carriages and fulfilled an army order for 57 mm M1 anti-tank gun carriages channeled through War Supplies Ltd. The firm produced 400 of these gun carriages for the US during the war.

Rheinische Metalwaaren-und Maschinenfabrik, Dusseldorf, Germany. German ordnance producer founded by engineer Heinrich Ehrhardt to fulfill rifle orders in 1889. So strong was this man's influence that in the early 1900s, the Ehrhardt name was synonymous with the firm and cannon it produced. The company developed and sold long-recoil field guns to Norway, Great Britain, and the United States. It also supplied fifty 3-inch Model 1902 guns, ammunition, carriages, limbers, and caissons to the US Army. It designed the 3-inch naval landing gun Mk VII, though the guns were fabricated and delivered by subcontractor American and British Manufacturing. In 1916, it began producing (along with several other German firms) the 10cm (105mm) howitzer LeFH-16 for the German army. Postwar, several hundred units of this gun ceded to the US were kept in reserve. Between the First and Second World Wars, the firm's name was shortened to Rheinmetall. Its 37 mm anti-tank gun influenced the design of the American 37 mm M3 anti-tank gun. The company still exists as Rheinmetall Defence.

Schneider et. Comp., Le Creusot, France. A large, private French cannon producer since 1782, founded by Joseph-Eugène Schneider. By the First World War, it offered a full range of castings, forgings, stampings, and complete guns, howitzers, and carriages of all sizes. The company developed the 75 mm M1897 field gun, though it was produced at the Puteaux government arsenal and other locations. It also manufactured the 155 mm Model 1917 howitzer. Many were supplied directly to the American AEF in France. The design was licensed and put into production in the US as Model 1918. The company supplied the US with additional carriages and recuperators for domestically produced gun tubes. It cooperated in the design and licensing of its patents for the US Army's 240 mm Model 1918 howitzer, though all were eventually produced in the US.

Vickers Sons and Maxim, Ltd., London, England. A British steel and shipbuilding firm that began designing and selling cannon when it acquired the Sheffield Steel and Gun Works at River Don Works. In 1897, Vickers acquired Maxim Nordenfelt Guns and Ammunition Co. Ltd. of London, changing the corporate name as above. Maxim's plant at Erith was kept for the manufacture of light guns and machine guns. The US purchased a small quantity of 1-pounder "Pom-Pom" guns from Maxim Nordenfelt starting in 1894. In 1899, thirty 2.95-inch mountain guns were purchased from Vickers Sons and Maxim, along with rights to manufacture the gun in the US. During the First World War, three types of heavy guns were purchased from Vickers: the 6-inch BL Mk 19 Field Gun, the 8-inch BL Mk 7 & 8 howitzer, and the 9.2-inch BL Mk 2 siege howitzer. In the latter two cases, some of these weapons were being produced under contract at American commercial firms (Bethlehem Steel and Midvale Steel). Consequently, some units were supplied by domestic firms through transfer or sale from Vickers. Vickers merged with Armstrong in the 1920s.

Sir W. G. Armstrong Whitworth & Co. Ltd., Newcastle upon Tyne, England. Founded by Sir William G. Armstrong in the mid-nineteenth century. A key subsidiary was the Elswick Ordnance Company, which specialized in designing and producing guns as early as 1855. In 1897, it merged with Joseph Whitworth Co., and with Vickers in 1927. It operated extensive naval ship construction facilities at Newcastle on Tyne for many years. The company was a long-time supplier of ordnance to the British military services and export markets. It supplied the US army with 200 5-inch, 60-pounder BL Mk I guns immediately after the First World War. The company survived as an ordnance and aircraft manufacturer until the late twentieth century.

Bibliography and Sources Consulted

Primary Sources:

US Army:

Annual Report of the Chief of Ordnance to the Secretary of War, various years 1880–1919, Government Printing Office, Washington.

Army Ordnance Department Publications:

No. 1035, Service Handbook of the 75- mm Gun Matériel, Model of 1916, 1921.

No. 1095, Service Handbook of the 37-Millimenter Gun Matériel Model of 1916, 1922.

No. 1098, Service Handbook of the 9.2-inch Howitzer Matériel Model of 1917, 1918, 1922.

No. 1659, Handbook of 3-inch Field Artillery Matériel, 1912.

No. 1660, Handbook of the 3.2-inch Field Battery, 1902.

No. 1661, Handbook of the 5-inch Siege Gun Battery, 1903, Revised 1914.

No. 1676, Table of United States Army Cannon, Carriages & Projectiles, 1904, revised Jan. 15, 1924.

No. 1680, Handbook of the 5-inch and 6-inch carriages Model of 1917 and 1917 A, 1918.

No. 1714, Handbook of the 3.6-inch and 7-inch Mortar Carriages Model 1895, 1915.

No. 1761, Handbook of the 2.95-inch Mountain Gun Matériel and Pack Outfit, 1912, revised 1918.

No. 1762, Handbook for the 1-Pdr. Maxim Q.F. Gun, 1902.

No. 1763, Instructions for Mounting, Using, and Caring for 2.24-inch (6-Pounder) Guns, 1903, Revised 1915.

No. 1771, Handbook of the 4.7-inch Gun Matériel Model of 1906, 1910, 1917.

No. 1773, Handbook of the 3.8-inch Gun Matériel, 1917.

No. 1779, Handbook of the 6-inch Howitzer Matériel Model of 1908 and 1908M1, 1917.

No. 1780, Handbook of the 4.7-inch Howitzer Matériel Model of 1908, 1913.

No. 1781, Handbook of the 3.8-inch Howitzer Matériel, 1916.

No. 1817, Handbook of the 75- mm Gun Matériel, Model of 1897M1, 1918.

No. 1851, Description and Instructions for the Care and Operation of the 155 mm Howitzer Model of 1915 (Schneider), 1917.

No. 1862, The Story of the 75, 1920.

No. 2016, Handbook of the 240- mm Howitzer Matériel Model of 1918, 1918.

No. 2033, Handbook of Artillery, May, 1920.

No. 2033, Handbook of Artillery, July 1921, revised May 1924, 1925.

No. 2042, American Coast Artillery Matériel, June 1922, 1923.

Ordnance Memoranda No. 27, Hotchkiss Revolving Cannon, 1886.

TM 9-246 37 mm Gun T32 and Tripod Mount T9, August 1944.

TM 9-319 75 mm Pack Howitzer M1A1 and Carriage M8, November 1948.

TM 9-332 3-in Gun M5 and Carriage M6, March 1943

TM 9-331B Howitzer M1 and Mount M114 and Motor Carriage M41, March 1953.

TM 9-335 8-inch Howitzer M2 and Carriage M1, May 1947.

TM 9-336 8-inch Gun M1 and Carriage M2, November 1943.

TM 9-338-1 280- mm Gun M131 and 280- mm Gun Carriage T72, 7 September 1952.

TM 9-340 240 mm Howitzers M1918 and M1918MA1 and Transport Wagons M4 and M5, April 1944.

TM 9-345 144 mm Gun Materiel, M1917 and M1918 and Modifications, July 1942.

TM 9-350 155 mm Gun M2; Carriage M1 and M1A1, May 1945.

TM 9-355A 76 mm Gun T124 and 76 mm Gun Carriage T66, April 1951

TM 9-375 90 mm Gun T8 and 90 mm Gun Carriage T5E2, February 1945.

TM 9-1025-200-35 Direct Support, General Support and Depot Maintenance Manual, Howitzer, Medium, Towed 155-MM, M114, April 1965.

TM 9-1305 Gun and Carriage 75 mm M1897 All Types, April 1942.

TM 9-1325 105 mm Howitzer M2 and M2A1, September 1944.

TM 9-1326 105 mm Howitzer M3, January 1944.

TM 9-2300 Standard Artillery and Fire Control Materiel, February 1944.

TR-430, Field Artillery, Service of the Piece, 8-inch Howitzer, 1924

TR-1305, Mobile Artillery Matèriel 155- mm Gun Model M1918, 1931.

Ordnance Files at the National Archives and Records Administration, Record Group 156, US Army Chief of Ordnance:

Entry 21, Chief of Ordnance Correspondence 1812–1894.

Entry 28, Chief of Ordnance Correspondence 1894–1913.

Entry 29, Chief of Ordnance Correspondence 1910–1915.

Entry 36A, Chief of Ordnance Correspondence, 1915–1931.

Entry 36B, Chief of Ordnance Correspondence, 1931–1941.

Entry 819, Historical Files:
    Condensed History 155- mm Howitzer—4.5" Gun.

Condensed History 240 mm Howitzer and 8" Gun.

Design, Development, and Production of 75mm. Howitzer, M2 & M.3

Program for 75 mm Howitzer Materiel.

Program for 105 mm Howitzer Wheeled and Self-Propelled.

Program for 240 mm Howitzer and 8" Gun.

Program for 155 mm Gun and 8" Howitzer.

Towed Antitank Guns of World War II.

History of Gun, 37mm, T32 and Mount, 37mm, T9.

Entry 1451, Registers of Guns Manufactured and Modified at Watervliet Arsenal 1891–1920.

US Navy

Annual Report of the Bureau of Ordnance to the Secretary of the Navy, various years 1870–1919, Government Printing Office, Washington.

Navy Bureau of Ordnance Publications:

Ordnance Pamphlet No. 77, 1-Pounder Case Guns, January 1903.

Ordnance Pamphlet No. 124, Assemblies 3-inch Mountain Gun, Mark XII, May 1923.

Ordnance Pamphlet No. 131, Assemblies 3-inch Naval Landing Gun, Mark XI with Carriage and Limber, July 1921.

Ordnance Pamphlet No. 147, 3-inch Landing Gun, Mark VII, November 1911.

Ordnance Pamphlet No. 148, 3-inch Field Gun Mark I, Mod 1 with Carriage and Limber, May 10, 1912.

Ordnance Pamphlet No. 149, The 3-inch Landing Gun Mark IV, August, 1912.

Ordnance Pamphlet No. 216, 7-inch Tractor Mount Mark V, April, 1919.

Ordnance Files at the National Archives and Records Administration, Record Group 74, US Navy Bureau of Ordnance:

Entry 25, Chief of Bureau of Ordnance Correspondence 1888–1941.

Entry 111, Record of Armament of Naval Vessels 1841–1903.

Entry 112, Registers of Naval Guns 1842–1900.

Entry 118, Record of Guns and Mounts Afloat 1860–1942.

Unpublished Sources:

Kirchner, David P. *Firepower for the Infantry: The Post-WW1 Program to Develop More Powerful Infantry Weapons*, Draft of September 2011, in author's collection.

Secondary Sources:

Anonymous. *Handbook of the Hotchkiss 2-Pounder Mountain Gun.* London: Harrison and Sons, 1894.

Anonymous. *History of Watervliet Arsenal 1813 to Modernization 1982.* Watervliet, NY: US Army, Watervliet Arsenal, n.d.

Anonymous. *Naval Ordnance, A Textbook.* Annapolis, MD: The United States Naval Institute, 1937.

Anonymous. *Navy Ordnance Activities World War 1918–1918.* Washington: Government Printing Office, 1920.

Barnes, G. M. *Weapons of World War II.* New York: D. Van Nostrand Company, 1947.

Bethlehem Steel Company. *Mobile Artillery Material.* South Bethlehem, PA, 1916.

Birnie, Capt. Rogers, Jr. *Gun Making in the United States.* Washington: Government Printing Office, 1907.

Bishop, Maj. Gen. H.G. *Field Artillery, The King of Battles.* Boston: Houghton Mifflin Company, 1935.

Boose, Donald W. Jr. *US Army Forces in the Korean War 1950-53.* Oxford, United Kingdom: Osprey Publishing Ltd., 2005.

Boyd, William B. and Buford Rowland. *US Navy Bureau of Ordnance in World War II.* Washington: Bureau of Ordnance department of the Navy, n.d.

Brown, Sevellon. *The Story of Ordnance in the World War.* Washington: James William Bryan Press, 1920.

Bruff, Captain Lawrence L., US Army. *A Text Book of Ordnance and Gunnery.* New York: John Wiley & Sons, 1896.

Buckner, Maj. David N. "WWI Tractor Gun Acquired by Museum." *Fortitudine* IX No. 4 Spring 1980: 16–17.

Canfield, Bruce N. *US Infantry Weapons of the First World War.* Lincoln, RI: Andrew Mobray Publishers, 1999.

Civilian Production Administration. *Official Munitions Production of the United States*, 1947.

Comparato, Frank E. *Age of Great Guns.* Harrisburg, PA: The Stackpole Company, 1965.

Crozier, Maj. Gen William. *Ordnance and the World War.* New York: Charles Scribner's Sons, 1920.

Crowell, Benedict. *America's Munitions 1917–1918.* Washington: Government Printing Office, 1919.

Dastrup, Boyd L. *King of Battle, A Branch History of the US Army's Field Artillery.* Fort Monroe, VA: Office of the Command Historian, United States Army Training and Doctrine Command, 1992.

De Weerd, H. A. "American Adoption of French Artillery 1917–1918." *The Journal of The American Military Institute* 3, No. 2, Summer, 1939: 104-116.

Dyer, Colonel A.B. *Handbook for Light Artillery.* New York: John Wiley & Sons, 1908.

Farrow, Edward S. *American Guns in the War with Germany.* New York: E. P. Dutton & Company, 1920.

Fullam, Commander William F. and Lieutenant Thomas C. Hart, US Navy. *Text-Book of Ordnance and Gunnery Second Edition.* Annapolis, MD: The United States Naval Institute, 1905.

Gaujac, Paul. *American Field Artillery 1941-45.* Paris: Histoire & Collections, 2009.

Hazlett, James C., Edwin Olmstead, M. Hume Parks. *Field Artillery Weapons of the Civil War.* Newark: University of Delaware Press, 1983.

Hayes, Colonel Thomas J. US Army. *Elements of Ordnance: A Textbook for Use of Cadets of the United States Military Academy.* New York: John Wiley & Sons, 1938.

Hodges, Maj. LeRoy. *Notes of Post-War Ordnance Development.* Richmond, VA: Richmond Press Inc.,1923.

Lissak, Lieutenant-Colonel Ormond M. US Army. *Ordnance and Gunnery.* New York: John Wiley & Sons, 1910.

Marolda, Edward J. *The Washington Navy Yard.* Washington: Naval

Historical Center, 1999.

McKenney, Janice. "More Bang for the Buck in the Interwar Army: The 105 mm Howitzer." *Military Affairs* 42, No. 2, April, 1975: 80–86.

Mellichamp, Robert A. *A Gun for All Nations, Volume I 1870-1913.* Self-published, 2010.

_____. *A Gun for All Nations, Volume II 1914-1926.* Self-published, 2012.

Mueller, Chester. *The New York Ordnance District in World War II.* New York: *The New York Post*, 1947.

Peck, Taylor. *Round Shot to Rockets, A History of the Washington Navy Yard and US Naval Gun Factory.* Annapolis, MD: United States Naval Institute, 1949.

Schreier, Konrad F. Jr. "US Army Field Artillery Weapons—1866 to 1918." *CAMP Periodical* Summer 1997: 20–41.

Snow, Maj. Gen William J. *Signposts of Experience.* Washington: United States Field Artillery Association, 1941.

The Morgan Engineering Co. *Our Contribution to Uncle Sam's War Program.* Alliance, Ohio: 1919.

The War Office. *Statistics of the Military Effort of the British Empire during the Great War 1914–1922.* London: Reprinted by the Naval & Military Press, 1999.

Thomson, Harry C. and Lida Mayo. *United States Army in World War II, The Ordnance Department: Procurement and Supply.* Washington: Center of Military History, 1991.

Tschappat, Lt. Col. William H., US Army. *Text-Book of Ordnance and Gunnery.* New York: John Wiley & Sons, 1917.

Warren, Kenneth. *Bethlehem Steel, Builder and Arsenal of America.* Pittsburgh: University of Pittsburgh Press, 2008.

Zaloga, Steven J. *US Anti-tank Artillery 1941-45.* Oxford, United Kingdom: Osprey Publishing Ltd., 2005.

_____. *US Field Artillery of World War II.* Oxford, United Kingdom: Osprey Publishing Ltd., 2007).

Index to Gun and Howitzer Types